**"中国法治论坛"编辑委员会**

主　任：李　林

副主任：陈　甦　孙宪忠

委　员（以姓氏拼音为序）：

　　　　陈欣新　冯　军　冀祥德　李明德
　　　　刘仁文　刘作翔　莫纪宏　田　禾
　　　　王敏远　谢鸿飞　熊秋红　薛宁兰
　　　　张广兴　周汉华　邹海林

学术秘书：张锦贵

中国法治论坛
CHINA FORUM ON THE RULE OF LAW

# 中国法治论坛
CHINA FORUM ON THE RULE OF LAW

# 法治发展与司法改革：
## 中国与芬兰的比较

**Rule of Law Development and Judicial Reform:**
**A Comparision between China and Finland**

主　编／〔中国〕李　林
　　　　〔芬兰〕尤拉·柳库恩
副主编／〔中国〕谢增毅

社会科学文献出版社
SOCIAL SCIENCES ACADEMIC PRESS (CHINA)

# 总　　序

　　故宫北侧，景山东麓，一座静谧的院落。蕴藉当年新文化运动的历史辉煌与典雅的土地上，流淌着中国法律理论的潺潺清泉，燃烧着法治思想的不息火焰。多年来，尤其是1978年中国改革开放以来，一代代法律学者在这里辛勤劳作，各领风骚，用他们的心血和智慧，谱写了许多可以载入史册的不朽篇章。

　　为了记载和激扬法治学问，推动法治，继往开来，中国社会科学院法学研究所设立"中国法治论坛"系列丛书。一方面，重新出版最近20余年来有重要文献价值的论文集，如始于20世纪70年代末的关于人治与法治、法律面前人人平等、起草新宪法以及法律阶级性等问题的专项讨论，90年代初以来关于人权、市场经济法律体系、依法治国、司法改革、WTO与中国法、环境保护、反酷刑、死刑存废等问题的专项讨论；另一方面，陆续编辑出版今后有足够学术含量和价值、比较成熟的国际国内相关研究项目和会议的论文集。

　　法律乃人类秩序规则。法治乃当世共通理念。"中国法治论坛"不限于讨论中国的法律问题,也并非由中国社会科学院的学者独自担当。我们期望,这个论坛能够成为海内外学者、专家和广大读者、听众共同拥有的一个阐解法意、砥砺学问的场所,一片芳草茵茵、百花盛开的园地。

夏 勇

2003 年 6 月 6 日

# Preface to China Forum on the Rule of Law

To the north of the Forbidden City and east of Jingshan Hill lays a peaceful courtyard. It is the seat of the Institute of Law of Chinese Academy of Social Sciences, the most prestigious national institute in China devoted to legal research and legal education. On this small piece of land, rich in historical splendor and elegance of the New Culture Movement of 1919, flows an inexhaustible spring of Chinese legal theory and rages an inextinguishable flame of the ideal of the rule of law. Since several decades ago, especially since the "reform and opening up" in 1978, generations of Chinese legal scholars have been working diligently on this small piece of land and, with their wisdom and painstaking efforts, composed many immortal masterpieces of law that will go down in history.

China Forum on the Rule of Law is a series of books published by the Institute of Law with a view to carrying on the past and opening a new way for the future in the research of the rule of law and promoting the development of the rule of law in China. In this series, we will, on the one hand, republish papers published in China in the past 20 years which are of great historical significance, such as those relating to the discussions since late 1970s on the rule of man and the rule of law, the equality of everyone before the law, the drafting of the new Constitution, and the class nature of the law and those relating to debates since early 1990s on human rights, the legal system under the market economy, ruling the country in accordance with the law, judicial reform, WTO and China, environmental protection, eradication of torture, and abolition of the death penalty. On the other hand, we will edit and publish papers from future research projects and academic seminars, both in China and abroad, which are relatively mature and of sufficiently high academic value.

The law is the norms of order for all mankind and the rule of law a universal ideal of all peoples in the contemporary world. China Forum on the Rule of Law is not limited to the discussion of the legal issues in China, nor will it be monopolized by scholars of the Institute of Law. We sincerely hope that it will be able to provide an opportunity for scholars, experts, as well as readers to freely express their ideas and exchange their views on legal issues, a forum for a hundred schools of thoughts to contend, and a garden for a hundred flowers to bloom.

Xia Yong<br>
6 June, 2003

# 目 录

前　言 ……………………………………………… 尤拉·柳库恩 / 1

## 上篇　司法体制及其改革

论我国刑事诉讼中的司法审查
　　——以侦查中强制性措施的司法审查为例 ……………… 王敏远 / 3
法院与行政机关：司法审查的定性因素 ………… 奥利·玛恩帕 / 11
中国法院司法公开制度与实践 ……………………………… 田　禾 / 29
法治与法院：作为法治基础之一的
　　获得司法公正的权利 ………………… 皮亚·勒托－瓦纳莫 / 42
论我国赦免制度的完善 …………………………………… 刘仁文 / 57
芬兰程序法的改革：一个成功的故事？ ……… 约翰娜·尼厄米 / 84
公益诉讼与中国的司法体制改革 ………………………… 贺海仁 / 101
北欧国家最高法院的异同 …………………… 迪特列夫·塔姆 / 112
审判中心：以人民陪审员制度改革为突破口 …………… 施鹏鹏 / 121

## 下篇　法治的新发展

法治中国建设与人权保障事业的新进展 …………………… 柳华文 / 133
法律保护：芬兰的一项进化中的基本权利？…… 艾达·科伊维斯托 / 144
员工参与：芬兰和欧盟的法律框架 …………………… 尤拉·柳库恩 / 161
中国职工参与公司治理的本土路径选择 ………………… 陈　洁 / 174
芬兰劳动法语境中的欧盟反歧视法 ………… 玛丽奥·伊尔哈伊南 / 190
社会性别主流化与我国反家暴立法中的相关问题研究 …… 徐　卉 / 205
我国见义勇为认定标准和程序的完善 …………………… 谢增毅 / 218
中国所得税制改革的走向及其制度完善 ………………… 席月民 / 230
互联网时代中国的电子政务与公民参与 ………………… 李　霞 / 255

# CONTENT

Preface                                            *Ulla Liukkunen* / 1

## Part I   The Judicial System and Its Reform

Judicial Review in Criminal Proceedings: Taking the Judicial Review of Compulsory Measures in Criminal Investigation as an Example     *Wang Minyuan* / 3

Courts and the Executive: Qualitative Elements of Judicial Review     *Olli Mäenpää* / 11

Institutional Arrangement and Practice of Judicial Openness of Chinese Courts     *Tian He* / 29

Rule of law and the Courts: Access to Justice as A Basis for the Rule of Law     *Pia Letto-Vanamo* / 42

On the Improvement of the Pardon System in China     *Liu Renwen* / 57

Finnish Reforms of Procedural law: A Success Story?     *Johanna Niemi* / 84

Public Interest Litigation and Judicial Reform in China     *He Hairen* / 101

Nordic Supreme Courts—Differences and Similarities     *Ditlev Tamm, Copenhagen* / 112

Adjudication Centralism: Taking the Reform of the People Assessor System as the Breakthrough Point     *Shi Pengpeng* / 121

## Part II  New Developments of the Rule of Law

New Developments in the Construction of the Rule of
　Law and Safeguarding of Human Rights in China　　*Liu Huawen* / 133
Protection under the Law—An Evolving Fundamental
　Right in Finland?　　　　　　　　　　　　　　　　*Ida Koivisto* / 144
Employee Participation—Observations on the Legal
　Framework in Finland and the EU　　　　　　*Ulla Liukkunen* / 161
Choice of Native Approaches to Employees'
　Participation in Corporate Governance in China　　　*Chen Jie* / 174
An introduction to the non-discrimination law of the
　European Union in the Finnish labour law context
　　　　　　　　　　　　　　　　　　　　　　　　*Marjo Ylhäinen* / 190
Gender Mainstreaming and Anti-domestic
　Violence Law in China　　　　　　　　　　　　　　　*Xu Hui* / 205
Improvement of the Standard and Procedure of
　Identification of Courageous Acts for a Just Cause in China
　　　　　　　　　　　　　　　　　　　　　　　　　*Xie Zengyi* / 218
Income Tax Reform in China: Trend of Development and
　Institutional Improvement　　　　　　　　　　　　*Xi Yuemin* / 230
E-Government and Public Participation in the Internet Era　*Li Xia* / 255

# 前　言

本书反映了中国社会科学院法学研究所和芬兰中国法与中国法律文化中心（中国法中心）下属机构共同举办的第六届和第七届中芬双边年度研讨会的成果。第六届中芬研讨会由图尔库大学法学系承办，于2014年在芬兰图尔库举行；第七届中芬研讨会由中国社会科学院法学研究所承办，于2015年在北京举行。

在本书中，中芬两国学者讨论了法治发展、行政法和劳动法等不同领域的专门问题。然而，读者不应将本书仅仅看作一本研讨会论文集。本书中的文章反映了两国学者的一个共同兴趣，即对不同实体法领域之间的联系开展比较研究。

芬兰中国法中心于2012年成立之时就被赋予了发展和协调芬兰有关中国法和中国法律文化的研究和教育的总体目标。该中心成立伊始就将其工作的出发点确定为寻找中芬法律学者共同感兴趣的研究领域。以年度双边研讨会形式开展的中芬合作表明，这些共同感兴趣的领域很容易确定。从中国和芬兰的视角分享经验有助于我们更好地了解法律在特定文化、社会和经济语境中的运作方式。信息和思想的交流使我们得以将共同的研究兴趣具体地体现在由芬兰科学院所资助的6个研究项目之中。而这些项目大多数是通过中国社会科学院法学研究所与芬兰大学之间的合作顺利完成的。

法律无法逃避全球性挑战。我们看到中国正处于一个由经济体制改革引发法律制度深层变革的转型时期。在改革开放初期，中国似乎很少关注不同法律制度之间的比较研究。但近年来这一情况发生了改变。随着中国社会的进一步开放，人们对不同规制模式日益增长的兴趣为比较法研究铺平了道路。而在芬兰，对全球化更为深入的理解使我们重新认识到有必要在面向国际的研究活动中更加重视比较法研究。全球化也使我们更加确信正在发展中的跨国法律规则的重要性。在这一语境中，比较研究可能会引发法律的新发展。

换言之，比较法是解决如何对待不同文化背景中的法律制度这一问题的一种前沿方法。类似的法律行为或者看似类似的法律规定所起到的作用和造成的影响在不同的法律制度中往往有着显著的差别。在中芬合作过程中，我们逐渐将关注焦点从单纯的法律规则和概念层面转向法律运作的文化和历史语境。这种研究合作不仅拓宽了我们对法律世界的了解，而且也使我们得以从新的角度观察我们本国的法律制度。

众所周知，比较法律研究往往在移植和引进外国法律模式和概念的过程中起着重要的作用。在芬兰，我们经常强调，与中方在比较法研究领域保持合作的目的之一就是向我们的中国同行们学习其应对全球性、地区性和跨地区性挑战的法律经验。在中芬双边研讨会中，我们发现中国同行们也有着在相关法律领域学习芬兰或北欧经验的类似的渴望。

所有这些都凸显了本系列丛书所提供的有关各种法律问题的比较研究材料的重要性。

尤拉·柳库恩（Ulla Liukkunen）教授<br>芬兰中国法与中国法律文化中心主任

2015 年 11 月 20 日于赫尔辛基

# Preface

This publication is based on the outcome of the sixth and seventh Annual Sino-Finnish Bilateral Seminars between the Chinese Academy of Social Science (CASS), Institute of Law and the member institutions of the Finnish Center of Chinese Law and Chinese Legal Culture (China Law Center). The sixth seminar in 2014 was hosted in Turku by the Faculty of Law of the University of Turku, and the seventh seminar in 2015 was hosted by CASS Law in Beijing.

In this volume, scholars from China and Finland have written articles about topical questions in different fields, such as developments in the rule of law, administrative law and labour law. However, this book should not be viewed merely as a collection of seminar papers. The articles reflect a shared interest in drawing legal comparisons in the connection between different fields of substantive law.

When the Finnish China Law Center was established in 2012, it was given the overall objective of developing and coordinating research and education in Finland on Chinese law and legal culture. From the beginning, the point of departure was to identify research areas of mutual interest. Collaboration between China and Finland in the form of Annual Bilateral Sino-Finnish seminars has demonstrated that these areas are easy to pinpoint. Sharing experiences from Chinese and Finnish perspectives helps us to better understand how law operates in its cultural and socio-economic context. Exchange of information and ideas has also enabled us to concretize our shared research interests in the form of six Finnish Academy-funded research projects, many of which have been successfully carried out in co-operation between CASS Law and Finnish universities.

Law cannot escape its global challenges. We have been witnessing a transitional period where economic reform in China has resulted in profound changes in the legal system. In the early stages of the opening of Chinese society little consideration appears to have been devoted to scholarly comparisons between different legal systems. However, the situation has changed in recent years. With the opening of Chinese society, growing interest in different regulatory models has paved the way to developing comparative law scholarship there. In Finland, too, a better understanding of globalization has resulted in a renewed emphasis on the need for comparative law to be more directly placed at the heart of internationally oriented research activities. Globalization has also reaffirmed our understanding of the relevance of cross-border, or transnational, legal rules, which are still largely under development. In this kind of context, comparative research may inspire new developments in law.

Put differently, comparative law belongs in the frontline of methods for tackling questions as to how to approach culturally different legal systems. Often, the roles and impact of similar legal actors-or seemingly similar legal provisions-can be strikingly different in different legal systems. In Sino-Finnish collaboration we have gradually been moving away from keeping solely to the level of legal rules and concepts to the cultural-historical context where law operates. This kind of research collaboration not only broadens our understanding of the legal world, but also enables a fresh insight to our own legal systems.

It is generally known that comparative legal studies have often played an important role in processes of transplanting and transporting legal models and ideas from abroad. In Finland, we have often emphasized that one of the purposes of maintaining comparative research with China is to learn from our Chinese colleagues more about their legal experience and solutions to global and local, or translocal, challenges. In the well-established Annual Bilateral Sino-Finnish Seminars, we have recognized a similar eagerness to learn about Finnishor

Nordicsolutions in various fields of law.

All this underlines the importance of comparative material on topical legal issues made available through the present publication series of CASS Law.

Helsinki, 20 November, 2015

Ulla Liukkunen

Professor, Director of the

Finnish Center of Chinese Law

and Chinese Legal Culture

# 上　篇
## 司法体制及其改革

# 论我国刑事诉讼中的司法审查

——以侦查中强制性措施的司法审查为例

王敏远[*]

**【摘要】** 刑事诉讼程序包括刑事审前程序和刑事审判程序及执行，刑事审前程序包括刑事侦查程序和刑事起诉程序。刑事诉讼中的司法审查主要是指司法机关对侦查措施的事前审查。我国刑事诉讼中司法审查的立法及实践的发展过程，反映了我国刑事程序法治发展的进程，体现了国家法治发展的水平。1979年制定的《刑事诉讼法》在1996年和2012年两次重大修改之后，虽然其他相关制度和程序均有明显的修改、完善，但刑事诉讼中的司法审查，变化却十分有限。深入研究我国刑事诉讼中侦查措施的司法审查制度的完善问题，除了加强、完善关于人身自由的强制性措施的司法审查，还需要研究增加关于涉案财产查封、扣押、冻结等措施的司法审查。

**【关键词】** 刑事诉讼　司法审查　拘留查封　扣押

# 引　言

我国刑事诉讼中司法审查制度的产生和发展，反映了我国法治发展的进程，体现了法治发展的水平。我国是在1979年制定《刑事诉讼法》之后，才开启了刑事诉讼中的司法审查之门。当然，这个门最初开得很有限，主要限于对逮捕（这种较长时间羁押）的司法审查。《刑事诉讼法》在

---

[*] 中国社会科学院法学研究所研究员。

1996年和2012年两次重大修改之后，虽然刑事诉讼其他相关制度和程序均有显著修改、完善，但刑事诉讼中对侦查措施的司法审查，变化却十分有限。深入研究我国刑事诉讼中对侦查措施的司法审查问题，探讨进一步予以完善的途径和方法，对继续推进我国的法治发展，具有积极的意义。

刑事审前程序包括刑事侦查程序和刑事起诉程序两个部分，而侦查对刑事诉讼来说，具有基础性的意义。刑事诉讼的实体公正和程序公正所出现的问题，主要产生于侦查阶段。因此，通过刑事侦查措施的司法审查以预防、控制其不公正，具有十分重要的意义。刑事侦查措施的司法审查是指：司法机关对侦查机关（人员）所采取的涉及人身、财产及公民相关权益的具有强制性的措施予以审查并确定是否予以批准、认可的制度。

侦查机关（人员）在刑事侦查中采取的上述强制性措施的司法审查问题，长期以来一直是学术界讨论的热门话题之一。在大量的讨论中，人们对侦查机关（人员）在侦查中采用的强制性措施的现行控制模式存在的弊端予以充分地揭示，并纷纷提出应予以重新调整的建议。本文并非意在重复已有的众多优秀论著的话题，[①] 而是试图为刑事侦查的司法审查这个现实问题的理论分析，提供一种新的思路，以期有助于进一步推动对该问题的讨论。

任何关于制度改革、完善问题的讨论，均源于现行制度所存在的弊端，因此，分析侦查机关（人员）强制性措施的现行审查模式存在哪些弊端，是进行讨论的基本前提。而欲深入研究这个问题，首先应当明确现行审查模式的种类及其特点，并且确定相应的判断标准，然后才能进行有的放矢的研究。因此，我们先从说明我国现行审查模式的种类开始，然后确定对其进行分析判断的相应标准，最后再分析进一步完善司法审查模式的方案应注意的问题。

## 一　现行侦查措施的审查模式

从我国《刑事诉讼法》及相关的规定来看，对公安机关侦查中的强制性措施并不缺乏审查。对这些审查予以分类，主要包括以下几个方面。

### （一）按照审查的不同来源，分为侦查机关内部审查和司法审查

所谓内部审查即来自于侦查机关内部的上级审查。例如，拘留、查封、

---

① 例如，由宋英辉、吴宏耀撰写的《刑事审判前程序研究》（中国政法大学出版社，2002）中就有对此问题的大量精彩的论述，有兴趣的读者可以阅读其中的相关章节。

扣押等强制性措施应当经过县级以上公安机关负责人的审查批准，监听等技术侦查措施应经过地市级公安机关负责人的审查批准等。所谓司法审查则是指来自于司法机关的审查。例如，公安机关提请的逮捕应当得到检察机关的批准，等等。我国现在刑事侦查中的强制性措施，多数经由内部审查批准。而来自于司法机关的审查，根据我国法律的规定，司法机关包括人民法院和人民检察院，因此，所谓司法审查，包括法院审查和检察院审查。

### （二）按照审查的不同方式，可以分为事前审查与事后审查

所谓事前审查是指在侦查中采用强制性措施之前进行的审查；所谓事后审查是指通过对侦查中的强制性措施（及其效果）进行事后审查以确定其是否被认可。前者如前述之内部审查及检察机关的批准逮捕等，后者如起诉、审判中对获取证据的方法进行审查以确定该证据是否应予以排除等。我国刑事侦查中的强制性措施，多数缺乏事后审查。

### （三）按照审查的不同效果，可以分为强审查与弱审查

所谓强审查是指审查效果具有强制意义的审查方式，例如公安机关执行的逮捕必须事先经过检察机关的批准（或法院的决定）；而弱审查则是指控制效果相对有限的审查方式，例如对非法取证行为的审查，其结果可能并不是排除该非法证据，而是要求其补正或做出合理说明。

需要说明的是，上述对侦查中的强制性措施的审查的分类，是相对而言的，且不同种类的审查并不相互排斥，各种不同类型的审查在现实中存在着交叉。例如：外部审查这种方式，既包含着如批准逮捕这样的事前审查，也包含着排除非法证据这种事后审查；而事后审查则既可能是（诸如由于严格排除非法证据而产生的）强审查，也可能是（只是要求补正或做出合理解释）因肯定非法证据的效力而出现的弱审查。另外，从上述分类中，我们只能看到（根据现行法律的规定）强制性侦查措施并不缺乏审查，并不能因此而直接得到何种审查更优或更劣的结论。至于这些审查的效率如何、是否存在着应予克服的弊端，却是另一个问题。对审查的上述分类研究只是分析这个问题的基础，进一步的研究则有待于对这些审查之优劣的分析、判断。

## 二　现行审查模式的分析、判断标准

人们在分析、评判一种法律制度的优劣及利弊得失时，必然要以一定

的标准作为衡量的依据。由于根据不同的标准进行衡量所得到的结论就会有差异，因此，如何确定衡量的标准，是我们准确分析、判断现行法律所规定的审查模式之利弊得失的关键。

就我国刑事侦查中的强制性措施的司法审查而言，衡量的标准可以有许多，概括来说，主要包括以下这些内容：第一，是否有助于我国刑事诉讼实现准确、有效、及时地发现、揭露、证实、惩罚犯罪的目标；第二，是否能够满足人们对刑事诉讼人权保障的需要；第三，是否符合刑事诉讼程序对公正的基本要求；第四，是否符合与刑事诉讼法律制度发展规律相适应的基本理念；第五，是否符合有关国际公约所确定的基本要求。

上述标准当然不是"原子"性的元标准，也就是说，它们是仍然可以做进一步分解的标准。例如"是否符合有关国际公约所确定的基本要求"这个标准，就包含着相关国际公约的若干条款的规定，而并不是单一的。又如，"是否能够满足人们对刑事诉讼人权保障的需要"这个标准，既包含着对刑事被告人的权利保障的需要，也包含着对其他诉讼参与人的权利保障的需要。再如，"是否符合刑事诉讼程序对公正的基本要求"这个标准，既包含着对刑事诉讼实体公正的要求，也包含着对刑事诉讼程序公正的要求。上述标准的可分解性，要求我们在依据其中的某一方面的标准进行分析、判断时，应当明确指出具体依据的是该标准的哪个方面的内容，而不能（不应）简单地"概括而言"。

另需要说明的是，在此列举这些标准，目的并不是求全，而在于为进一步的分析奠定一个基础。而所谓的进一步的分析则是指：应当如何确定衡量标准的权重，即以哪个（些）衡量标准为主进行判断，以哪个（些）衡量标准作为判断的基础。笔者以为，研究如何确定衡量标准的权重，面临着两个不能回避的问题：其一，不同层面的衡量标准的侧重点之选择问题；其二，不同价值趋向的衡量标准之选择问题。下面予以具体分析。

其一，不同层面的衡量标准的侧重点之选择问题。

所谓不同层面的衡量标准，是指基于不同层面的需要所确定的衡量标准，例如，根据刑事诉讼中人权保障的需要所确定的衡量标准，根据有关国际公约的规定所确定的衡量标准，等等。由于不同层面的需要本身存在着差异，由于人们对不同层面的需要的不同认识，确定衡量标准的权重问题成为十分复杂的难题。例如，基于有利于发现、揭露、证实、惩罚犯罪的需要所确定的衡量标准，不同于基于人权保障的需要所确定的衡量标准，如何在这两者之间做出选择？以其中的何者作为主要判断依据，以哪个作为基本的衡量标准等问题，就是一个十分复杂难解的衡量标准的权重问题。

由于人们在各个衡量标准之间的关系问题上的基本共识，即基于不同层面的需要所确定的各个衡量标准之间的关系，并不是绝对的矛盾对立关系，更不能说是绝对的排斥关系，因此，如今在讨论不同层面的衡量标准的权重问题时，鲜见绝对化的立场、观点，常见的是在两个衡量标准之间有无主次之分、何者为主等方面存在的观点差异。在此，笔者无意对这类问题表明观点，而是要说明，解决衡量标准的权重问题，目的是解决现实问题，对解决现实问题并没有价值的分析，即使说得头头是道，也不具有科学性。[①]

当然，对衡量标准权重问题的探讨，并不能代替对不同价值趋向的衡量标准之选择问题的探讨。

其二，不同价值趋向的衡量标准之选择问题。

所谓不同价值趋向的衡量标准之选择问题，是指在分析具体问题时，如何在基于不同价值趋向所确定的衡量标准之间进行选择。在上述各个衡量标准之间，既存在着价值趋向相同的现象，也存在着价值趋向相异的问题；有的衡量标准之间，甚至存在着价值趋向的对立问题。由于只有在不同的衡量标准之间存在着价值趋向相异或对立的情况时，才会发生如何进行选择的问题，因此，是否存在相异或对立，是研究如何进行选择的基础。

如果说在相异或对立的衡量标准之间进行价值趋向的选择问题，是个主观性的判断问题，因而其正当性只能说明而难以证明，那么，在不同的衡量标准之间是否存在着价值趋向的选择问题，则是个相对来说具有客观性的问题，是个需要并且能够证明的问题，而且，我们应当将其置于刑事诉讼程序中进行分析。

之所以这么说，并非无的放矢，例如，经常被提及的在被告人和被害人双方对立的需求中如何进行价值趋向的选择，是否应当影响诉讼程序的设计，就是一个问题。显然，刑事诉讼中的被告人和被害人的需求经常处于对立状态，然而，我们不应将这种实体权益上诉求的差异，作为诉讼程序选择时的价值根据。换句话说，我们不能将保障被害人权益的需要作为

---

[①] 笔者曾撰文批判对不同判断标准采取不分彼此予以"并重"的观点，主要原因就是这种理论对解决现实问题并无意义。参见拙文《论刑事司法程序的改革》，载信春鹰主编《公法研究》第3卷，法律出版社，2001。

在诉讼程序中限制被告人权利的理由。因此，分析刑事侦查强制性措施的审查模式在价值需求层面的冲突，应当十分慎重。

## 三 设计新的司法审查方案的目的

依据一定的判断标准，不仅可以对现行的刑事侦查强制性措施的审查模式进行评判（当然，这并不是主要目的），而且可以为设计新的审查模式提供依据。在此所要讨论的并不是如何具体设计对刑事侦查进行司法审查的新模式，[①]而是要说明，在人们一致认为应由司法权对刑事侦查进行审查的时候，还应当考虑到如何使司法权对刑事侦查的审查满足改革的需要，符合相应的判断标准。在笔者看来，司法权对刑事侦查的审查本身并不是目的，而只是达到目的的手段。只有认识到这一点，才能使新的审查模式最大限度地满足现实的需要，并有效避免可能发生的问题。

例如，人们提出"拘留、搜查、查封、扣押、监听等强制性（技术）侦查措施的采用实行公安机关内部审查不能保证侦查活动的合法性、公正性"[②]，因而主张应由司法权对此进行审查的时候，需要进一步考虑到：由法院（法官）进行审查，使审查主体与执行主体分离，虽然有助于"保证侦查活动的合法性、公正性"，但并不意味着因此而当然地实现了"侦查活动的合法性、公正性"。一方面，从实体层面来看，如果法院（法官）对刑事侦查机关并不符合法定要求的申请同样予以批准，那么，审查主体的身份即使由侦查机关自己改为法院（法官），也并不会因此而有助于实现"保证侦查活动的合法性"；另一方面，从程序层面来看，如果法院（法官）在审查相应的强制性措施（如逮捕、查封、扣押）之申请时，本应按照公正程序的要求，保障辩护方（犯罪嫌疑人）相应的程序性权利，但却不给其提供行使这种权利的机会，以至于审查程序并无公正可言，那么，审查主体的身份改为法院（法官），对于刑事诉讼程序公正的实现又有何意义呢?![③]

---

① 关于这个问题，从公开发表的论著来看，学术界几乎一致认为，在新的审查模式中，司法权的作用应予以充分考虑。不仅如此，实务界也有人赞同这种主张。参见马荣春等《论公检法刑事诉讼关系之重构》，人民法院出版社，2002，第145~146页。

② 谢佑平、万毅：《刑事诉讼法原则：程序正义的基石》，法律出版社，2002，第147~148页。

③ 当然，从符合国际公约的规定来说，这种改革仍然是有意义的；不仅如此，如果将审查主体的改变视为一种形式变化，那么，这种形式变化或多或少，或早或晚，肯定会对相关的实质变化产生影响。

正如有论者所言:"我国立法所确立的刑事审判前程序构造的格局,只是表明人民法院在审判前程序中不承担裁判职能,不能因此而否定我国刑事审判前程序的构成中存在裁判职能,甚至不能因此而否定我国刑事审判前程序中存在裁判主体。"① 因此,在讨论改革刑事侦查强制性措施的审查模式时,重要的问题并不是原有的审查模式中有无裁判职能,而是由谁承担裁判职能的问题。② 而"由谁承担裁判职能"的问题,绝不仅仅是效果如何的问题,而且还是正当性如何的问题。这个在现代法治国家并无争议的问题,在中国之所以是个问题,当然是由具有中国特色的公、检、法三机关的关系原则所决定的。

根据我国《宪法》和《刑事诉讼法》的规定,刑事诉讼中承担侦查职能的公安机关与主要承担起诉职能的检察机关、承担审判职能的法院,三个机关是"平行关系",即各机关"分工负责、互相配合、互相制约"。在这样的体制下,如何对侦查机关的强制性措施进行司法审查,显然是个问题。由此可见,我国在对侦查中的强制性措施的司法审查体制的完善过程中,需要研究的问题还很多。③

# Judicial Review in Criminal Proceedings: Taking the Judicial Review of Compulsory Measures in Criminal Investigation as an Example

*Wang Minyuan*

【Abstract】 Criminal procedure includes pre-trial procedures, trial procedures and execution procedures. Pretrial procedures can be further divided into criminal

---

① 宋英辉、吴宏耀:《刑事审判前程序研究》,中国政法大学出版社,2002,第104页。
② 当然,对侦查中不同的强制性措施进行控制的方式也有所不同,这个问题也同样重要,只是因为该问题争议不多,故不在此讨论。
③ 2014年12月30日中央全面深化改革领导小组第八次会议审议通过的《关于进一步规范刑事诉讼涉案财物处置工作的意见》,要求各地区各部门要尽快探索建立涉案财物集中管理信息平台,这与我们在此所讨论的主题有相关性,但与本文所讨论的对侦查中涉案财产的查封、扣押、冻结等措施的司法审查,并不相同。

investigation procedures and criminal prosecution procedures. Judicial review in criminal proceedings mainly refers to the pre-review of criminal investigation measures by judicial organs. The development of the legislation and practice of judicial review in criminal proceedings in China reflects the development of rule of law in the field of criminal procedure and embodies the level of general development of rule of law in the country. The Chinese Criminal Procedural Law was first adopted in 1996. Although, after the two major revisions in 1996 and 2012, there have been great improvements in various systems and procedures provided for in the Law, little changes have been made to the system of judicial review in criminal proceedings. To further improve the systems of judicial review of investigation measures in the criminal proceedings, China not only needs to strengthen the judicial review of compulsory measures against personal freedom, but also needs to intensify the judical review of compulsory measures against property, such as seal up, seizure, and freezing of property, in the criminal proceedings.

【**Key words**】 Criminal; Procedure; Judicial Review; Detention; Seal Up and Seizure

# Courts and the Executive: Qualitative Elements of Judicial Review

*Olli Mäenpää*\*

【Abstract】 The role of the courts performing the judicial review of administrative action varies in different legal systems due to context and traditions, juridical cultures, divergent perceptions of the proper functions of the courts, the value accorded to judicial protection and other related factors. In this article the role of the courts and judicial review are explored as guarantees of the rule of law in the exercise of executive powers. Special emphasis is given to the interrelationship between the judiciary and the executive in implementing the rights and obligations as defined by the legislative power. The presentation will also touch upon the division of state power between the judicial, executive and legislative powers.

The objectives of the presentation are threefold. First, an attempt is made to situate more precisely on the judicial map the role of courts in proceedings concerning administrative cases, i. e. cases where executive action is challenged in courts. Second, a mapping exercise also includes a description of the characteristic features of judicial procedure in administrative cases. Third, a qualitative assessment of the basic elements of judicial review is introduced with specific attention to the relationship between the courts and the administration.

## 1. Introduction

A distinct and fruitful tension can be identified in the relationship between the

---

\* Professor, Faculty of Law, University of Helsinki.

courts and the executive with respect to their different functions in exercising public power. The courts exercise judicial power and have a central role in offering legal protection to individuals affected by administrative decision-making. The basic function of the executive, on the other hand, is to exercise administrative power in order to make rights and obligations real within the framework defined by the legislature.

The tension is engendered by the fact that judicial review can be a constraint on the exercise of executive power because of its emphasis on adherence to law and legal principles. On the other hand, judicial review can also support administrative activity since the courts and the executive share the function of guaranteeing the rule of law both in individual cases and in the implementation of legislative intent.

This presentation will focus on the judicial review of administrative action and the role of courts in supervising legality in the exercise of executive power. The role of the courts and judicial review are explored as guarantees of the rule of law in the exercise of executive powers. Special emphasis is given to the interrelationship between the judiciary and the executive in implementing the rights and obligations as defined by the legislative power. In this respect the presentation will also touch upon the division of state power between the judicial, executive and legislative powers.

The objectives of the presentation are threefold. First, an attempt is made to situate more precisely on the judicial map the role of courts in proceedings concerning administrative cases, i. e. cases where executive action is challenged in courts. Second, a mapping exercise also includes a description of the characteristic features of judicial procedure in administrative cases. Third, a qualitative assessment of the basic elements of judicial review is introduced with specific attention to the relationship between the courts and the administration.

Two assumptions are inherent in the discussion of these three topics. It will be taken for granted that the interrelationship between the courts and the executive is significantly different from judicial proceedings concerning conventional civil or criminal cases. It will also be assumed that the basic reason for the judicial and procedural differences can be found in the specific qualities of the executive exercise of public authority. The executive possesses both the capacity and the capability to use power that can be unilateral and regulatory in nature. It is argued that these particular features should be taken seriously into consideration when the subject of judicial review is the executive – private relationship.

## 2. The judicial review of the executive action

### The rule of law and the role of the courts

Judicial control of the executive is one of the cornerstones of the rule of law. Why does the control exercised by an independent judiciary play such an essential role in this respect? One of the key reasons can be found in the very definition of the rule of law. It is conventionally understood as denoting that law acts as a constraint on both individual and public action. Therefore, government and governors must also be subjected to law, and their actions must be independently reviewable.

Protection of individual basic, human and ordinary legal rights can be seen as the nucleus of the rule of law. In this respect, the right to challenge administrative decisions on legal grounds is a central warranty of individual rights. This can also be understood as one of the central reasons for imposing independent judicial control and review on government and executive action. The courts' chief role in this dimension is negative and restrictive. The courts act as a constraint on the exercise of administrative power and as a provider of judicial relief in cases of an administrative encroachment on private rights as well as an abuse of executive power.

But the law also imposes obligations to be complied with and sets down objectives to be achieved. It is the task of the executive to implement legislation and to make rights, obligations and goals real. This is the basis for a constructive and even creative role of the court. Furthermore, since the actualization of rights and obligations can be taken to be one of the basic functions of the executive within the framework created by the legislature, judicial review should also reinforce this task. Consequently, the court's chief role can be characterized as that of a positive guarantor that the legislative intent is carried through and that duties are observed.

### The judicial constellation: the court and the parties

All judicial procedures may be illustrated in the same triangular constellation.

The court is placed at the top of the triangle since it exercises judicial power in the individual case. The adversaries, whether parties in a civil dispute or in criminal proceedings, are placed on opposite sides of the lower corners of the triangle. The opposing parties are considered to occupy equal positions in the procedure and they must also be treated equally.

Equality of arms is the powerful metaphor that the European Court of Justice uses to characterize the parties' positions. It requires each party to be given a reasonable opportunity to present his or her case under conditions that do not place him or her at a substantial disadvantage vis-à-vis the opponent. That right means, in principle, the opportunity for the parties to a trial to have knowledge of and comment on all evidence adduced or observations filed, with a view to influencing the court's decision.

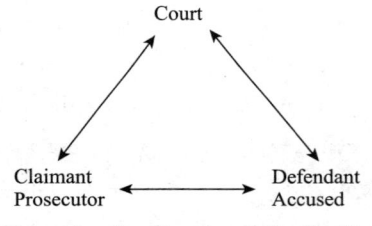

**Figure 1  the Court and the Parties**

## The court and the executive: specific characteristics

The judicial constellation is identical when the court is reviewing executive action. The adversarial parties—the private subject and the executive-are in formally equal positions before the court. Correspondingly, equality of arms between the executive and the private party is also an essential procedural requirement. In reality, however, the constellation is not necessarily similar. It takes on special features as a consequence of the specific characteristics of the relationship between the administrative authority on one hand and the subject of the exercise of public powers on the other.

A variety of specific issues emerge from the characteristics of the judicial constellation in administrative cases. To start with, the focus of the court's review is in most cases on a power relation, a regulatory relationship between the public authority and the private party. As a consequence of its regulatory character, the

## Courts and the Executive: Qualitative Elements of Judicial Review

```
                         Court
                Judicial procedure, Fair trial

   judicial review                      Access to court
   powers of the court                  Judiclel Protection


   Administrative  ◄─────────────►  Private party
   authority         Rule of low     ( Individual, Company )
                  Exercise of public power
```

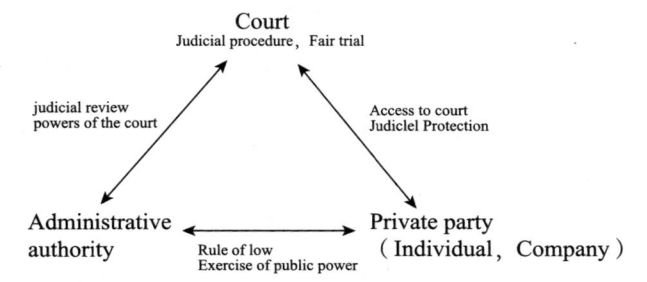

**Figure 2 the Court and the Executive**

administrative relationship is unilateral without consensual or contractual elements. Therefore the court is charged with the challenging duty of guaranteeing the fairness of the trial in the conduct of the procedure. More specifically, how can procedural fairness and equality of arms be guaranteed when one of the parties has unilateral executive powers and the other party is subject to the exercise of that power?

Since law governs the relationship between the executive and the private subject, legality and the rule of law are particularly central requirements in administrative decision-making. It is the court's task both to judge the legality of the decision and to provide judicial protection to the private party. Due to the varying effects of the administrative decision, the private party's access to the court is governed by specific rules of standing, which are more complex than in civil or criminal procedures.

The court needs to assess the action ( or possibly in action) of the administrative agency or official in order to provide judicial protection. Both the scope and intensity of the court's review therefore become central issues. The powers of the court are also of significance: how far and to what degree of detail can or should the court interfere into the area of the executive by exercising its judicial powers in order to produce effective protection and redress.

In this article, these specific features of the judicial constellation will be characterized with particular reference to the accessibility and quality of judicial protection. The focus of the analysis will be on the relationship between the courts and the executive action in five dimensions:

(1) Access to justice—Individual access to court in administrative cases.

(2) The scope of judicial review—Judicial reviewability of executive action and

deference accorded to administrative decision-making.

(3) Procedural fairness—Guarantees of a fair hearing in proceedings concerning administrative cases.

(4) The effectiveness of judicial remedies—Effective remedies for unilateral administrative action.

(5) The independence of the judiciary—Guarantees of the independence and impartiality of the court hearing administrative cases.

## 3. Access to a court in administrative cases

### Three components of access

Access to justice is based on three main components: personal, substantive and procedural. In civil and criminal processes these components are fairly clear-cut and unproblematic, whereas in administrative cases all the components are central. They can significantly either limit or extend the jurisdiction of the courts and the scope of judicial review with respect to administrative action.

Personal access determines who can initiate the judicial procedure by challenging an administrative action in a court, while substantive access defines what kind of administrative actions can be reviewed by a court. Procedural access is a term that becomes applicable once the hurdles of personal and substantive access have been surpassed. It denotes the procedural rules and requirements governing the conduct and course of the procedure. All these components are more or less regulated in procedural legislation and usually, in a more nuanced manner, by case law.

The basis of all three components is regulated, albeit in a fairly general manner, in European law, thus forming a general European standard on access to judicial procedure. According to Article 6 (1) of the European Convention of Human Rights (ECHR) on the *Right to a fair trial*:

> In the determination of his civil rights and obligations or of any criminal charge against him, everyone is entitled to a fair and public hearing within a reasonable time by an independent and impartial tribunal established by law.

Similarly, *the Charter of Fundamental Rights of the European Union* lays down the basic access rules with respect to the application of EU law. Pursuant to Article 47 defining the *Right to an effective remedy and to a fair trial*:

> Everyone whose rights and freedoms guaranteed by the law of the Union are violated has the right to an effective remedy before a tribunal in compliance with the conditions laid down in this Article. Everyone is entitled to a fair and public hearing within a reasonable time by an independent and impartial tribunal previously established by law. Everyone shall have the possibility of being advised, defended and represented.

## Personal access

Personal access (standing) is in the first place accorded to the direct subject of an administrative action. This includes persons whose rights or obligations are determined or whose rights and freedoms are violated by an administrative decision. The person to whom the administrative decision is directly addressed or who is directly affected by its outcome is entitled to challenge the administrative decision. For example, an applicant whose application for a license or a social benefit has been totally or partially rejected or a person on whom an obligation to pay taxes has been imposed has standing as a party and may thus challenge that decision.

Gradually, standing has been extended to those who are only indirectly but factually or substantially affected by a decision, e.g. to competitors in cases involving the application of business legislation and neighbors in environmental regulation cases. In this respect, special attention may be given to the harmful effects of decisions implementing environmental legislation. If such effects are of direct concern to the actual neighbors and those living in the neighborhood, they may appeal, for instance a siting permit for an industrial plant, which can be hazardous to health.

## The reviewability of administrative action

Substantive access defines what kind of administrative action can be challenged before the court and to what extent they can be reviewed. In other words, substantive access is about the reviewability of administrative action. With respect to substantive access, the right to challenge executive action usually extends to administrative decisions determining or pertaining to rights or obligations. The right to challenge the legality of such decisions can be regarded as a fundamental element of the system of legal protection and judicial review.

More concretely, the access right would encompass decisions of administrative authorities particularly concerning administrative regulation (administrative licenses, land-use planning etc.), taxation, public services and social welfare entitlements. In these areas of administrative action, an appeal may be directed against any final act or measure of an administrative authority. A problematic gap can still exist in the reviewability of executive action. If an authority remains passive, delays the matter, or completely fails to act without making a decision, an appeal is not necessarily available against such conduct or omission. If inaction cannot be challenged in a court, an administrative complaint can usually be lodged with an Ombudsman.

## Procedural access

Procedural access is an important supplement to personal and substantive access. It determines how the procedure is conducted and what should be expected of the parties once they have gained formal access to the procedure. Central issues include the kind of procedural obligations the parties must comply with and the kind of procedural rights they are entitled to exercise.

Procedural access may be seriously hampered if the emphasis is solely on procedural formalities and strict compliance with them. The procedural requirements should not overshadow the actual purpose of the procedure, which after all is to provide judicial protection for the private party. Rigorous observation of due process should not pose an obstacle to attaining this goal. This is why the procedural rules should be designed so as to facilitate access to justice rather than to hinder it.

Since a considerable gap usually exists between the information and procedural skills of the private party and the administrative authority, the procedural rules should be simple, transparent, easily compliable with and foreseeable. In addition, the court should actively oversee that the individual is not left at a disadvantage because of his or her inferior procedural skills or informational abilities.

## 4. The scope of judicial review

An essential element defining the relationship between the court and the executive is the court's ability to perform inclusive and wide-ranging judicial scrutiny. Since judicial review interferes with the executive, at least whenever an administrative authority can be shown to have acted illegally, the range of that review is a measure of the judicial power vis-á-vis the executive power. Consequently, to the extent that courts can investigate the lawfulness of the administrative action, they can also affect the separation of powers between the judiciary and the executive. In this sense, the scope of judicial review also has constitutional dimensions.

### Deference and the range of review

With respect to the range and depth of review, one of the central questions is how much deference the court can or should concede to the executive authority. Should the court be an active investigator or only a neutral or passive referee? Should the scope of review be limited only to the formal and procedural requirements of the exercise of administrative powers, or should the court have the authority to also scrutinize and judge the use of discretionary powers? In other terms, should the court's default approach be to give a "green light" to administrative decision-making unless the decision is manifestly unlawful or based on grave unreasonableness, or should the court apply a more stringent and in-depth degree of scrutiny, amounting to a "red light" approach?[1]

In common-law jurisdictions judicial deference usually means that courts should primarily give effect to the legislative intent and its implementation by the executive.[2] Therefore the courts should also be deferential to administrative decision-making and accord administrative decision-making a variable degree of

---

[1] The traffic-light theory was first introduced by *Carol Harlow & Richard Rawlings*, Law and Administration, London, 1997, pp. 29 – 127, 1st ed. 1984.

[2] Paul Daly, *A theory of deference in administrative law*, Cambridge, 2012.

deference.① A deferential treatment of the executive power may also imply that the courts restrain from examining the discretion used by an administrative authority with the exception of clearly unreasonable interpretations. The U. S. Supreme Court's Chevron case law suggests that the court must "give effect to the unambiguously expressed intent of Congress". If the statute is silent or ambiguous, the court must defer to any reasonable interpretation made by the administrative authority.②

Continental European jurisdictions apply more varied standards of deference. For instance, in Finland, Sweden and France the use of the discretionary powers of the executive is subject to judicial review even though the standards of review may vary. For instance, the Finnish administrative courts have (and use) the power to investigate whether the authority has complied with general administrative principles (e. g. objectivity, equality, impartiality, proportionality, the protection of legitimate interests and the prohibition to abuse power) when exercising its discretionary powers. Even if the administrative authority has wide discretionary powers, the conformity of the use of those powers with these legal principles comes under the scope of the review of legality. The review of legality should also be extended to how the authorities comply with constitutional rights.③

## The limits of judicial power

Even though the standard and scope of judicial review may vary in different jurisdictions, it is normally focused only on whether the administration acted in a legal manner and within the powers defined by law and legal principles. Courts should show reticence in other issues that are not directly connected to the evaluation of legality. Policy issues and the actual exercise of executive power are especially considered to limit judicial review.

Administrative policies are considered to remain in the exclusive domain of the executive. Therefore the investigation of the advisability and expediency of an

---

① See in general Paul Daly, *A theory of deference in administrative law*, Cambridge, 2012.
② Chevron U. S. A. Inc. v. Natural Resources Defence Council Inc., 467 U. S. 837 (1984), pp. 843 – 844.
③ See e. g. E. Spiliotopoulos (ed.), *Towards a Unified Protection of Citizens in Europe* (?), London, 2000.

administrative decision falls outside the jurisdiction of the courts, and policy issues should be left outside of judicial review. However, the border line between administrative policy and discretion is difficult to draw, and the limits of judicial review in this dimension are open to interpretation.

Another limit of judicial power is based on constitutional principles, more precisely on the separation of powers doctrine. According to that doctrine, the actual adoption of an administrative decision belongs to the exclusive sphere of executive power. Because the courts are judicial organs, they lack the power to exercise executive power and to make original administrative decisions. Consequently, a court should not substitute itself for the administrative authority which has adopted the contested decision. This limitation can only be indicative since the courts are commonly considered to have the power to amend administrative decisions, at least under some criteria.

## Judicial activism

In addition to the scope of judicial review, another testing stone of the character of the court—executive relationship is the degree of judicial activism. How dynamic should the court be? An active court is required to conduct the procedure in an active manner, to investigate on its own initiative, and the court is also empowered to take a detailed stand on the contents of the case. In this manner, the court is thought to be able to enhance the equilibrium between the inherently unbalanced relationship between the executive and the private party.

Particularly continental jurisdictions with separate administrative courts attribute an active role to the courts. [1]The administrative courts are under a general obligation to actively conduct the procedure. The procedure is characterized by an investigation principle, according to which the court is responsible for comprehensively scrutinizing the contested decision. Although the burden of proof lies with the parties, the court may also obtain evidence and factual information on its own initiative, if this is deemed necessary to supplement the evidence supplied by the parties and to guarantee the fairness of the procedure.

---

[1] S. Galera (ed.), *Judicial review: a comparative analysis inside the European legal system*, Strasbourg, 2010.

An alternative procedural model is applied in common-law jurisdictions. It relies more clearly on the activity of the parties, who are expected to obtain and present the substantive evidence. Since the parties share the burden of proof, the court usually does not act on its own initiative. In fact, the court is expected to base its decision only onthe evidence put forward by the parties, the executive party and the private party.

## 5. Procedural fairness

### Fair trial in administrative cases

Guarantees of procedural fairness must apply also in judicial proceedings concerning administrative cases. These guarantees include the right to be heard, the procedurally equal status of the parties and a public hearing in addition to the essential right of access to a court.

### Equality of the parties

A key measure of fairness in judicial procedure is equality. Only equal treatment of the parties and their equal procedural rights and obligations are capable of guaranteeing a procedural balance that will put neither party at a disadvantage. In the judicial review of administrative action, the requirement of procedural equality can be approached from two angles, formal and material. Formal equality can be accomplished by treating both parties—both the executive and the private party—in exactly the same manner. On the other hand, a prerequisite of material equality mandates that the actual differences of the parties are accounted for without compromising the equilibrium of the procedure.

In administrative decision-making the administrative authority usually has a *de facto* superiority of power compared to the private party. The executive's superior position is based on several factors, usually including the right to exercise unilateral public power, sophisticated expertise in legal and administrative issues, and broader access to government-held data and information. Of significance is also the administrative authority's general proficiency in conducting the decision-making procedure and participating in a judicial procedure. It is rarely and perhaps only in the case of large companies or organizations that the private party is actually capable of matching the government in all these areas.

As a consequence of these and similar factors, a considerable gap usually lies between the information and procedural skills of the private party and the administrative authority. Therefore the procedural rules must be simple, transparent, easy to comply with and foreseeable. The court conducting the procedure must also actively oversee that the private party is not left at a disadvantage because of his or her inferior procedural skills or informational abilities. Similarly, the European Court of Human Rights has stressed that the requirement of equality of arms implies that "each party must be afforded a reasonable opportunity to present his case-including his evidence-under conditions that do not place him at a substantial disadvantage vis-à-vis his opponent". [1]

Against this backdrop, material equality as a supplement to formal equality is stressed in the Finnish law governing judicial proceedings in administrative courts. To start with, the administrative authority is not considered to have its own, individual rights that it should defend as an adversary of the private party. Since public authority belongs to the public domain and is exercised in the general interest, the agency or official does not possess the administrative authority. Procedurally, the agency is a party, but it is bound to the principles of legality, objectivity and impartiality as well as to the obligation to protect the general interest. Its position as a procedural party neither relieves the agency of its official duties nor does it authorize partial action.

That is why the administrative authority must act in a detached and impartial manner in the judicial procedure. For instance, the authority must provide all the evidence at its disposal even if it might be compromising for the authority's case. Further, the official statements submitted by the authority must be based on a neutral and objective evaluation.

## The hearing and contradictory procedure

The gist of the judicial control of executive action is the hearing conducted by the court. Both the private party and the public authority have a right to be heard.

---

[1] Vilén v. Finland, ECHR 2009, § 21; Helle v. Finland, ECHR 1997, § § 53 – 54.

Both parties (or all the parties, as the case may be) must be presented an opportunity to comment on the demands of the other parties. They are also entitled to give their opinions on all the factual evidence that may affect the resolution of the matter.

In order to exercise the right to be heard, the private party to an administrative judicial procedure enjoys considerable right of access to the case documents. The private appellant usually gains access also to classified documents if they may be or may have been of influence in the processing of the case.

According to the European Court of Human Rights, the adversarial nature of the procedure must be guaranteed so that "each party must in principle have the opportunity not only to make known any evidence needed for his claims to succeed, but also to have knowledge of and comment on all evidence adduced or observations filed with a view to influencing the court's decision."[1] Such a contradictory nature of the procedure is necessary since "the very purpose of adversarial procedure…is to prevent the Court from being influenced by arguments which the parties have been unable to discuss".[2]

**Due process**

Due process denotes the rights and duties of the parties involved, but it also imposes duties on the court. Since the rule of law applies also to courts, due process is a guarantee of both the procedural predictability and fairness of the proceedings. The minimum requirements for due process are clearly defined procedural rules, their regulation in law and their vigorous application in individual proceedings. All cases and parties must be treated equally and with equal fairness.

## 6. The effectiveness of judicial review

The judicial review of administrative action can only be successful if it is sufficiently effective to provide redress and to reinstate the status quo. Important factors in measuring effectiveness are the extensiveness and intensiveness of the

---

[1] Mantovanelli v. France, ECHR 1997, § 33.
[2] See generally Kress v. France, ECHR 2001.

judicial review. In other words, how wide-ranging are the judicial powers of the court to reconsider the administrative action, and can the judicial remedy enable the restoration of the status quo?

The effectiveness of the judicial powers can be measured in a number of dimensions. One can assess, for instance, the remedial, reformatory, constructive, compensatory, constitutional and interim powers of the court.

*Remedial powers* define the main foundations of any judicial remedy. In short, the court has the power to uphold or annul the challenged administrative decision. The court may also refer the case back to the administrative authority for reconsideration.

*Reformatory powers* refer to the court's power to substantially amend or otherwise modify the administrative decision subject to review. For instance, in cases concerning the application of environmental legislation or other regulatory decisions, the courts may have the power to amend a positive decision by supplementing it with more stringent conditions or limitations.

*Constructive powers* refer generally to the court's power to mandate new obligations, restrictions or positive objectives on the administrative authority. Such powers are situated squarely in the problematic boundary between the judiciary and the executive. As a principle, the court cannot assume executive functions, but on the other hand, it must provide effective judicial protection. How far does the objective of remedial effectiveness empower the court to extend its jurisdiction into the realm of the executive in a constructive manner? The established doctrine and case law tend to favor considerable reservation in this respect. However, even a more practical and extensive interpretation is possible if more emphasis is put on the corrective outcome of the review.

*Compensatory powers* refer to the court's power to hear restitution claims arising from a violation of rights or duties under administrative law and to award compensation for damages caused by the activity (or failure to act) of an administrative agency. In some jurisdictions (e. g. Germany and Finland) the compensatory powers of the administrative courts are limited since in most cases only the ordinary civil courts can award damages against the administration. In principle, the powers of administrative courts could quite as well comprise compensatory powers since there are no fundamental reasons to limit their remedial powers in this respect.

*Constitutional powers* define the boundary between the judiciary and the legislature. A critical yardstick is whether the courts are empowered to declare a legal provision null and void on the basis that it is contrary to the constitution. The ordinary courts are usually considered to lack the power to invalidate an act of parliament even if they find it to be in conflict with constitutional provisions. Similarly, the courts are generally not empowered to declare a legal provision null and void on the basis that it is contrary to the constitution. If the conflict between a legal norm and the constitution is clear, however, the courts may be under an obligation to refuse to apply the law and, instead, give precedence to the constitution in a concrete case.

With respect to delegated legislation and different kinds of administrative norms and instructions, the powers of the courts are normally not limited. The courts may thus misapply government decrees and similar administrative norms of an inferior normative rank to the extent that they conflict with the constitution or an act of Parliament.

*Interim powers* refer to the court's power to issue injunctions to the administrative agencies and to stay the execution of an administrative decision. Since the duration of a judicial procedure can vary and proceedings can be delayed, interim powers may offer significant, albeit provisional protection.

## 7. The independence of the judiciary

A fair trial is possible only in independent courts of law. With specific respect to the courts reviewing the legality of administrative cases, it is of paramount importance that the administration cannot wield an influence on how the courts handle the cases. Courts are not an extension of the executive, nor can they receive any instructions from administrative agencies or officials. Integrity, authority and legitimacy are of the highest significance in the judicial decision-making when reviewing the legality of the executive arm of the state.

As a general requirement, the division of state powers mandates that the courts act independently of the executive, the legislative power and other courts. The courts must also be able to conduct the procedure without interference from the media, political organizations and other external actors. The only legitimate and lawful method of influencing the decision-making of the court is by way of procedural action by the parties. Therefore it is both legitimate and essential that the authority whose decision is challenged can produce evidence and specify the grounds that support its decision.

## 8. Concluding observations

A well-functioning judicial review and effective remedies are necessary guarantees of legal protection for the subject of executive power. They are also needed to ensure compliance with law in administrative action. Even in an ideal situation in which laws are correctly observed and implemented by the administration in a proactive and practical manner, the possibility of judicial review would still be needed for preventive reasons.

The role of the courts performing the judicial review of administrative action varies in different legal systems due to context and traditions, juridical cultures, divergent perceptions of the proper functions of the courts, the value accorded to judicial protection and other related factors. For these reasons, it is difficult to generalize and to define a generic standard of the judicial constellation with respect to the relationship between the courts and the executive.

What probably can be accomplished, however, is to analyze and describe the central dimensions and qualitative elements of such a standard. It can be argued that foremost on the list of indispensable elements are adequate access to a court, guarantees of procedural fairness, a sufficiently broad scope of judicial review, effective remedies and the independence of the courts.

The chief purpose of this article has been to chart some of the principal factors defining the role of both the court and the parties in this relationship. The focus has been on traditional nation states, their constitutional systems and administrative law regimes. The emergence and growth of trans-national and global administration will be likely to complicate the role, scope and procedure of judicial review, but these issues will need to be addressed separately and in more detail.

# 法院与行政机关: 司法审查的定性因素

奥利·玛恩帕

**【摘要】** 由于受到不同的语境和传统、法律文化、对法院功能的理解、司法保护被赋予的价值等相关因素的影响,负责对行政行为进行司法审查的法院在不同的法律系统中所扮演的角色各不相同。本文探讨了在行政权力的行使过程中,法院和司法审查所起到的作用,重点讨论了在实施立法机关所界定的权利和义务的过程中司法机关与行政机关之间的相互关系,并简要阐述了国家权力在司法、行政和立法机关之间的分配。本文的目的有三个。首先,力图在司法系统中为法院在行政案件——对行政行为提出挑战的案件——中起到的作用找到一个更为准确的定位。其次,这种定位还包括对行政案件中司法程序的特征的描述。第三,本文还对司法审查的基本要素,特别是法院和行政机关之间的关系进行了定量评估。

# 中国法院司法公开制度与实践

田 禾*

**【摘要】** 司法公开制度是人民法院必须严格遵循的一项宪法原则，也是一项重要的司法制度。司法公开是中国司法改革的重要内容，近年来，无论从制度安排和实践上都有较大的推进。本文首先分析了中国司法公开的时代背景。随着经济的发展，中国社会利益的分化对司法提出了较高的要求，司法公信力和司法权威受到了挑战，司法公开是法治社会的基本要求，有助于提升司法公信力，也可以满足公众对知情权的需要。司法公开制度的发展演进体现出由表及里的态势，尽管如此，不同社会群体对司法公开的推进看法仍然不一。本文还讨论了最高人民法院实际督促领导全国法院推进司法公开的情况，以及第三方学术机构对司法公开的测评情况，分析了司法公开取得的成绩和改进的方向。

**【关键词】** 司法 司法公开 第三方测评

司法公开制度是人民法院必须严格遵循的一项宪法原则。[①] 《中共中央

---

\* 中国社会科学院法学研究所研究员。
① 中国《宪法》第125条规定："人民法院审理案件，除法律规定的特别情况外，一律公开进行。"《刑事诉讼法》第11条规定："人民法院审判案件，除本法另有规定的以外，一律公开进行。"第183条规定："人们法院审判第一审案件应当公开进行，但是有关国家秘密或者个人隐私的案件，不公开审理；涉及商业秘密的案件，当事人申请不公开审理的，可以不公开审理。不公开审理的案件，应当当庭宣布不公开审理的理由。"第274条规定："审判的时候被告人不满十八周岁的案件，不公开审理。"第196条规定："宣告判决，一律公开进行。"《民事诉讼法》第10条规定："人民法院审理民事案件，依照法律规定实行合议、回避、公开审判和两审终审制度。"第134条规定："人民法院审理民事案件，除涉及国家机密、个人隐私或者法律另有规定的以外，应当公开进行。离婚案件，涉及商业秘密的案件，当事人申请不公开审理的，可以不公开审理。"第148条规定："人民法院对公开审理或不公开审理的案件，一律公开宣告判决。"第156条规定："公众可以查阅发生法律效力的判决书、裁定书，但涉及国家秘密、商业秘密和个人隐私的内容除外。"《行政诉讼法》第7条规定："人民法院审理行政案件，依法实行合议、回避、公开审判和两审终审制度。"第54条规定："人民法院公开审理行政案件，但涉及国家秘密、个人隐私和法律另有规定的除外。"

关于全面深化改革若干重大问题的决定》明确提出，要"深化司法体制改革，加快建设公正高效权威的社会主义司法制度，维护人民权益，让人民群众在每一个司法案件中都感受到公平正义"。《中共中央关于全面推进依法治国若干重大问题的决定》也提出，要"构建开放、动态、透明、便民的阳光司法机制，推进审判公开、检务公开、警务公开、狱务公开，依法及时公开司法依据、程序、流程、结果和生效法律文书，杜绝暗箱操作"。近年来，最高人民法院发布了一系列司法公开的文件，推动了中国各级法院的司法公开工作，司法透明程度明显提升。本文将就中国司法公开的制度安排和公开实践做出分析。

## 一　中国司法公开的制度安排

近年来，司法公开一直是中国司法体制改革的重要内容。自20世纪90年代以来，最高人民法院先后多次下发推动司法公开的文件，包括《关于严格执行公开审判制度的若干规定》（法发〔2009〕3号）、《关于人民法院执行公开的若干规定》（法发〔2006〕35号）、《关于加强人民法院审判公开工作的若干意见》（法发〔2007〕20号）、《关于进一步加强民意沟通工作的意见》（法发〔2009〕20号）、《关于司法公开的六项规定》（法发〔2009〕58号）、《关于确定司法公开示范法院的决定》（法〔2010〕383号）、《关于人民法院在互联网公布裁判文书的规定》（2010年11月21日发布，2013年11月21日修改）、《关于推进司法公开三大平台建设的若干意见》（2013年11月21日发布）、《关于公布失信被执行人名单信息的若干规定》（2013年7月19日发布）等，这些规定大力地推动了中国的司法公开实践。

上述文件中，《关于加强人民法院审判公开工作的若干意见》（以下简称《意见》）系统规定了人民法院司法公开的原则和要求。《意见》提出要准确把握人民法院审判公开工作的基本原则，做到依法公开、及时公开、全面公开。《意见》要求人民法院以设置宣传栏或者公告牌、建立网站等方便查阅的形式，公布本院管辖的各类案件的立案条件、法律文书的样式、诉讼费用的收费标准及缓、减、免交诉讼费的基本条件和程序、案件审理与执行工作流程等事项。为了方便当事人及其委托代理人及时了解与当事人诉讼权利、义务相关的审判和执行信息，人民法院还应建立和公布案件办理情况查询机制，有条件的人民法院对于庭审活动和相关重要审判活动还应当录音、录像，建立审判工作的声像档案，并允许当事人查阅和复制。

《意见》对裁判文书的公开也做出了相关规定。各高级人民法院应根据本辖区内的情况制定通过出版物、局域网、互联网等方式公布生效裁判文书的具体办法，逐步加大生效裁判文书公开的力度。裁判文书的制作应当符合最高人民法院颁布的裁判文书样式要求，繁简得当、易于理解，内容应包含裁判过程、事实、理由和裁判依据等要素。

《关于司法公开的六项规定》则从立案公开、庭审公开、执行公开、听证公开、文书公开和审务公开6个方面，对人民法院依法公开、及时公开、全面公开做出了详细规定。

在立案方面，各类案件的立案条件，立案流程，法律文书样式，诉讼费用标准，缓、减、免交诉讼费程序，当事人重要权利义务，诉讼和执行风险提示以及可选择的诉讼外纠纷解决方式等内容，应当通过适当的形式向社会和当事人公开。

在庭审方面，各级人民法院应建立健全有序开放、有效管理的旁听和报道庭审的规则，消除对公众和媒体知情监督的障碍。

在执行方面，法院应当将执行的依据、标准、规范、程序以及执行全过程向社会和当事人公开，但涉及国家秘密、商业秘密、个人隐私等法律禁止公开的信息除外。为此，法院应进一步健全和完善执行信息查询系统，扩大查询范围，为当事人查询执行案件信息提供方便。

在审务方面，人民法院的审判管理工作以及与审判工作有关的其他管理活动因与审判活动密切相关，也应向全社会公开。各级人民法院应逐步建立和完善互联网站和其他信息公开平台，通过便捷、有效的方式及时向社会公开关于法院工作的方针政策、各种规范性文件、审判指导意见以及非涉密司法统计数据及分析报告，公开重大案件的审判情况、重要研究成果等。

在裁判文书方面，所公开的裁判文书应做到说理公开，充分表述当事人的诉辩意见、证据的采信理由、事实的认定、适用法律的推理与解释过程。除涉及国家秘密、商业秘密、个人隐私以及其他不适宜公开的案件和调解结案的案件外，人民法院的裁判文书应当在互联网上公开发布。为了满足公众对裁判文书公开的需求，最高人民法院于2010年发布了《关于人民法院在互联网公布裁判文书的规定》。2013年，最高人民法院根据信息化发展和司法公开工作的形势，对该规定做了较大修改，明确了裁判文书公开的范围、方式，强调裁判文书以公开为原则、不公开为例外，并要求各级法院的裁判文书统一上传到中国裁判文书网，集中对社会发布。

2013年,最高人民法院还发布了《关于推进司法公开三大平台建设的若干意见》,将司法公开浓缩为三大内容,即审判流程公开、裁判文书公开、执行信息公开,要求全力推进与上述三大公开内容相关的平台建设。

2015年2月,最高人民法院发布《关于全面深化人民法院改革的意见——人民法院第四个五年改革纲要(2014—2018)》。纲要对司法公开提出了更高的要求,如完善庭审公开制度,完善审判信息数据库,加强中国裁判文书网网站建设,整合各类执行信息等。

从制度演进来看,司法公开的制度演进呈现由粗略公开到精细化公开,由形式公开到实质性公开的发展过程,公开工作层层递进,由表及里,逐渐"变被动公开为主动公开,变内部公开为外部公开,变选择性公开为全面公开,变形式公开为实质公开"[1]。从公众的反应来看,司法公开受到普遍欢迎,并成为公众了解司法制度运行的重要途径。法律职业人员对司法公开的反应则出现一定的分化。律师群体认为公开还应该加速,而目前司法公开的步伐仍显缓慢。法学工作者则肯定司法公开的意义,但对司法公开的成效表现出疑虑。法官们则有不少人对司法公开持抵触态度,这是因为现有司法环境不好,案多人少,法官压力过大,司法公开无疑加大了法官的工作量。此外,司法公开的范围界定模糊,法官无所适从,也是其抵触的重要原因之一。

## 二 司法公开在中国的现实意义

改革开放以来,我国的经济总量上升到今天的世界第二位,人民的生活水平大大提升,国家综合实力和国际影响力也不断提升。但是,随着经济的发展,社会利益分化也比较明显,生态环境、食品安全、医疗纠纷、经济纠纷等方面的矛盾不断增加,这些问题都对国家的司法制度提出了较高的要求。司法是国家专门机关依照法定职权和法定程序,运用法律处理特定案件,解决特定纠纷,维护当事人权利的活动。司法的功能是定纷止争,通过将法律适用于特定案件,达到解决当事人纠纷、维持社会秩序的目的。但现实生活中,由于个别法官的徇私枉法,也由于司法公开的不足,人们怀疑法官"暗箱操作"、"吃了原告吃被告",司法公信力受到了很大的

---

[1] 引自最高人民法院院长周强在2013年11月27日全国法院司法公开工作推进会上的讲话《筑牢司法公开的基石 以公开促公正 以公开树公信》,人民法院网,http://www.chinacourt.org/article/detail/2013/11/id/1151559.shtml,最后访问日期:2016年5月1日。

质疑，司法权威一落千丈。

司法制度是现代法治社会的重要制度之一。司法公开是现代社会司法文明状况的重要判断标准，[①] 其对于法治的实现，乃至对于当今中国的司法制度运行都具有重要的推动作用。

第一，司法公开有助于防止司法腐败，实现司法正义。司法机关是维护社会正义的最后一道防线，正义不仅要实现，而且要以人们看得见的方式实现。[②] 当前，实践中存在的"司法不公"、"司法腐败"、"司法过程不透明"、"暗箱操作"等现象，是人们质疑司法公正性的主要原因，因此，提升司法过程和结果的透明程度是治理司法腐败、纠正司法不公的重要路径。法院向公众全面、准确地公开所掌握的各类信息，不仅有利于公众了解专业性很强的司法程序、法官行使自由裁量权的考量因素、司法裁决结果，并有效地监督司法行为，督促法官慎重从事，也有利于堵塞各种徇私枉法和腐败的渠道，切断法官与当事人之间非正常联系的途径，使司法腐败行为无处遁形。

第二，司法公开有助于提高司法公信力，维护司法权威。公信力和权威是法院司法活动的出发点和落脚点，是法院的生命所在。近年来，由于司法体制上的一些弊端，[③] 加上个别法官的枉法裁判，公众对司法判决的认可度不高，一些案件不能做到案结事了，一些生效判决得不到有效执行，即便经过终审或再审，当事人仍拒绝接受案件判决，而选择信访等诉讼外的渠道寻求进一步的救济，涉法涉诉信访案件的数量逐年增多。个案的司法公信力欠缺可能演化成普遍的社会信任危机，这对一个国家的司法系统而言是极为危险之事，故提升司法公信力、维护司法公正是当前中国司法机关的当务之急。司法公正不能依靠司法机关的自我标榜，只有得到公众的认可，司法才能具有公信力和权威性。司法要获得公众的认可，必须让公众尽可能详细地了解司法的全过程，使公众最大限度地了解司法权力的运作方式和运行结果，消除公众对司法机关的猜疑，减少当事人信访、拒

---

[①] 周功满：《论司法公开之度》，《理论观察》2010 年第 2 期。
[②] 〔英〕丹宁：《法律的正当程序》，李克强、杨百揆、刘庸安译，法律出版社，2011，第 23 页。
[③] 例如，目前中国地方各级人民法院隶属于各级行政管辖区域，在人事管理和组织关系方面适用的是地方主管、上级司法机关协管的方式，经费由同级财政负担，法院行政化趋势严重，不仅出现了司法地方化现象，也导致党政部门干预司法的现象增多。

不履行判决等情况的发生，使司法正义变成看得见、摸得到的正义。

第三，司法公开有助于提升法官的能力，提高司法水平。司法公开对法官提出了很高的要求，因为司法公开使法院的司法活动置于社会的全时空监督之下，司法机关及其司法人员的任何行为都将接受公众的评论与判断，任何有悖常理的事实认定、法律适用都可能受到最严厉、最直接的质疑和批判。以审判信息公开为例，如果要求法院将案件的开庭日程、庭审过程以及裁判文书等内容向全体公众公开，法院在司法过程中就会更加注重庭审程序的合法性、案件证据的充分性、法律适用的准确性以及裁判文书写作的规范性。法官会更加审慎地对待司法参与人的意见，认定事实和适用法律会更慎重，以便对案件争议得出符合法律规定和客观事实的正确结论。因此，可以说，司法公开实际上可以倒逼司法机关及其司法人员提高办案水平和办案质量，提升司法能力。

第四，司法公开有助于保障公众知情权和当事人的合法权益。司法活动是公权力活动的一部分，除国家安全、商业秘密和公民隐私等内容外，公民有权知晓其运行的全部信息。即便是涉及上述几方面的内容，公民也有权知晓其判决信息。司法公开便于社会公众参与司法活动，监督司法活动，是实现司法民主的重要路径。

司法公开的主要内容是法院向诉讼参与人及社会公众公开以审判为核心的相关司法信息，以促进和实现司法公正。

司法机关公开的工作信息、诉讼指南、审判信息、执行信息可以使当事人充分了解自己的诉权、诉权的行使方式及行使诉权过程中可能面临的法律风险，了解司法活动的内容和进程，进而正确、及时地行使自己的权利，采取合法手段维护自己的权益。

## 三 中国司法公开的实践进展

司法有广义和狭义之分，狭义的司法是指国家审判机关——法院依据职权和程序处理案件、解决纠纷的活动，即法院的审判活动。[①] 司法公开的信息不限于审判活动的信息，一切与审判活动相关的信息都应该公开。本文探讨的是狭义的司法及司法公开。

---

① 广义的司法机关包括检察机关，司法活动为法院的审判和检察机关的侦查、公诉以及法律监督活动。

### (一) 最高人民法院推动的司法公开取得了很大的成效

首先，审判全流程公开。2014年11月，中国审判流程信息公开网正式开通，人们可查询最高人民法院以及北京、浙江、重庆等20个省（区、市）地方法院的案件审判流程信息和进展情况。中国审判流程信息公开网还向案件当事人及诉讼代理人提供了庭审笔录、庭审录像和电子卷宗的查询服务。

其次，裁判文书公开。2013年12月，最高人民法院上线中国裁判文书网，并要求全国3000多家各级法院在中国裁判文书网公开裁判文书，接受公众监督。截至2014年11月底，中国裁判文书网发布生效裁判文书近300万份。

再次，执行方面推进有力。最高人民法院建立了全国法院失信被执行人名单信息公布与查询平台、被执行人信息查询平台和执行案件流程信息公开平台。截至2014年12月，最高人民法院公布失信被执行人超77万名，其中自然人66.6万余名，法人及其他组织10万余个。①

最后，司法公开形式创新。科学技术推动了人民法院的司法公开形式创新。各级法院加快科技法庭建设，以浙江法院为例，其1783个审判法庭全部建成数字化法庭，并在全省90个看守所建成92个远程视频提讯室，所有开庭案件都实现了全程同步录音录像、同步记录、同步显示。② 此外，新媒体推动了司法公开，一些大案要案，如国家发改委原副主任刘铁男受贿案、刘汉黑社会案和多地官员腐败案，均通过微博进行了直播，彰显了科技对推动司法公开的巨大威力。

### (二) 第三方学术机构对司法公开的推进作用

由第三方评估机构对法院司法公开的成效进行评估，创新了司法公开监督的形式。2011年起，中国社会科学院法学研究所（以下简称"社科院法学所"）对高级人民法院和全国较大的市的中级人民法院的司法公开进行测评并每年发布《中国政府透明度年度报告》，2013年最高人民法院的司法公开也被纳入测评范围。2013年开始，社科院法学所受浙江省高级人民法

---

① 《2014年里的司法公开八项举措 你感受到了吗？》，新华网，http://news.xinhuanet.com/legal/2015-01/16/c_1114027442.htm，最后访问日期：2015年3月9日。

② 周斌、袁定波：《司法公开全面提速公平正义触手可及》，《法制日报》2014年12月26日。

院的委托，对浙江省3级103家法院①开展3年期的阳光司法指数测评。测评内容包括审务公开、立案庭审公开、裁判文书公开、执行公开和保障机制5个板块。课题组通过查询法院网站、现场考察立案大厅、抽查法院案卷、进行电话验证、法院自报数据等方式，对法院审判全流程的公开情况进行了全方位测评。与社科院法学所自行开展的中国司法透明度测评不同的是，浙江阳光司法指数在方法上更为综合，不仅有网络测评，还有实体测评。由于阳光司法指数测评是司法实务部门与国家最高法学研究机构合作完成的，在国内尚属第一次，该测评在推动司法公开工作和法学研究方面都具有十分重要的意义。

社科院法学所的两类司法公开测评具有以下几个特点。

第一，测评是研究机构的学术行为，具有独立性。中国司法透明度测评和浙江阳光司法指数测评②从指标设定、测评到报告发布，均由社科院法学所独立完成，未有任何机构干预。浙江阳光司法指数测评也是如此。浙江法院曾经开展过类似的考核工作，具体做法是各地区的法院交叉进行评估，评估结果普遍成绩良好，由于这种测评是一种自说自话的自我评价，缺乏公信力。社科院法学所课题组对其独立开展测评时，做到了全省法院"四不"，即不提前通知、不提前布置、不做动员、不告知测评科目。

第二，依法设定测评指标，指标具有法定性。阳光司法指数测评意在评价法院落实司法公开工作的现状、分析其存在的问题，只有做到于法有据，才能使评估不会成为无源之水、无本之木。测评指标包括审务公开、立案庭审公开、裁判文书公开、执行公开和保障机制等内容，其核心指标均是现行法律、司法解释等有明确要求的，如开庭公告的公开、对诉讼当事人的权利义务告知等。

第三，测评指标重点突出。"法治"涉及公权力运行的方方面面，司法公开的内容也纷繁复杂，包括司法权运行的各个环节，对其全部进行测评既不现实且会迷失重点。立足于信息化环境下推进司法公开的要求以及公众对司法公信力的期望，社科院法学所设定的评估指标体系以立案庭审、裁判文书公开和执行信息公开三个核心的环节为主要内容。

第四，排除测评的主观随意性。指标设计和评分标准必须最大限度地

---

① 浙江省高级法院下辖105家法院，2013年只测评了103家，未测评刚移交的杭州铁路运输法院和新成立的杭州经济技术开发区法院。2014年起，上述两家法院也进入测评序列。
② 浙江阳光司法指数测评前期是浙江大学光华法学院与浙江省高级法院研发的，法学所接受浙江省高院的委托后，对指标体系进行了可量化修改。

排除主观随意性，才能有效掌控评估活动，防止测评结果出现明显偏差。为此，课题组在设计阳光司法指数指标时注意排除主观判断的空间，把各种价值判断转化为明确且无自由裁量空间的标准。所有的指标设计都只允许测评人员去判断有没有，如某一类信息是否公开了，而不是去判断它公开得好不好，只有这样才能保障测评结果不受测评人员主观好恶的影响。

第五，注重公开实际效果。司法公开测评的目的不仅仅在于得出总排名和各测评板块的排名，更是通过每个测评指标的数据，分析相关制度的实施情况，让法院了解自身存在的问题。如此，我们方能明确究竟是制度设计存在不足，还是制度落实不到位，为进一步推进司法公开工作提供有价值的参考，为司法公开工作更为精细化提供必要的智力支持。

以下是《2014 年中国司法透明度指数报告》显示的中国司法公开的进展。

1. 网站是司法信息公开的重要平台

以 2013 年司法透明度调研为例，课题组调研了 31 个省级法院、49 个较大的市的中级法院以及最高人民法院共计 81 家法院的司法公开情况。调研结果显示，法院的门户网站正在成为法院公开信息的重要平台。截至 2014 年年初，31 家高级法院中有 29 家省、直辖市的高级法院建立了门户网站，① 49 个中级法院中，有 46 个中级法院建立了门户网站。很多法院网站设置了"法院概况"、"诉讼指南"、"裁判文书"、"法院公告"等栏目，方便公众获取有关信息。2013 年，为了集中统一发布裁判文书，方便公众参阅，最高人民法院开通了裁判文书网。此外，最高人民法院还开通了官方微博、微信，利用新媒体向公众推送重要的司法信息。

不少法院重视运用高科技手段提供便民服务，这也是一些法院创新司法透明方式的重要手段。比如，上海市高级人民法院提供的在线服务平台（http://www.hshfy.sh.cn/shfy/gweb/zxfw.jsp）分为"当事人服务区"和"公众服务区"。在公众服务区设有三维诉讼引导系统，其中包括法院的地图及乘车路线，进入法院之后的角色模拟，方便公众身临其境地了解诉讼、立案、旁听、查阅、拍卖等程序信息。深圳中级人民法院用动画解说的形式，帮助公众了解相关信息，非常具有特色。

2. 裁判文书上网稳步推进

2013 年，最高人民法院推出司法公开三大平台（即立案庭审、裁判文

---

① 在 2013 年的测评中，宁夏高级人民法院的网站不能打开，西藏自治区高级人民法院的网站正在改版。

书和执行信息三大信息平台)建设,其中最重要的一项就是建设中国裁判文书网,并将其作为全国统一的裁判文书网上平台。为统一裁判文书公开标准,最高人民法院出台了新的裁判文书上网规定。在功能上,中国裁判文书网增加了打印和下载链接,方便公众获取信息。

地方法院随后创新了裁判文书上网形式:南京中院、郑州中院、武汉中院等做到了裁判文书及时上网,不少文书能够在裁判做出之后30日内上网公开;广西法院新建立了统一的裁判文书公开平台,公开裁判文书统计表;江苏高院推出的典型案例,附有裁判文书;邯郸中院公开的裁判文书还附有对案件的点评。上述这些形式创新使公开的裁判文书具有较强的学术研究和司法参考价值。

**3. 司法行政信息的公开范围逐年扩大**

司法行政信息是司法公开中阻力较大的领域。尽管如此,2013年的数据显示,司法人员的信息透明度有所提升。与2011年、2012年相比,2013年不少法院全面公开了法院领导的信息。在被测评的81家法院中,有14家法院公开了法院领导包括学习工作经历在内的全部信息,有35家法院公开了法院领导的部分信息。最高人民法院、广西高院、甘肃高院、郑州中院、徐州中院、兰州中院、成都中院等均公开了法院领导详细的学习工作经历。珠海中院除了公开法院领导的照片、姓名、分管工作之外,还公开了审判委员会①专职委员的姓名、照片、出生年月、籍贯、学历。

2013年,有10家法院公开了审判人员的信息,占81家被测评法院的12.3%。其中,有6家法院公开了包括学习工作经历在内的法院领导的详细信息。徐州中院和宁波中院公开了人民审判员信息。成都中院在法院执行网公开了执行法官的照片、姓名、职务、电话。2012年,有5家法院公开了审判人员的信息,占被测评的69家法院②的7.2%。

2013年,法院财务信息公开呈上升趋势。法院作为公权力机构,其预算支出应该满足纳税人的知情权,以便公众监督。司法财务信息包括年度预算信息、前一年度的决算信息和"三公"经费信息三项内容。调研结果显示,与2012年相比,2013年法院的预算信息公开率提高了10个百分点。2012年,提供预算信息的中级人民法院和高级人民法院分别占38%和

---

① 审判委员会是中国各级人民法院内部的最高审判组织,它的任务主要是总结交流审判经验、讨论决定疑难、复杂案件以及研究与审判工作有关的问题。
② 2012年测评的69家法院不包括民族地区的高级法院及民族地区较大的市的中级人民法院,也不包括最高人民法院。

15%，2013年有48%的高级人民法院和25%的中级人民法院公开了本年度预算信息。2012年，所有被测评的高级人民法院均未公开决算信息；2013年，中级人民法院公开决算信息的比例保持不变，而23%的高级人民法院公开了上年度决算信息。总的来说，虽然预决算信息的公开比例仍然不高，但呈年度上升趋势。

法院的公务接待费用、公务用车费用、公务出国（境）费用等信息逐步走向透明。2012年只有青海高院1家法院公开了"三公"经费信息，2013年有18家高级人民法院公开了"三公"经费信息，占被测评法院的58%。2013年公开"三公"经费信息的中级人民法院有7家，在49个中级人民法院中的比例为14%。海南高院、苏州中院和厦门中院还在网站上专门开设司法政务公开或财务公开目录，凸显对司法财务信息公开的重视。

由上可见，不论是由最高人民法院推进的司法公开，还是由第三方学术机构推动的司法公开，都表明尽管还存在些许不情愿，但司法公开在中国已经不是问题。在政治层面和学术层面的双重推动下，司法公开成为司法制度运行的规定动作，这无疑对司法公信力和司法权威的重塑具有重要作用。

## 四 司法公开的展望

在中国新一轮的司法改革工作中，司法公开被作为重要的切入点，各级法院成效明显，但存在的问题同样不容忽视。存在的问题当前主要有：认识上还不够统一，如人事信息应如何公开，看法不一；司法公开平台建设和信息化建设滞后，一些法院信息化投入不足，还没有建设网站；现有司法平台建设较为混乱，或是建立统一平台，或是建立分散平台，[①]之间的关系缺乏协调，重复建设严重；法院网站的定位不准，不少法院公开的主要是新闻、领导行踪、法官风采等信息，而公众关注的办事信息、司法过程信息公开不够；司法信息的公开标准不明确，虽然很多法律法规有明确要求，但具体公开什么、向谁公开、在哪里公开等还有不少模糊之处；裁判文书可以不公开的范围还有待进一步明确；司法公开不均衡现象明显，不同地区之间以及同一法院在不同信息的公开上都存在不均衡现象。

今后的司法公开需要从以下几个方面进行改进。

---

① 除门户网站外，各法院还纷纷建立专门网站，但由于缺乏统一标准，网站五花八门，信息不协调不一致的情况比比皆是，公开效果差。

首先，应提升司法公开意识。司法信息属于公共资源，不能由任何机构垄断。因此，凡属于与司法权运行有关的信息，如人员信息、财务信息等，除非涉及国家秘密、商业秘密、个人隐私，一律都要公开。

其次，进一步明确司法公开的标准，对公开内容、公开对象、公开方式、公开时限等做出更具体、明确的要求，以使司法公开更具有可操作性。

最后，加强网站建设。在互联网时代，门户网站必然是法院司法公开的主要平台，为此，必须对网站建设做好规划，防止重复建设，对网站功能要定位明确，应以满足公众办事需求为导向。

总之，司法公开是提升司法公信力和保证司法公正的重要制度安排，司法公开可以有效地监督司法制度的运行状况。虽然导致司法不公和司法公信力下降的原因有许多，比如司法体制导致的法院行政化问题、经费保障问题、司法审判受多重因素干扰的问题，但司法公开在促进司法公正和提升司法公信力方面的确具有不可替代的作用。司法公开是司法改革的马前卒，以其万钧之力，破釜沉舟，将司法制度中的体制沉疴一一暴露在阳光下，让司法人员和公众都能看到前进的方向，这是其他制度安排所难以完成的，正因如此，中国才把司法公开作为司法改革的重中之重。

# Institutional Arrangement and Practice of Judicial Openness of Chinese Courts

*Tian He*

【Abstract】Judicial openness, as an important component of the judicial system and a major content of the judicial reform in China. is a constitutional principle to be strictly followed by people's courts. In recent years, China has made major progresses in developing this system, both in institutional arrangement and in practice. This article analyzes the historical background of judicial openness in China. With the development of the economy, the differentiation of social interest has raised higher demand on the administration of Justice, and challenged the public confidence and the authority of the. Judicial openness represents one of the basic requirements of a society under the rule of law and is conducive to improving public confidence in the judiciary and safeguarding citizens' right to know. Although the development of the system of judicial openness has displayed a tendency of proceeding from the exterior to the interior, different social groups have different opinions on this development. This article also analyzes the role played by the Supreme Court in supervising over the implementation of the system of judicial openness by people's courts throughout the country, the open evaluation of judicial openness by a third party of academic institution, as well as the results achieved by and the direction of future reform of the system of judicial openness in China.

【Key words】 Administration of Justice; Judicial Openness; Third Party Evaluation

# Rule of law and the Courts: Access to Justice as A Basis for the Rule of Law

*Pia Letto-Vanamo* [*]

[Abstract] In the article the relationship of the principle of rule of law to the principle of access to justice is discussed. Rule of law development depends heavily on availability of justice, reasonable costs of proceedings, clarity of procedure, and quality of decisions. First, the status and role of courts in guaranteeing citizens' access to justice is analysed. Many other institutions resolving disputes and producing legal services play today an important role in the access to justice approach, too. Thus, the article discusses not only court litigation but also its alternatives, such as arbitration and ombudsmen. The increasing role of alternative means of dispute resolution (ADR) at least partly reflects the problems and low standard of court services and court proceedings. For this reason, ideas are also taken up for developing the daily practice of the courts, especially the idea of the "participation" by the parties. Reliable and qualified judges are needed for the sake of trust among people in the courts and the quality of their work: Issues of the independence of the courts and of individual judges, as well as training and recruitment of judges, are discussed at the end of the article.

## 1. Introduction

The principle of rule of law is closely related to another principle guaranteeing justice and democracy in society. This is the principle of access to justice: the functionality of the rule of law is understood expressly through particular legal

---

[*] Professor, Faculty of Law, University of Helsinki.

conflicts. It can be said that rule of law development depends heavily on availability of justice, reasonable costs of proceedings, clarity of procedure, and quality of decisions. In human rights doctrine, the concept of fair trial is used, while access to justice is understood as a fundamental element of the right to a fair trial.

It is not easy to define the concept of access to justice succinctly. ①Nevertheless, a consensus exists as to the central role of the court system in guaranteeing individuals access to justice. ② It has been said that access to the courts is a necessary part of access to justice, even of an effective democracy, while access to justice begins with a just society. The courts protect our rights and freedoms against arbitrary interference, at the same time, ensuring that we do not unlawfully interfere with the rights and freedoms of others. Implicit in this responsibility is the duty of the courts to ensure equality of access.

Today, a common consensus also exists on access to justice as a constitutional right. More widely, the concept of access to justice is closely related to the concept of human rights. The central rules of international human rights conventions seem to belong to the articles providing for the right to a fair trial. ③ Thus, it is the right to a fair trial that is generally understood as a human right. This can also be seen in national fundamental/human rights systems. We can say that an individual should have the right to bring their legal issue to an independent court, which should handle the matter fairly. The concept of fairness, however, is multifaceted. In Europe, the jurisprudence of the European Court of Human Rights on the application of Article 6 (right to a fair trial) of the European Convention on Human Rights has been crucial to development of the concept of fair trial and its implementation in national legal practice. ④

---

① On elements of the concept of access to justice see Letto-Vanamo, Pia, *Access to Justice: A Conceptual and Practical Analysis with Implications for Justice Reforms*, Voices of Development Jurists, International Development Organisation, Rome, 2015.

② See also the chapter by Olli Mäenpää in this volume.

③ The right to be heard stands at the centre of the idea of the right to fair trial. See for instance the *African Charter on Human and Peoples' Rights*, Article 7.

④ Leanza, Piero&Pridal, Ondrej, *The right to a fair trial: article 6 of the European Convention on Human Rights*, Kluwer Law International, 2014, and Gagu, Camelia, "The right to a fair trial—distinct interpretation from the sense outlined by the art", 6 of the European Convention on Human Rights, *Utrecht Law Review*, 2013, pp. 90–108.

In the following, I will discuss the status and role of courts in guaranteeing citizens' access to justice. Many other, public and private, institutions resolving disputes and producing legal services play an important role in the access to justice approach, too. Thus, the discussion will cover not only court litigation but also its alternatives, such as arbitration and ombudsmen. The increasing role of alternative dispute resolution (ADR) at least partly reflects the problems and low standard of court services and court proceedings. For this reason, ideas are also taken up for developing the daily practice of the courts, especially the idea of the "participation" by the parties. Reliable and qualified judges are needed for the sake of trust among people in the courts and the quality of their work: Issues of the independence of the courts and of individual judges, as well as training and recruitment of judges, will be discussed at the end of the article.

## 2. Access to the courts

The status and role of ordinary court procedure in dispute resolution reflect the legitimacy and trust that courts enjoy among people in a particular society. Clearly, an increase in differentiation or fragmentation in society may weaken the position of the judiciary: today, in our western "post-modern" society, it seems to be quite difficult to speak of one idea of justice: indeed, various meanings are attached to it. At the same time, justice as defined or guaranteed by the ordinary courts does not automatically enjoy acceptance among the members of society. In general, awareness is growing that the traditional court system is no longer adequate to meet the needs of citizens in a complex modern society.

Often, all that citizens can achieve in the courts is an imperfect remedy that provides, at best, some level of compensation. Actually, a court will normally be able to determine who is right and who is wrong according to the law, but it may not always be able to provide a meaningful remedy for the party found to be right. That is why mere access to an independent, impartial, and incorruptible system of courts (or justice in the thin sense) does not always result in substantive justice (or justice in the thick sense). Resources are required to vindicate claims of rights, and from a broader perspective, access to justice does not begin with adequate regulation and law enforcement: it begins with equal access to the political process for all citizens.

In spite of the centrality of the judicial system and associated procedures, the trend in Europe is towards increasing use of various methods of ADR. This trend, also actively furthered by the European Union e. g. in consumer disputes,① includes withdrawal of disputes from the official justice system, and reduced competitiveness of the courts in the long run. Actually, for the position of the courts in society but also for the development of the law, it is important that the courts hear and decide a wide and comprehensive variety of disputes that arise from every sector of society. But it seems to have been difficult to develop the working and legal procedures of the courts so that court litigation would have remained a competitive alternative to arbitration or other extrajudicial methods of conflict resolution.

Thus, alternatives to traditional court litigation reflect not only the mistrust that courts may suffer among people but also concrete problems of ordinary court services, their low standard or narrow scope, or the high costs and long duration of court proceedings. ②Arbitration has for a long time been a typical dispute resolution method in business relations. Cases are taken out of the courts and submitted to arbitration for the reason that court proceedings are perceived as too slow and devoid of expertise. The option of non-public proceedings plays an important role here, too.

The Nordic Countries have both a long tradition of using various non-judicial means such as boards and ombudsmen for guaranteeing individuals' access to justice and a general trend of increasing the role of conflict resolution outside the courts. ③ At the same time, a transformation has occurred from a system with numerous "all-inclusive" local courts to a system of fewer but rationalized and effective courts with specialist judges. Registration matters pertaining to real property have been transferred to the administrative authorities, and undisputed money claims

---

① See for instance Directive, 2013/11EU of the European Parliament and of the Council of 21 May 2013 on alternative dispute resolution for consumer disputes and amending Regulation (EC) No 2006/2004 and Directive 2009/22/EC.

② For instance, several cases against Finland at the European Court of Human Rights have dealt with the requirement of Article 6 of the European Convention on Human Rights that a court decision must be made within a reasonable time.

③ See Ervo, Laura &Nylund, Anna (eds), *The Future of Civil Litigation. Access to Courts and Court-annexed Mediation in the Nordic Countries*, Springer, 2014.

(summary matters) to enforcement authorities.

In courts, again, more emphasis has been placed on alternative procedures, with court annexed mediation as the latest example, while the personality and professional skills of judges and their personal responsibility for decisions have been accented. Moreover, the idea of procedural justice has been emphasised. One can speak of a client-centred approach, which emphasises the judge's communicative skills and the parties' subjective experience of (procedural) justice[①] as well as the interaction between the judge and the parties. Thus, important aspects of the perception of justice are not only the impartiality and the high professional and ethical standards of the judge but also an opportunity for the parties to "participate" in the proceedings, and the manner in which they are treated during the court procedure.

## 3. Quality of court procedure

Hence, the mere existence of independent and impartial courts does not alone guarantee individuals' access to justice. Courts must earn trust and legitimacy among citizens but must also have the procedural and substantive capacity to handle disputes. Actually, citizens' rights related to access to justice are more often guaranteed by national constitutions. The right to defence, for instance, is one of those rights but meets obstacles in real life.[②] One of the major obstacles to access to justice, in addition to a lack of resources, is a lack of information. In many countries, this results, at least partly, from strong resistance by members of the legal profession, who often want to make access to justice available only through lawyers. As already mentioned, it is also commonplace for proceedings to be long-lasting, while only a small proportion of actions end in a judgment on the merits of the case. The excessive duration of smaller claims makes costs exorbitant, and, as far as other kinds of dispute are concerned, has led to movements aimed at

---

① See e. g. Ervasti, Kaijus, "*Conflicts before the Courts and Court-annexed Mediation in Finland*", *Scandinavian Studies in Law*, 2007, pp. 186 – 199.

② See more examples e. g. in Chiarloni, Sergio "Civil Justice and its Paradoxes, Civil Justice in crisis", in A. A. S. Zuckerman (ed.), *Comparative Perspectives of Civil Procedure*, Oxford University Press, 1999, pp. 263 – 290; the problems analysed by Chiarloni are from Italy, but most of them are common to many other industrialized countries.

promoting alternative models of dispute prevention and dispute resolution. The duration of proceedings may also explain the number of waived claims, which is often high.

The problems of the court system and court proceedings are apparent in northern, as well as southern, Europe. For example, a State Commission was appointed by the government in 2001 to analyze and inquire into the court system in Finland, a country with 5.5 million inhabitants. However, many problems of the Finnish court system, described and analyzed in the final report of the Commission, are by nature common European, even global, problems. [1] According to the Commission report, two viewpoints of the court system —the internal and the external— should always be taken into consideration when developing the work of the courts. The internal viewpoint concerns court working practices. However, the position of the judiciary in society, as well as the daily work of the courts, is influenced by social changes, such as changes in economic and demographic structures, the fragmentation of society, and increasing legal regulation. This external viewpoint also takes into account the parties, who are the clients of the courts. Therefore, individuals' access to justice is a prominent theme in the Commission report: in order to improve access to justice, the needs and expectations of the courts' clients should receive sufficient emphasis. It is essential to the very functioning of the whole legal system and its credibility that the rights guaranteed by the legal system can also be realized in practice.

Hence, the Commission put forward two views of judicial proceedings. The first was the "rule of law" view, in which the focus was on the end result of the proceedings, that is, on the judgment. Here, the main task of the courts is to apply the law in individual cases, thereby concluding the proceedings. Secondly, the proceedings must be fair (just). Thus, it is important in all judicial reform work to consider the fairness of the proceedings as perceived by the parties: they should be taken as active participants, rather than mere objects of the courts' operations. Thus, the work of the courts and court procedure should be developed from the premise that a party should be able to follow how their case is being dealt

---

[1] The Report was published in December 2003, with an English summary. See http://www.om.fi/23391.htm. The author of this article was one of the members of the Commission.

with by the court, as well as to participate in and influence the proceedings. In this way, the parties can experience the proceedings as open, fair, and credible.

## 4. Institutions other than courts promoting access to justice

Most jurisdictions need to increase the openness of proceedings, to make procedures more flexible and simpler, and to develop alternatives to traditional court litigation. Not only arbitration or (extra-judicial and court-annexed) mediation but also legal advisory services and the ombudsman system are examples of alternatives. In this context, access to legal assistance as well as the high quality of that assistance ought also to be mentioned.①As far as the capacity and quality of the judiciary are concerned a significant element consists of investment in the professional competence and skills of individual judges, which will be discussed later in the article.

For a long time, various conflict resolution methods other than court litigation have been in use in Finland as well as in other Nordic countries. Legal advisory services (in the wide sense) play an important role not only in preventing conflicts but also in resolving them. Legal advisory services are multifaceted, with many of them organized by state or municipal authorities and funded from the public purse. Public legal aid offices and local (municipal) consumer rights advisers can be mentioned as examples. Moreover, different boards issuing various types of recommendation, opinion, instruction or resolution belong to the Nordic—lay and corporatist—legal tradition and occupy a central role in promoting access to justice. Boards are used, for instance, in insurance, labour, consumer and competition law disputes. The institution of ombudsman with the Parliamentary Ombudsman and specialised ombudsmen exists first and foremost for general oversight of legality but in all Nordic countries plays an important role in conflict resolution as well.②

---

① Letto-Vanamo, Pia, Judicial Dispute Resolution and Its Many Alternatives. The Nordic Experience, In Zekoll, Joachim et al. (ed.), *Formalisation and Flexibilisation in Dispute Resolution*, Brill, 2014, pp. 151–163.

② For a further comparison between the Nordic countries, see Michael, "The Danish Ombudsman, a national watchdog with selected preferences", *Utrecht Law Journal*, 2010, pp. 33–50.

The Swedish ombudsman is the oldest in the world, dating back to 1809. Subsequent ombudsman institutions were created in Finland in 1920, in Denmark in 1955, and in Norway in 1962. The general framework is that the holder of the office is appointed by the legislator and enjoys independence from both the executive and the judiciary. The task of the institution is to inquire into administrative decisions and to safeguard the interests of citizens by ensuring administration according to the law, discovering instances of maladministration and eliminating defects in administration. The main task of this ordinary-so-called Parliamentary-Ombudsman is to oversee that the authorities and officials observe the law and discharge their duties. ① Supervision is carried out on the basis of complaints—by examining complaints received from citizens who believe that a public authority has made mistakes. For instance, in Denmark (a country without special ombudsmen), the Ombudsman receives 4000 – 5000 complaints every year. The Ombudsman can also intervene in perceived shortcomings on their own initiative, issuing statements and opinions, and can recommend that the authorities reopen a case and perhaps change their decision, but cannot as such make decisions. In addition, the Ombudsman carries out inspections at offices and institutions.

In Sweden and Finland, however, there are-mainly for historical reasons-two supreme overseers of legality, the Chancellor of Justice, who reports to the Government and to the Parliament, and the Parliamentary Ombudsman. Their tasks and powers are largely the same. Both oversee the legality of the actions of authorities and officials. The Finnish Chancellor of Justice also oversees the actions of lawyers. ② In principle, a complaint can be made either to the Chancellor of Justice or the Ombudsman. However, small differences in the division of tasks between them determine which of them ultimately investigates a complaint.

---

① In Sweden and Finland the Ombudsman pays special attention to the implementation of fundamental and human rights; the Danish ombudsman, however, enjoys a more autonomous role in developing legal principles of good administration; Danish legislation e. g. includes no explicit duty to consider fundamental rights.

② Alongside investigating complaints, the Chancellor of Justice has the task of overseeing the legality of the Government's actions and for that reason is present at cabinet sessions and examines the relevant documents beforehand.

There are also ombudsmen for special sectors or matters, e. g. the ombudsman for data protection, for children and for equality. Sweden and Norway have an Equality Ombudsman called the "discrimination ombudsman", which is a government agency that seeks to combat discrimination and promote equal rights and opportunities for everyone. Thus, the Ombudsman ensures compliance with anti-discrimination legislation that prohibits discrimination related to a "person's sex, transgender identity or expression, ethnicity, religion or other belief, disability, sexual orientation or age". Finland has an ombudsman for equality and another for minorities. The task of the Ombudsman for Minorities is to advance the status and legal protection of ethnic minorities and to prevent and tackle ethnic discrimination. The Ombudsman targets its services at immigrants, foreigners living in Finland, and Finland's traditional ethnic minorities such as the Roma and Sami peoples.

The Finnish Ombudsman for Equality supervises compliance with legislation on equality between women and men-and gender minorities-against discrimination, and prohibition of discrimination and discriminatory job advertising, as well as promoting equality by means of initiatives, advice and counselling, and monitoring implementation of equality between women and men in different sectors of society.

The most powerful actor in consumer affairs in the Nordic countries is the Consumer Ombudsman. The Nordic Consumer Ombudsman is part of the consumer authority, a state authority[①] dealing with consumer protection as well as disputes between consumers and business. Besides the Ombudsman, consumer dispute boards and local consumer rights advisors take care of consumer law matters.

## 5. Independent courts, independent judges

The capabilities of the court system as a whole, and the judiciary especially, should be sufficient to guarantee individuals' access to justice. One of the essential elements characterizing modern court systems and court procedures is

---

① In Finland consumer law matters belong to the recently founded Finnish Competition and Consumer Authority (Denmark and Finland have a joint agency for consumer and competition affairs).

independence; indeed, this is the main qualification of the judiciary. The judiciary has to be structurally, and individual judges personally, free from external interference. The independence of the judiciary is based on the idea of the separation of powers structurally, meaning that the organs of the judiciary must function independently from the organs of the legislative and the executive. ① Furthermore, the judge must also be independent from the parties to each case. ②

Judicial independence is also defined as freedom from interference in individual decision-making, as a principle of impartiality in administering justice. This definition, however, raises problems in identifying its practical implications: the appointment or dismissal of judges comes easily to mind. Even training or performance appraisal could be seen as an external influence. Indeed, the very purpose of training is to influence the practices of judges in their day-to-day work. But if we analyze judicial independence as a constitutional requirement arising from the need to ensure impartiality in decision-making, then the tension between training and judicial independence appears rather slight.

Many international conventions include provisions on independence. The overall starting point is the Universal Declaration of Human Rights. ③ Several efforts have been made by international, intergovernmental and non-governmental organizations to identify, develop, and promote common standards of independence and impartiality for national judges and judicial systems. The concept of the independence of courts and judges has also been developed by the jurisprudence of internationaland European courts. In particular, the European Court of Human Rights has elaborated the concept of judicial independence through its practice. One typical formulation can be found in the case of Findlay v. UK (1997), which states that in order to establish whether a tribunal can be considered as "independent", due regard should be given to the manner of appointment of its members, as well as their term of office, and the existence of guarantees against outside pressures. The Court has also developed the concept of independence by considering the

---

① Judges, as a branch of the State, play a role in balancing competing interests at a constitutional level, so that the principle of judicial independence exists despite the distribution of powers.
② See Malleson Kate, "Judicial Training and Performance Appraisal: The Problem of Judicial Independence", *The Modern Law Review*, 1997, Vol. 60, pp. 655 – 667.
③ Adopted and proclaimed by the General Assembly resolution 217 A (Ⅲ) of 10 December, 1948.

relationship between the court and the judge in question, on the one hand, and the executive and the parties, on the other hand. Thus, a judicial body must be independent in its functions and as an institution. Furthermore, it has to appear independent and impartial in the eyes of citizens- and also those of the parties concerned. ①

It is interesting to note that rules, standards, and ideas also exist concerning the independence of judges in the international courts. Generally, the statutes of the international courts proclaim that members of the courts are independent. That independence is guaranteed by requirements applicable to the appointment of judges, the duration of their office, their status, and the manner in which the courts are organized and function in practice. ②Other studies conducted on the behaviour of judges at the International Court of Justice show that the main element of independence is the judges' character: A judge who wants to be independent is in fact independent in their practical work.

However, a less familiar aspect of judicial independence, one that may have relevance for training and performance appraisal, is freedom from internal interference. Actually, although training has often been kept within the control of the judiciary in order to avoid external interference, the danger of internal interference is prima facie strong. A judicial career is normally based on a promotion system. This means that the prospect of promotion can strongly influence individual behaviour. So it is in this area that performance appraisal and training may have the most significant impact. A judge who performs poorly—or differently—in training may not face dismissal but may not be promoted.

However, the development of a judicial career includes not only structural but also cultural elements. The daily work of judges has traditionally been solitary and relatively isolated, dependent on a culture of individualism. This idea still lies at

---

① See also Council of Europe Recommendation R (94) 12 on the independence, efficiency and role of judges.

② Every judge has to be, and appear, independent. This principle has been set, for instance, by the Rules of Procedure (1998) of the European Court of Human Rights. According to these principles, in certain situations a judge may or must withdraw from a case: of their own motion (proprio motu) with the President's agreement; after a decision taken by the President or, in case of disagreement, by the competent chamber; or after a party has made an objection concerning the judge, and that objection has been accepted by the President or the Chamber (Rule 28).

the centre of the two most important debates about the judiciary: 1) the extent to which judges play a creative role in shaping the law (especially with the system of judicial review), and 2) whether or not the political views of judges direct their decisions. In every case, the expansion in size and the formalization of a career structure-of which training is one part—may undermine the culture of individualism that has been understood as a prerequisite of strong judicial independence. This can be true even when the introduction of teamwork is concerned.

## 6. To appoint "righteous" judges

Except in times of political crisis, the independence of the judiciary has seldom been questioned in the Nordic countries. No separate institutions exist for educating judges, and all judges are educated by the law faculties of (state funded) universities. On the other hand, discussions of the central administration of the courts have also touched issues of independence: In Denmark and Sweden, the foundation of a central administrative agency for the courts, separate from the Ministry of Justice, was partly motivated by the aim of emphasizing the independence of the courts. In Finland, one of the main themes during the last decades of the $20^{th}$ century was the recruitment and background of the members of the judiciary. In legal-political debates of the 1970s, judges were deemed socially and politically distanced from citizens, which gave rise to a lack of trust in the courts. Attempts to tackle this problem were made, for example, through reforms to legal education, with approximation of legal science to other social sciences. [1]

The final and concrete changes in the recruitment base, however, began with the change over to a salary system and with the establishment of the positions of district judges. Ever since the late 1970s, the number of first instance judges has increased considerably, and at the same time the proportion of women in the judiciary has begun to rise. In 1950, the Finnish judiciary consisted of 557 judges, 45 of whom were women. In 1970, the corresponding numbers were 699 and

---

[1] See Letto-Vanamo, Pia, "Finnish Judges between Tradition and Dynamism", in Turenne, Sophie (ed.), *Fair Reflection of Society in Judicial Systems—A Comparative Study*, Springer, 2015, pp. 157 – 167.

84. According to statistics for 1990, the numbers had grown to 1981 and 914. In 2013 the numbers were 1962 and 998. ①

Actually, no clear data are available about differences in attitudes and conceptions among the current crop of judges and their predecessors. In contrast, a study was carried out in 1995 where district judges were asked about what constitutes "a good life" and about their relationship to work, money, leisure and family. It was found that, in the main, judges are no different from anyone else in Finland. Also in more general terms, the symbolic self-differentiation of Finns—unlike that of for example the French—is not linked to the formation of social classes over time and to any concomitant values or conceptions. In contrast, the Protestant work ethic, a kind of "pioneer spirit", has indeed been important for the definition of commonly accepted and desired values. This is not to say, however, that Finnish judges would not be clearly a part of the middle class, characterised by expertise gained through education, and enjoying a respected and legitimate status as a part of the community. It is not uncommon that the profession of the law is "inherited"; it is only very seldom that a judge would have a working class background.

After the 1970s, reasons for judicial reform have been somewhat distanced from political considerations. Reforms have mainly been justified by reference to promptness and efficiency. At the same time, the "competitiveness" of the ordinary courts as an institution of conflict resolution has been pointed out, while "opening a judicial career" -having been closed especially when the appellate court judiciary is concerned-has been enhanced. This can clearly be seen in the provisions on judicial appointments in 2000.

Provisions on judicial selection in Finland can be found in *The Constitution of Finland* (731/1999) and in the *Act on Judicial Appointments* (205/2000). Appointments to tenured positions in the judiciary are made by the President of the Republic.②Temporary judicial appointments are regulated by the *Judicial Appointments Act*, but there are variations in the appointment procedure depending

---

① For statistics on recent developments see http://www.coe.int/t/dghl/cooperation/cepej/evaluation/2014/Finland_2014.pdf.

② See Section 102 of the Constitution of Finland, and Section 2 of the *Act on Judicial Appointments*.

on the positions concerned. In general, all Finnish judges are appointed by the President of the Republic on the basis of a draft decision submitted by the Government. The draft or recommendation comes from the Minister of Justice but today the role of the Minister is quite formal.

Since 2000, an independent body, the Judicial Appointments Board, arranges to fill positions in the judiciary. One of the main reasons for the foundation of the Board was to promote "a more open judicial career". At the same time, the independence of the judiciary was also pointed out. A reasoned proposal from the Board is delivered to the Government in order for a draft decision on the appointment to be presented to the President of the Republic. However, the Board has no jurisdiction regarding the appointment of President or Justice to the Supreme Court or to the Supreme Administrative Court. These are also only positions which can be filled without first being announced as vacant. The courts of final instance make their own appointment proposals to the President of the Republic, who is also the final decision-maker in these matters. However, the Board may present-and does present-an opinion on the appointment of a Justice of the Supreme or Supreme Administrative Court upon a request from the proposing Court. [1]

The Judicial Appointments Board[2] is expected to promote the recruitment of judges from all walks of legal life. During recent years it has quite successfully recruited judges not only from among temporarily appointed judges, but also from the legal profession and civil service. The Board, having a term of five years, is composed mainly of members of the judiciary, but three members come from outside the profession. One is a practicing lawyer nominated by the Finnish Bar Association, another is a prosecutor nominated by the Prosecutor General, and the third is an academic nominated by the Ministry of Justice after hearing the law faculties. [3]

However, the basic qualification requirements for all judicial positions are similar, and these can be found in the *Act on Judicial Appointments*. The applicant

---

[1] Section 6 (2) of the *Act on Judicial Appointments*.
[2] The Board has a president, a vice president and ten other members.
[3] See Section 7 of the *Act on Judicial Appointments*.

must be a "righteous Finnish citizen who has earned a Master's degree in law and who by his or her previous activity in a court of law or elsewhere has demonstrated the professional competence and the personal characteristics necessary for successful performance of the duties inherent in the position." In addition, the President or Justice of the Supreme Court or the Supreme Administrative Court must be "an eminent legal expert". Judges having positions of president or chief justice must also have leadership skills. No exemptions can be granted, and before being appointed, a person proposed by the Judicial Appointments Board for a tenured position must declare his or her interests.

# 法治与法院：作为法治基础之一的获得司法公正的权利

皮亚·勒托-瓦纳莫

**【摘要】** 本文讨论了法治原则与获得司法公正原则之间的关系。法治的发展在很大程度上取决于司法公正的可获得性、诉讼费用的合理性、诉讼程序的清晰程度和司法决定的质量。本文首先分析了法院在保障公民获得司法公正权利方面的地位和作用。许多其他解决争端和提供法律服务的机构如今也在保障获得司法公正的权利方面起着重要的作用。因此，本文不仅讨论法庭诉讼，而且还讨论诸如仲裁和监察专员制度等替代性机制。替代性争端解决机制的日益重要至少在某种程度上反映了法庭服务和法庭程序存在的问题和低标准。由于这一原因，本文还讨论了有关发展法庭日常实践的问题，特别是有关诉讼当事人"参与"的问题。为提高法院及其工作的公信度，我们需要可靠和合格的法官。因此本文在最后一部分讨论了有关法院和法官的独立性以及法官培训和招聘方面的问题。

# 论我国赦免制度的完善

刘仁文*

【摘要】 我国对于赦免制度只是在《宪法》、《刑法》和《刑事诉讼法》的相关条款中做了零星规定，这种立法现状在法治日益健全的今天几乎注定了这一制度被悬置的命运。完善我国的赦免制度，首先要从实体上丰富赦免的种类，包括大赦、特赦、赦免性减刑和赦免性复权四部分。其次要从程序上予以完备，以保证赦免制度的规范运行。在特别赦免中，死刑案件特别赦免程序值得专门研究。关于赦免的立法模式，就我国的实际情况来看，制定一部专门的《赦免法》，明确赦免实施的各项实体和程序条件，比较科学可行。

【关键词】 赦免 实体程序 死刑案件立法模式

法律之所以为人信仰，并不仅仅在于它的苛严与威仪，更在于它正义的慈悲心。

——〔意〕托马斯·阿奎那

## 一 为何赦免重新受到关注

从 1959 年为庆祝中华人民共和国成立 10 周年而对在押的确已改恶从善的蒋介石集团和伪满洲国的战争罪犯、反革命罪犯和普通刑事罪犯实行特赦，到 1975 年第 7 次特赦对全部在押战争罪犯实行特赦并给予公民权，特赦曾经作为一项重要的刑事政策措施而受到决策者的重视和青睐。但从 1975 年后，由于我国再未实行过特赦，因此该制度逐渐被虚置，在蓬勃发

---

* 中国社会科学院法学研究所研究员、刑法室主任。

展的法学研究中,赦免制度反而成了被人遗忘的角落。正如有学者所观察指出的:"赦免作为介乎刑法与宪法之间的冷僻话题,无论刑法学界还是宪法学界对之均鲜有涉及。"①

进入新世纪以来,赦免这一在中国法学界长期被冷落的话题重新受到关注。据笔者初步统计,近年来光这个领域的专著就出版了6本,而有关这方面的公开发表的论文,更多达30余篇,这还不包括那些未公开出版的以此为题的博士和硕士学位论文。虽然这些专著和论文在内容上存在不同程度的重复,但仍然说明了有越来越多的学者开始关注赦免制度这一事实。从作者队伍来看,最初主要是刑法学者,涉及的内容也多为实体法的内容,但后来逐渐扩展至刑事诉讼法学者,内容也从实体法扩展至程序法,最近两三年来更有宪法学者从宪政的角度进行阐述,这反映了赦免制度本身所具有的跨学科特点和学界研究的逐步深入。

在理论界关注赦免制度的同时,赦免话题也不断被推向社会,例如:2007年底《南方周末》发表《2008,能否成为中国特赦年?》的署名文章,②呼吁国家在改革开放政策实施30周年及奥运会举办之际搞一次特赦,引起广泛讨论;③ 2009年,就新中国成立60周年要否搞特赦,又引发热议;④ 2010年底至2011年初,媒体大量报道了尚在监狱服刑的"中国最后一个流氓犯人",就其是否应被特赦展开讨论,引起强烈反响。⑤

另外,近年的"两会"上,也频频出现这方面的提案,如来自福建华侨大学的全国人大代表戴仲川于2008年向全国人大提出《关于尽快制定一部〈特赦法〉的立法建议》,⑥来自重庆西南政法大学的全国人大代表陈忠林于2009年向全国人大提出《关于建国60周年实行特赦的建议》,⑦来自重庆发改委的全国政协委员吴刚先后于2008年、2009年两次提出《关于建国

---

① 阴建峰:《现代赦免制度论衡》,中国人民公安大学出版社,2006,第6页。
② 参见刘仁文《2008,能否成为中国特赦年?》,《南方周末》2007年12月13日。
③ 反对意见参见封利强《别把奥运与刑事司法挂钩》,《检察日报》2008年1月2日。
④ 主张特赦的意见参见高铭暄《建议国庆特赦》,《南方人物周刊》2009年第9期;赵秉志:《赦免制度 适时而行》,《法制日报》2009年2月25日。反对意见如周光权《不要轻率实行国庆特赦》,《南方周末》2009年2月26日。
⑤ 参见马守敏、孟会玲《最后的"流氓"能否被特赦》,《人民法院报》2011年1月15日。1997年新刑法已经废除了流氓罪,这是此次讨论的基本背景。
⑥ 参见中国律师观察网,http://www.ccwlawyer.com/center.asp?idd=1453,最后访问日期:2011年7月30日。
⑦ 参见《重庆商报》2009年3月9日的报道。

60 周年大庆之际进行大赦的建议》，① 来自上海复旦大学的全国政协委员葛剑雄也于 2009 年提出关于在新中国成立 60 周年大庆之际实行特赦的提案。②

赦免制度为何重新受到关注？笔者认为，这一问题可以从以下诸视角做出分析。

首先是构建社会主义和谐社会的政治背景。从 1999 年全国人大通过宪法修正案，明确"中华人民共和国实行依法治国，建设社会主义法治国家"，到 2004 年全国人大再次通过宪法修正案把"国家尊重和保障人权"写入宪法，从 2003 年中共中央总书记胡锦涛提出"坚持以人为本"的科学发展观，到 2004 年中国共产党第十六届四中全会提出"构建社会主义和谐社会"的理论，这些文件的制定和理念的提出均记载了当代中国建设社会主义政治文明的轨迹。"以人为本"必然带来宽容、人道的文化，"和谐社会"必然要求摈弃单一的斗争哲学。在这样的背景下，体现宽容价值的赦免制度自然会受到重视，③ 例如，2007 年，时任最高人民法院院长的肖扬在全国哲学社会科学规划办公室编发的一期关于刑事政策的《成果要报》上曾批示："我完全赞成（该成果）对赦免制度的研究。赦免是国家的一项政策性重大措施，也是社会文明进步的重要体现。我国现行宪法第 67 条和第 80 条对特赦作了规定，但是自从 1975 年最后一次特赦全部战争罪犯以来的 30 多年里，我国再没有实行过特赦……当前，全党全国人民正投身于构建社会主义和谐社会的伟大实践，充分发挥特赦制度的作用，对于营造和谐稳定的社会环境，增进人民内部的团结，必会产生良好的巨大的影响。"④ 事实上，一些论文的标题就直接反映了这一背景，如《和谐社会呼唤现代赦免制度》、《构建和谐社会应当完善现代赦免制度》。

其次是"宽严相济"取代"严打"的社会背景。"宽严相济"刑事政策的确立，一方面是党中央围绕"构建社会主义和谐社会"而在社会治安领域做出的重要工作思路调整；另一方面也应当看到，经过 20 多年的改革开放，新旧体制的转轨尽管还没有最终完成，但已经度过了最混乱的时期，

---

① 参见《重庆晨报》2009 年 3 月 2 日的报道。该提案中的"大赦"应为"特赦"，因为目前我国宪法中只有特赦、没有大赦，因而在立法修改之前实行大赦没有宪法根据。
② 参见《东方早报》2009 年 3 月 7 日的报道。
③ 美国学者巴西奥尼指出："赦免……本质上是政府针对违反公共利益的罪行而给予的一种宽恕。" See Cherif Bassiouni, *Introduction to International Criminal Law*, Transnational Publishers, Inc., Ardsley, New York, 2003, p. 705.
④ 参见《法学院谢望原教授研究成果获最高人民法院院长肖扬重要批示》，中国人民大学新闻网，http://news1.ruc.edu.cn/102392/49854.html，最后访问日期：2011 年 7 月 21 日。

国家治理社会和管理经济的经验也在不断丰富,在这种情况下,也就具备了对"严打"进行反思的条件。也就是说,社会治安的相对稳定和刑事犯罪态势的相对平稳为转变"严打"这一刑事政策创造了条件。① 从"严打"到"宽严相济",不言而喻,"以宽济严"是其中的一项重要内容。在探求"以宽济严"的制度措施时,赦免成为顺乎逻辑的一个选项。② 这方面,中外历史均有例可循,例如,美国学者弗里德曼就曾经指出:"现代制度不安地摇摆于严惩理论与宽宥理论之间。这种紧张关系并不新鲜……18 世纪英国的刑事司法以大批量的宽赦缓和了它血腥的法典:在王座和高等法院法官们的宽恕和恩惠下实行特赦和减刑。它因此就获得了两种极端形式都不能获得的一定的功效……在我们的时代,宽宥甚至更为广泛。"③

再次是依法治国深入发展的法治背景。"文化大革命"结束后,我们国家逐渐走上了法治的道路,毫无疑问,这是正确的选择。但也应当承认,我们在法治进程中,曾经出现过一些不太科学的认识,如把调解的优良传统简单地与法治对立起来,以致在一个时期里把调解打入了"冷宫",直到近年,我们才重新认识到调解的价值,并通过制度使调解与法治有机地结合起来。在赦免这个问题上,我们也经历过类似的认识。由于过去的历次特赦都是在没有刑法、刑事诉讼法的情况下实施的,带有浓厚的政策色彩,所以在重建法制后,就很容易把赦免看成法制的对立物。其实,现代意义上的赦免已经不再是法制的对立物,而是依法行赦、依宪行赦。换句话说,现代国家为什么还会继续保留发源于专制时代的赦免制度?其原因除了赦免制度本身所蕴藏的刑事政策的意义外,④ 还在于赦免制度在现代被赋予了

---

① 最新研究指出:近年全国社会治安形势总体稳定,公众的社会安全感上升,严重暴力犯罪呈下降趋势。参见靳高风《2010 年中国犯罪形势分析及 2011 年预测》,载李林主编《中国法治发展报告 (2011)》,社会科学文献出版社,2011,第 153 页及以下。
② 参见蒋娜《宽严相济刑事政策下的死刑赦免制度研究》,《法学杂志》2009 年第 9 期。
③ 〔美〕弗里德曼:《选择的共和国》,高鸿钧等译,清华大学出版社,2005,第 164 页。
④ 中外学者均将刑事政策上的考量作为赦免制度的重要目的,如德国学者李斯特认为:"赦免的目的在于,相对于法律的僵化的一般性,提出公平要求(但总是有利于被判刑人,决不会反过来);它还可以纠正(事实上的或被认为的)法官的误判,或者达到刑事政策上之目的。"(参见〔德〕李斯特《德国刑法教科书》,徐久生译,法律出版社,2000,第 487 页。)意大利刑法学者帕多瓦尼在谈到赦免制度时,甚至指出:"只有从刑事政策的角度考虑,才可能以宽大为由对这种不平等作出解释。"(参见〔意〕杜里奥·帕多瓦尼《意大利刑法学原理》,法律出版社,1998,第 395 页。)一般认为,赦免制度的刑事政策意义主要体现在以下几方面:1. 化解国家祸乱,缓和国内外矛盾;2. 调节利益冲突,平衡社会关系;3. 弥补法律不足,缓和刑罚严苛;4. 彰显国家德政,昭示与民更始;(转下页注)

新的内涵，即经过近、现代国家统治者或主权者的承继和改造，其已经成为被吸纳进近现代宪法的一项规范内容，并被构建成为一项宪政制度。正如美国的霍姆斯大法官所指出的："赦免，在我们这个时代，不再是个人拥有权力发生的私人恩典，而是宪政的一部分。当实行赦免时，它是基于更好地服务于公共福利……"[①]可见，现代意义上的赦免是法治的产物，它必须在宪法和相关法律的规定之下实施，赦免法案的主旨在于"使从前的法外行动得以依法处理，或在于使已触犯法律的责任之个人得以依法救济"[②]。对赦免的这种辩证认识，无疑有助于在法治的层面激活对这一制度的讨论。

法谚云："没有恩赦的法律是违法的。"作为一项在当今世界范围内通行的治国之术（尽管各个国家和地区法律规定的内容不完全相同，实际适用的频率和幅度也有差异），我国不可能长期对赦免制度弃之不用。事实上，有学者就指出：尽管党和国家基于综合考虑最终没有在新中国成立60周年之际采纳特赦的建议，但不可否认的是，应否适时行赦以及如何行赦，已经成为关涉国家法治发展和社会进步的一个重大现实问题。[③]诚然，赦免的施行需要慎重论证，但在此之前，找出我国现有赦免制度存在的不足，把我国有关赦免的法律制度尽可能地加以完善，以便从实体和程序上为必要时依法行赦提供法律基础和法治保障，应是一件有意义的事情。

## 二 我国现有赦免制度的不足

我国现行法律对赦免制度的规定主要体现在以下三个方面。

第一，《宪法》第67条在规定全国人民代表大会常务委员会的职权时，第17项规定其有"决定特赦"的权力；第80条在规定中华人民共和国主

---

（接上页注④）5. 鼓励犯人自新，增强社会的凝聚力；等等（参见高铭暄、赵秉志、阴建峰《新中国成立60周年之际实行特赦的时代价值与构想》，《法学》2009年第5期）。当然，在现代法治社会，刑事政策和刑法的关系也不是简单对立的关系，相反，刑事政策的刑法化（如将赦免纳入刑法）和刑法的刑事政策化（如缓刑、假释等刑法制度的确立）正体现了二者相辅相成的关系。法治社会并不排斥政策的运用，只不过政策需在"法治的篱笆内"活动。

① Clifford Dorne, Kenneth Gewerth, "Mercy in a Climate of Retributive Justice: Interpretations from a National Survey of Executive Clemency Procedures", *New England Journal on Criminal and Civil Confinement Summer*, 1999.
② 〔英〕戴雪：《英宪精义》，雷宾南译，中国法制出版社，2001，第127页。
③ 参见阴建峰、王娜《现代赦免制度重构研究》，中国人民公安大学出版社，2011，第486页。

席的权力时，现定国家主席有根据全国人民代表大会常务委员会的决定"发布特赦令"的权力。

第二，《刑法》第 65 条和第 66 条关于累犯制度的规定涉及赦免，其中第 65 条针对一般累犯做出如下规定："被判处有期徒刑以上刑罚的犯罪分子，刑罚执行完毕或者赦免以后，在五年以内再犯应当判处有期徒刑以上刑罚之罪的，是累犯，应当从重处罚，但是过失犯罪和不满十八周岁的人犯罪的除外。"① 该法第 66 条关于特别累犯的规定指出："危害国家安全犯罪、恐怖活动犯罪、黑社会性质组织犯罪的犯罪分子，在刑罚执行完毕或者赦免以后，在任何时候再犯上述任一类罪的，都以累犯论处。"②

第三，《刑事诉讼法》第 15 条规定，"有下列情形之一的，不追究刑事责任，已经追究的，应当撤销案件，或者不起诉，或者终止审理，或者宣告无罪"，"下列情形"包括 6 种，其中第 3 种是"经特赦令免除刑罚的"。

由上可见，我国关于赦免制度的法律规定零散而粗糙，③ 只是在《宪法》、《刑法》和《刑事诉讼法》的相关内容中有所涉及，这与当今许多国家和地区对赦免制度进行专门而系统的立法形成了鲜明对照。具体而言，我国赦免制度的法律规定存在以下不足。

一是从赦免的种类看，我国目前有明确的宪法依据的仅特赦一种，但从其他国家和地区关于赦免制度的规定来看，赦免制度一般应包括大赦、特赦、减刑和复权四种类型。④ 从下文的分析我们可以看出，大赦、减刑和复权也有存在的必要。

二是即便特赦，宪法也是点到为止，只规定全国人民代表大会常务委员会有决定特赦的权力，但到底什么叫特赦，特赦的法律效果如何，全无规定。举个例子，关于特赦的法律效果，我国学界通说认为特赦只能免除刑罚的执行，而不能使被特赦者的有罪宣告归于无效。由此出发，特赦也就只能在法院判决之后实行。但正如下文将要指出的，世界上的特赦其

---

① 关于不满 18 周岁的人犯罪不构成累犯的规定系 2011 年 2 月 25 日全国人大常委会通过的《刑法修正案（八）》所新增。
② 恐怖活动犯罪、黑社会性质组织犯罪的犯罪分子构成特别累犯的规定系《刑法修正案（八）》所新增。
③ 例如，《宪法》和《刑事诉讼法》都使用"特赦"一词，但《刑法》却使用"赦免"一词，这种用词的不统一也说明了不同法律在这个问题上缺乏共识。
④ 有的国家还不止这些，如日本还有对刑罚执行的免除，美国还有对罚金或没收的免除，韩国还有对纪律处分或行政处罚的免除等。

实并不只有一个模型，有的国家和地区就规定特赦既能免刑又能免罪，因而在适用时间上也就可以先于判决确定之前。由此可见，特赦的内涵最终还得取决于法律的规定。

三是我国关于特赦的程序规定付之阙如。现代法治背景下的赦免制度特别强调程序的完备和周密，这也是防止滥赦、保证赦免制度妥当运行的最重要环节。但我国无论是赦免（特赦）的启动、申请与决定，还是赦免（特赦）的机构，乃至赦免令（特赦令）的颁布、执行与监督，都缺乏相应的法律规定。

上述缺陷使得我国以往的赦免实践带有很大的随意性和不规范性，[①] 例如，现在学界一般把1959年的特赦作为新中国首次特赦来阐述，其实这并不准确，因为早在1956年，最高人民检察院就根据全国人大常委会《关于处理在押日本侵略中国战争犯罪分子的决定》第1条第1项，即"对于次要的或者悔罪表现较好的日本战争犯罪分子，可以从宽处理，免予起诉"，先后分3次"免予起诉并立即释放"了1017名日本战犯。[②] 这一名为"免予起诉"的做法，其实就是赦免（类似特赦，但它又是针对尚未判刑的人，与我国关于特赦的通说有异），因为按通常做法，免予起诉只能适用于那些情节轻微的犯罪人，而战犯绝对谈不上情节轻微。

又如，我国1975年的特赦，如果按照过去6次的特赦标准（有改恶从善表现），有一批战犯无论如何通不过，但后来经毛泽东批示，所有战犯一律"特赦"。[③] 这其实是以特赦之名行大赦之实。正因此，有学者指出：我国从1959年到1975年的7次特赦，虽然同时具备通常所谓大赦和特赦的某些特点，却又有所不同，是一种具有中国特色的较为特殊的形式。[④]

如果说在法制不健全的年代，上述赦免实践并不存在多大的合法性危机，那么随着我国法制的健全和法治的进步，赦免制度的这种事实上处于

---

[①] 当然，当时的法治不彰、人治盛行是更大的时代背景，但具体制度的付之阙如无疑也为这种随意性大开了方便之门。

[②] 参见郭金霞、苗鸣宇《大赦·特赦——中外赦免制度概观》，群众出版社，2003，第186~188页。

[③] 当时，毛泽东在看了公安部《关于第七次特赦问题的报告》和准备给全国人大常委会的说明后做出批示，"这些批示，几乎出乎所有人的预料。很长时间准备的分类处理材料全部作废，所有战犯一律特赦，待遇一律相同，复杂的事一夜之间变得异常简单"。参见郭金霞、苗鸣宇《大赦·特赦——中外赦免制度概观》，群众出版社，2003，第209页。

[④] 参见马克昌主编《刑罚通论》，武汉大学出版社，1999，第705页。

空白状态的立法现状,① 几乎就注定了其被悬置的命运。笔者注意到,在近年来要否实行特赦的争论中,许多反对意见其实并不是反对特赦本身,而是出于对赦免无程序可循的担忧。例如,有人就指出,30 年前,我们还是"政策治国",一声令下,即可实行特赦,并不一定要经过严格的司法程序;如今,依法治国已经深入人心,特赦不仅要有法律渊源,更要有相应的规章制度和司法程序。然而,对于特赦,《宪法》虽然有此一说,但这只是一个原则性的规定,特赦的具体内容是什么?它有哪些类型?其范围和效力又是怎样?特赦由什么部门主管,又该如何执行?特赦出现问题后如何救济?在这些问题没有解决之前,仓促特赦,欲速则不达,搞不好还会沦为腐败的温床。②

这种担忧不无道理。其实,主张特赦的不少人士也看到了这一点,例如,有论者就遗憾地指出,关于特赦的条件和程序,我国《宪法》及法律没有进行具体的规定,如何操作成了实践中的一个难题,这也许是 30 多年来我国一直未有特赦的法律层面上的原因。因此,要实行特赦,就要根据《宪法》的规定,制定一部完整、统一的《特赦法》,对于特赦的主体、特赦的对象、特赦的条件以及特赦应当遵循的法律程序等做出明确的规定。③

## 三 赦免制度的实体完善

完善我国的赦免制度,首先要从实体上完善赦免的种类。如前所述,我国《宪法》中规定的赦免制度仅限于"特赦"一种,这较之其他国家和地区,涵盖面太窄。从其他国家和地区关于赦免制度的规定来看,赦免制度一般包括大赦、特赦、减刑和复权四部分。在这方面,我国还需要在《宪法》及相关法律上补充资源,使我国的赦免制度内容更加丰富。④

### (一) 关于大赦

我国 1954 年《宪法》明确规定了"大赦",在全国人民代表大会行使

---

① 说赦免制度在立法事实上处于空白状态,是因为《宪法》只规定了全国人民代表大会常务委员会有决定特赦的权力,就如我们说《宪法》规定了人民法院有定罪判刑的权力,但如果没有相应的《刑法》、《刑事诉讼法》,等于定罪判刑还是无法可依。
② 参见彭兴庭《"特赦"前提是制度化和程序化》,《华商报》2009 年 2 月 18 日。
③ 参见吴情树《特赦,我们准备好了吗?》,《检察日报》2008 年 1 月 2 日。
④ 具体而言,在宪法上赋予赦免制度以正当性之后,可以专门制定《赦免法》。依据《宪法》对赦免的规定,既可以把现在的"特赦"改成"赦免",而在《赦免法》中再明确我国的"赦免"包括大赦、特赦、减刑和复权四种类型,也可以将大赦、减刑和复权明确规定到《宪法》中,与特赦一起作为我国赦免的具体种类。

的职权中，其中之一即"决定大赦"；而该法在"中华人民共和国主席"一节中规定："中华人民共和国主席根据全国人民代表大会的决定和全国人民代表大会常务委员会的决定……发布大赦令和特赦令。"1975 年《宪法》既没有规定大赦，也没有规定特赦，此后 1978 年和 1982 年《宪法》（即现行《宪法》）都只规定了特赦而没有规定大赦。①

笔者认为，在宪法上增设大赦制度是必要的，主要理由如下。

第一，当今世界许多国家和地区的宪法都有大赦制度，如美国、法国、德国、俄罗斯等。我国从清末颁布的《钦定宪法大纲》，到《中华民国临时约法》，再到后来的《中华民国宪法》，也都规定有大赦制度。现在我国台湾地区的"宪法"及"赦免法"中也仍然有大赦制度。有关国际公约中也有大赦的内容，如我国已经签署的《公民权利和政治权利国际公约》，其中第 6 条第 4 项就规定："任何被判处死刑的人均有权要求赦免或减刑。对一切判处死刑的案件，均得给予大赦、特赦或减刑的机会。"又如，我国于 1983 年加入的《日内瓦四公约关于保护非国际性武装冲突受难者的附加议定书》（第二议定书）第 6 条"刑事追诉"的第 5 款规定：在敌对行动结束时，当局对参加武装冲突的人或基于有关武装冲突的原因而被剥夺自由的人，不论被拘禁或拘留，应给予尽可能最广泛的赦免。对于这里的"尽可能最广泛的赦免"，理解为"大赦"比较适宜。此外，《联合国有条件判刑或有条件释放犯罪人转移监督示范条约》第 12 条规定：缔约国双方均可根据本国宪法或其他法律给予特赦、大赦或减刑。《联合国关于移交外国囚犯的模式协定》第 4 节"执行和赦免"中也规定：判决国和执行国均应有权特赦和大赦。②

第二，虽然是否实行大赦是一个政治考量和决策的问题，需要结合一国的具体形势经过慎重决策而定，但这并不妨碍在宪法上为大赦预留一席之地。确实，随着社会的发展和法制的进步，基于频繁大赦所固有的诸多

---

① 也有学者指出：宪法没有明确规定大赦并不意味着该制度已经被取消，因为宪法在列举全国人民代表大会的职权时，有一个兜底条款，即"全国人民代表大会认为应当由它行使的其他职权"。据此，可将"大赦"解释为包括在"其他职权"之内（参见阴建峰、王娜《现代赦免制度重构研究》，中国人民公安大学出版社，2011，第 43 页）。但通说认为我国宪法没有规定大赦（参见高铭暄、马克昌主编《刑法学》，北京大学出版社、高等教育出版社，2000，第 327 页）。笔者认为，由于 1954 年宪法曾将大赦与特赦并列规定，而现在的宪法去掉了大赦，只规定了特赦，因而不能认为现在的宪法可以包含大赦，否则连"特赦"也没有必要规定，都用"其他职权"来解释就得了。

② 参见陈东升《赦免制度研究》，中国人民公安大学出版社，2004，第 110 页。

弊端，现代社会对大赦的适用呈现出越来越严格的趋势。但这并不意味着大赦就彻底丧失了存在的根据，相反，作为一项制度，它被大多数国家和地区的宪法所保留，并适时在实践中加以运用。① 毕竟国家治理宜备有多个选项，以便形势需要时可用。诚如有学者所言："将大赦确定为今人即未来的先人处理或调节社会矛盾的一个选项，是一个不容回避和有极高价值期待的政治技术乃至政治艺术。"②

第三，事实证明，我国社会由于正处在转型时期，有些问题通过大赦来解决效果可能会更好，如针对民营企业的"原罪"问题，我国从中央到地方，相继颁布过一些政策性文件，强调"政法机关为完善社会主义市场经济体制创造良好环境"，对民营企业经营者在创业初期的犯罪行为，应尽量从宽处理。有学者就指出，若能通过大赦来解决此类法律难题，则更为理想。③ 作为一个对照，我们可以看一下俄罗斯的做法：2005 年 3 月，时任俄罗斯总统的普京针对一些所谓的寡头的"原罪"，通过大赦实现了重大的政策调整。④

第四，有人认为，大赦存在诸多弊端，如不问犯罪人的悔过情况，只是根据政治的需要在一定时刻宣布一概消除罪与刑，会削弱法律的稳定性，降低刑罚的一般预防作用，使一部分尚有社会危害性的犯罪人回到社会，威胁社会治安，等等。⑤ 大赦制度存在的一些弊端，其实有些也存在于包括特赦制度在内的所有赦免制度之中，正因为有弊端，所以自古以来，就不乏对赦免制度持批评态度的学者，但为何赦免制度从未消失呢？就因为它利弊互存，简单地取消它无法解决一定社会形势下的特殊问题。所以，多数学者认为，不能因噎废食，应当留出制度空间，将大赦制度作为一种"国家紧急避险行为"规定下来，以便在必要时适用之，以保全社会公共利

---

① 据《新京报》2012 年 1 月 15 日报道，1 月 14 日，缅甸政府依据总统吴登盛签署的大赦令，释放了 651 名在押人员，其中包括至少 200 名政治犯。另据《法制日报》2013 年 1 月 8 日报道，2013 年元旦，捷克总统克劳斯宣布，为纪念捷克共和国独立 20 周年实行大赦，大赦对象包括刑期不足 1 年的罪犯和刑期不到 10 年且年龄超过 75 岁的罪犯；同一天，邻国斯洛伐克总统也宣布实行大赦，不过大赦对象仅限于因非故意犯罪入狱或健康有问题的囚犯。
② 陈云生：《重建大赦制度的现实基础》，《法治研究》2010 年第 3 期。
③ 参见阴建峰《现代赦免制度论衡》，中国人民公安大学出版社，2006，第 279、391 页。当然，即使实行大赦，也不能由地方政府来实施，而应通过中央政府。
④ 参见陈云生《大赦经纬》，《国家检察官学院学报》2010 年第 1 期。
⑤ 参见陈东升《赦免制度研究》，中国人民公安大学出版社，2004，第 265 页。

益。当然,由于大赦范围广,对其适用要采取十分慎重的态度,竭力避免滥用,在这方面,许多国家和地区正是这样做的,如对大赦规定了更严格的程序等。另外,需要指出的是,大赦制度本身,也并不是一成不变的,而是可以随着时代的变化和结合本国的国情,对其做出一些改进和完善。有的国家出现了附条件的大赦,如法国,往往给获得大赦者附加一定的条件或义务,① 还有的国家在实行大赦时,越来越多地考虑犯罪的性质和社会危害程度、所处刑种以及犯罪人的个人情况(如是否有过恶意违反服刑程序的行为等)。②

第五,还有人说,原本适用大赦的情况可以通过特赦来处理,而不用依赖大赦来完成。③ 诚然,传统意义上的大赦与特赦之间的界限在有的国家或地区确实逐渐消失了,如传统上认为,大赦罪刑皆免,特赦免刑而不免罪,但现在有的国家或地区的立法例规定,特赦在必要时也可以免罪,④ 而大赦也未必就罪刑皆免。⑤ 但这并不是说,大赦和特赦就是一回事了,一般而言:特赦的对象相对特定,而大赦的对象则不特定;特赦的规模较小,而大赦的规模要大;特赦只针对已判刑的人,大赦则可以针对尚未判刑的人。因此,特赦并不能完全取代大赦。如果仅仅是取消大赦之名,而将其内容渗入特赦,则反而不如明文规定大赦的好,因为大赦制度由于其范围和效力不同于特赦而往往在程序上规定了更严格的限制条件。

## (二) 关于减刑

赦免性减刑不同于刑法典中的普通减刑。根据我国《刑法》的规定,普通减刑是指在刑罚执行过程中,对那些确有悔改表现或者有立功表现的犯罪人,依法对原判刑罚予以减轻的一种制度。也许有人会说:既然我国《刑法》中已有对减刑制度的规定,何必还要有赦免性减刑呢?这里,先不

---

① 参见〔法〕卡斯东·斯特法尼等《法国刑法总论精义》,罗结珍译,中国政法大学出版社,1998,第671页。
② 参见〔俄〕库兹涅佐娃、佳日科娃主编《俄罗斯刑法教程(总论)》(下卷·刑罚论),黄道秀译,中国法制出版社,2002,第825页。
③ 参见于志刚《刑罚消灭制度研究》,法律出版社,2002,第468页。
④ 如我国台湾地区的"赦免法"第3条规定:"受罪刑宣告之人经特赦者,免除其刑之执行;其情节特殊者,得以其罪刑之宣告为无效。"
⑤ 如意大利《刑法》就将大赦区分为免罪性大赦和免刑性大赦;韩国《赦免法》也规定,大赦在大总统令有特别规定的情况下,可不免罪。

论我国刑法中的减刑制度是否合理,① 就以现有规定论,刑法中的减刑制度也不能替代赦免性减刑。二者的主要区别在于以下三方面。首先,刑法中的减刑是针对特定的个别犯罪人的,不能对不特定的人适用;而赦免性减刑则既可以针对特定的个别犯罪人,也可以对不特定的全部犯罪人或者某一类或某几类的全部犯罪人适用。其次,即使赦免性减刑可以针对特定的个别犯罪人,其也与刑法中的减刑不同,后者以犯罪人有悔改表现或者立功表现为前提,主要从犯罪人本身的状况出发,而前者则主要从刑事政策出发,根据国家政治形势的需要和社会发展之情状而定。再次,刑法中的减刑只能在犯罪人开始服刑后才能适用,而赦免性减刑则既可以在犯罪人服刑一段时间后适用,也可刑罚一经宣告就予以减刑。而且,刑法中的减刑有幅度上的限制,如按照我国《刑法》第78条的规定,经过一次或几次减刑后实际执行的刑期,判处管制、拘役、有期徒刑的,不能少于原判刑期的1/2,判处无期徒刑的,不能少于13年。但赦免性减刑没有这种限制,其政策灵活性更大。

赦免性减刑可分为一般减刑和特别减刑。一般减刑又称全国性减刑或普遍性减刑,是指对不特定的犯罪人实施减刑的制度。一般减刑与大赦的性质有相通之处,一般依照大赦的程序颁行。特别减刑又称个别减刑或特定减刑,是指对特定犯罪人实施减刑的制度。特别减刑与特赦的性质有相通之处,一般依照特赦的程序颁行。

赦免性减刑的内容包括同一刑种内刑度的减轻和不同刑种的变更两种,也有的国家分别对一般减刑和特别减刑规定了不同的减刑内容,如韩国《赦免法》就规定:一般减刑,法律没有特别规定的,变更刑种;特别减刑,只减轻刑的执行,有特别理由的才可变更刑种。

在我国过去的赦免实践中,往往把赦免性减刑包含在特赦中,如1959年为庆祝新中国成立10周年,当时的国家主席刘少奇根据我国人大常委会

---

① 国外刑法普遍规定有假释制度,但鲜有规定减刑制度(当然在赦免法中则普遍规定有减刑制度)。笔者认为,在刑法中规定减刑制度的理论正当性值得斟酌,因为宣判刑是基于审判时犯罪人的犯罪行为及其主观恶性和人身危险性而确定的,在执行阶段减轻,从刑事责任的根据、罪刑相适应的原则等角度来看都不太合适,如果犯罪人表现好,可采"假释"这样一种变更执行方式的制度,这样既不伤害原来的判决,又避免刑罚浪费,同时也鼓励犯罪人往好的方向改造。而且,由于假释给从监禁状态向自由状态过渡提供了一个缓冲期,因而更具有合理性。

《关于特赦确实改恶从善的罪犯的决定》发布的《中华人民共和国主席特赦令》中,除了宣布释放一批战争罪犯、反革命罪犯和普通刑事罪犯外,还规定对符合条件的死缓犯、无期徒刑犯予以减刑。① 在理论上,不同的学者有不同的理解,如高铭暄教授认为,特赦包括减刑,但张文显教授对特赦的理解就不包括减刑。② 笔者认为,把赦免性减刑笼统地包含在特赦里,至少是不准确的。虽然我们过去的赦免实践是这么做的,但应当看到,那是法制不完备时期的产物。从世界其他国家和地区的通行做法来看,特赦不能包含减刑:韩国《赦免法》规定,本法规定有关赦免、减刑和复权的事项,其中赦免分为一般赦免(即大赦——作者注)和特别赦免(即特赦——作者注),减刑分为一般减刑和特别减刑;我国台湾地区的"赦免法"规定,本法称赦免者,谓大赦、特赦、减刑及复权。从规范赦免的角度看,把赦免性减刑独立出来是有必要的。

### (三) 关于复权

赦免性复权,是指国家对因受到有罪判决而终身或定期丧失或者停止某些权利或资格者,经过法定的程序恢复其权利或资格的一种制度。它也分为一般复权和特别复权两种:一般复权是指针对符合条件的不特定多数人实施的复权;特别复权是指针对特定人实施的复权。

许多国家和地区的刑法也有复权制度,③ 虽然我国《刑法》中没有复权制度,但近年来也有不少学者主张增设该制度。④ 需要指出的是,赦免性复权与刑法上的复权在性质上有所不同:刑法上的复权是作为一种刑罚制度出现的,其目的在于消除刑罚过剩,奖励犯罪人积极悔过和自我改造;而赦免性复权则是作为一种赦免制度出现的,其目的在于调节利益冲突、衡

---

① 参见郭金霞、苗鸣宇《大赦·特赦——中外赦免制度概观》,群众出版社,2003,第 196~198 页。
② 参见王媛《特赦就是让百姓看到国家还是有它的"仁政"》,《南方人物周刊》2009 年第 9 期。
③ 正如同自由刑需要有缓刑与假释等制度来对其弊端提供救济一样,对于因受到有罪判决而终身或定期丧失或者被停止某些权利或资格者,若其经过一段时间而能洁身自好,法院应依职权或申请,有条件地提前恢复其权利或资格,以激励受刑人自新,此为刑法上的复权制度之价值。
④ 参见刘德法、王冠《论刑法中的复权制度》,《河南师范大学学报(哲学社会科学版)》2003 年第 6 期;彭新林:《略论刑法中的复权制度》,《中国青年政治学院学报》2006 年第 2 期。

平法律关系、弥补法律的不足。①

我国的赦免制度中虽然没有明确规定复权制度,但在过去的赦免实践中存在过类似复权的做法,如 1975 年 3 月 17 日,全国人大常委会决定,对全部在押战犯一律特赦,并给予公民权。当时,国务院副总理兼公安部部长华国锋在代表病重的周恩来总理向全国人大常委会做专题说明时指出:"遵照毛主席的指示精神,对这次特赦释放的全部在押战犯,每人都给公民权;有工作能力的,安排适当的工作;有病的,和我们干部一样治,享受公费医疗;丧失工作能力的,养起来;愿意回台湾的,可以回台湾,给足路费,提供方便,去了以后愿意回来的,我们欢迎。释放时,每人发给新制服装和一百元零用钱,把他们集中到北京开欢送会,由党和国家领导人接见,并宴请一次,然后组织他们参观学习。"② 据此,有学者认为,这里的给予公民权,即恢复他们的政治权利,实际上属于赦免性复权,只不过它与特赦是一同实施而不是单独实施罢了。③ 笔者同意这一看法,同时也认为,有必要在我国的赦免制度中,专门把复权制度拿出来研究并加以规定。④

综上,鉴于中国现行《宪法》仅规定了特赦这一单一的赦免类型,而立法过于简略,赦免实践中的特赦又兼具传统大赦、特赦的双重特点,且有时与赦免性减刑、赦免性复权等混为一体,⑤ 为了规范赦免的具体类型,避免赦免法定类型与实践类型的脱节以及由此导致的赦免适用的随意性,并根据各种复杂的案情对被追诉人和被判刑人适当、合理地适用不同类型的赦免,有必要在我国《宪法》和相关法律中将赦免类型法定化。⑥ 具体而言,我国的赦免种类至少应当包括大赦、特赦、减刑和复权四种,其中减刑又分为一般减刑和特别减刑,复权也分为一般复权和特别复权。在此前

---

① 参见阴建峰《现代赦免制度论衡》,中国人民公安大学出版社,2006,第 259 页。
② 郭金霞、苗鸣宇《大赦·特赦——中外赦免制度概观》,群众出版社,2003,第 211 页。
③ 参见高铭暄主编《刑法学原理》第 3 卷,中国人民大学出版社,1994,第 687 页。
④ 像"公民权"这种提法其实是不严谨的,因为即使是犯人,他们也还是国家的公民,除法律明确规定并通过判决加以剥夺的某些公民权利外,他们仍然享有其他公民权利。顺便说一句,复权中的"权"到底包括哪些权利(资格),各个国家和地区的规定也多有不同。如我国台湾地区的"赦免法"中将其界定为"所褫夺之公权",即"为公务员之资格"和"为公职候选人之资格",这比起我国《刑法》中的"剥夺政治权利",范围要窄,后者还包括剥夺言论、出版、集会、结社、游行、示威等权利。
⑤ 并不是说不同种类的赦免不可以同时适用,而是要有法可依、名正言顺。
⑥ 参见陈春勇《赦免及其程序问题研究》,中国人民公安大学出版社,2010,第 226~227 页。

提下，法律可再分别规定其法律后果、① 适用范围、② 附加条件③等。

## 四 赦免制度的程序完善

赦免制度本身是一把双刃剑，用得好，可以收到积极的刑事政策效果，但若被滥用，其消极效果也不容忽视。古今中外，对赦免制度的批评和担心其实也就集中在滥赦上。因此，建构科学完备的赦免程序，对于保证赦免制度的规范运行，具有重要意义。④

如何完善我国的赦免程序，有以下几个问题需要重点考虑。

### （一）关于赦免的启动、申请与决定

根据不同的赦免类型设置不同的赦免程序，这是世界各国的通例。在此，先不妨将大赦、一般减刑和一般复权统称为一般赦免，⑤将特赦、特别减刑和特别复权统称为特别赦免。一般赦免特别是大赦，因其适用范围广，社会影响大，各国一般都将其交给议会等最高权力机关以自上而下地启动：韩国规定，大赦除经过国务会议（由大总统主持的一种政府会议）的审议、并以大总统令限定所适用的罪名外，还须得到国会的同意；法国的大赦要经国会审议；俄罗斯的大赦由俄罗斯国家杜马审议。因此，我国在赦免制度的设计中，应将一般赦免的启动权赋予中共中央或国务院，由其向全国人民代表大会建议，再由全国人民代表大会来决定是否要实行一般赦免。

与一般赦免自上而下的启动模式不同，特别赦免在许多国家和地区均主要采取自下而上的启动模式，通常由当事人或其亲友、律师等申请启动，或由检察官和监狱等机关依职权提请启动，例如：日本的个别恩赦（即特

---

① 赦免的法律后果，亦称法律效力，如：规定大赦既免罪又免刑（也可规定特别情况下只免刑不免罪），特赦只免刑，必要时也可以免罪；又如，各种赦免对前科消灭、累犯成立等的影响，也都属于这一范畴。

② 从总体而言，"赦免恩德，如同甘霖普化"，其应可以对一切犯罪和犯罪人适用，但具体而言，每次赦免时可以有一定范围的限制，如我国台湾地区从20世纪50年代以来的3部"全国性"减刑条例，均规定对"重大犯罪"不予赦免，但在个案中，仍然可以对"重大犯罪"予以赦免，如1957年对黄百韬之子黄效先的赦免即属此例。参见阴建峰《现代赦免制度论衡》，中国人民公安大学出版社，2006，第271页。

③ 无论对一般赦免者还是特别赦免者，均可附加一定的条件，以便更好地实现刑罚目的，维护社会秩序。这些附加条件必须是法定的，但在具体适用时可以视情况而定。

④ 说到程序对法治的意义，人们常常引用美国联邦最高法院大法官威廉·道格拉斯的如下名言："权利法案的大多数规定都是程序性条款，这一事实绝不是无意义的。正是程序决定了法治与恣意的人治之间的基本区别。"

⑤ 需要注意的是，在有的国家如韩国，赦免即专指大赦。

赦）启动于当事人申请，或由教导所所长等依职权提请；俄罗斯特赦可由被判刑人或其亲友申请或社会团体、刑罚执行机关提请；美国特赦的启动主要源于当事人的申请。①

据有的学者考证，中国古代当事人自下而上地启动赦免也比皇帝及其他官员定期或不定期的录囚更为常见。② 但新中国成立以来的 7 次特赦实践，都是自上而下的启动模式，即由全国人大常委会根据党中央或国务院的建议来审议决定，并由国家主席颁令实行（第 7 次没有国家主席颁令这一环节）。当然，如前所述，这几次特赦中有的本来就带有大赦的性质，即使属于特赦性质的，也不是个别特赦，因而采取自上而下的启动模式，未尝不可。

但从完善特别赦免程序的角度来看，我国应该借鉴国外和我国古代的做法，在特别赦免中实行自上而下和自下而上相结合的启动模式，亦即在保留自上而下的启动模式的同时，③ 增加自下而上的启动模式。具体而言，可分为以下两种情形。

一是司法行政机关可以作为特别赦免提请主体，向中央赦免机构提出特别赦免建议，并负责提供相关调查材料。这一类自下而上的启动主要针对符合特别赦免条件的特定多数被判刑人，也就是说，根据国家形势的需要，觉得有必要对这些人实行特别赦免的，可以提出建议和申请。如我国 1997 年新《刑法》已经废除了投机倒把罪、流氓罪等罪名，那么过去因这些罪而被判刑如今仍然关押在监狱中的到底还有多少人，假如针对这些人认为有必要提请特赦的，就可以由刑罚执行机关上报司法行政机关提请特赦。

二是被判刑人本身或者其近亲属或者其委托的律师，可以作为特别赦免的申请主体，在符合条件的情况下提出申请。这其中，凡是被判处死刑的，一律赋予其无条件的申请特别赦免权（关于死刑案件的特别赦免程序，后文将专门阐述）；至于被判处其他刑罚的，则可以在满足一定条件的情况下赋予其申请权（如判决后已经服刑达到一定期限的，或赦免申请被驳回后必须经过一定的期限才可重新申请等）。

至于有学者指出："总体上看，一般赦免程序较之特别赦免程序规定相对粗略。"④ 对此，笔者的理解是：除了《宪法》和《赦免法》或者《刑

---

① 陈春勇《赦免及其程序问题研究》，中国人民公安大学出版社，2010，第 249 页。
② 参见陈春勇《赦免及其程序问题研究》，中国人民公安大学出版社，2010，第 250 页。
③ 如为了外交的需要，国家主动特赦某一国的间谍等罪犯。
④ 陈春勇：《赦免及其程序问题研究》，中国人民公安大学出版社，2010，第 241 页。

法》、《刑事诉讼法》规定的一般程序外，每次在实行一般赦免时，还要由议会等立法机关通过专门法令来施行，因此详细的一般赦免程序其实是在此类专门法令中得以体现的；而特别赦免由于在实践中施用更为频繁，且在许多国家和地区均体现为行政权，由国家元首决定和颁行（联邦制的国家在州一级还可由州长直接行使），因而需要事先加以详细规制。

我国现行《宪法》规定，特赦由全国人大常委会审议决定，国家主席发布特赦令。从今后完善的角度考虑，宜把个案的特别赦免和多案的特别赦免分开，[①] 后者仍然可由全国人大常委会来审议决定，但前者应通过修改《宪法》，将特别赦免的决定权由目前的立法机关（即全国人大常委会）转移到国家元首（即中华人民共和国主席）上来。也就是说，个案的特别赦免申请经由一定程序上达国家主席后，国家主席便可咨询相关机构和人士，如决定特别赦免，就可以特别赦免令的形式颁行，这样可以更好地保证特别赦免制度适用上的快捷、迅速，以及时回应社会关切和犯罪人的个人情状。[②]

### （二）关于专门赦免机构的设立

专门赦免机构主要针对特别赦免而言。世界上许多国家都设有专门的赦免机构，如俄罗斯总统办公厅设有特赦局，其负责起草和准备有关特赦问题的实质性文件和材料，拟成后送交俄罗斯联邦总统特赦问题委员会，该委员会负责审议并提出解决的办法、建议。这些建议通过总统办公厅呈报总统，最后由总统对特赦及其性质做出最终的决定。[③] 美国的联邦赦免申请由司法部下属的赦免事务办公室受理和审查，而各州的赦免则由州赦免事务委员会审查。日本也专设有"中央更生保护审查会"来处理赦免事宜，为法务大臣下属机关，一般由5名委员组成，委员都须经国会两院同意，法务大臣任命，其主要工作之一即调查犯罪人资料并初步决定可赦之人，呈

---

[①] 考虑到多案的特别赦免社会影响要大些，因而通过全国人大常委会来决定是比较妥当的。此外，国外还有这样的立法例，即对赦免高官设置更加复杂的程序，如希腊就规定：对于部长以上的高官必须通过更复杂的程序才能获得赦免，之所以这样规定，是因为该国立法机关认为，过去针对高官有滥用赦免的种种弊端。（参见崔康锡、刘仁文《韩国赦免制度及其改革方案》，载《亚洲法论坛》第1卷，中国人民公安大学出版社，2006，第310页。）不管我们是否要借鉴这一立法例，总之，特别赦免的程序可以根据不同情况做不同设计，并不是说特别赦免就只能有一种程序。

[②] 参见陈东升《赦免制度研究》，中国人民公安大学出版社，2004，第278页。

[③] 参见〔俄〕库兹涅佐娃、佳日科娃主编《俄罗斯刑法教程（总论）》（下卷·刑罚论），黄道秀译，中国法制出版社，2002，第830页。

报法务大臣,还接受"监狱长"、"保护观察所所长"及"有罪判决宣告法院检察处之检察官"提出的赦免申请。其他如法国,也在司法部下设有特赦事务司。①

由专门的赦免机构来处理赦免的相关事宜,有助于集中专门的业务人员和力量,有针对性地解决赦免申请的受理、审查、建议、通知、执行等有关赦免的各个环节的问题,提高处理赦免问题的专业性和效率,也是使赦免常态化的必要之举。我国没有这类专司赦免申请的受理与审查的机构,为健全赦免制度,应当设立这样的机构,具体设想如下。

第一,在全国人大常委会下设赦免事务委员会,该委员会的组成人员应来自公安、检察、法院、律师、法学教授以及其他民意代表,② 可以设立办公室作为日常运转机构。

第二,委员会的主要职责是:负责大赦等一般赦免的调查、建议和咨询;负责受理特别赦免的提请和申请;负责审查特别赦免的可行性,并上报有关调查材料;起草特别赦免建议要点;等等。

第三,审查赦免个案申请的基本步骤如下:首先,应看是否已是最后补充救济途径,即是否已穷尽法律内的一切救济渠道;其次,应考察是否有适宜特别赦免的因素,如查明原审判决所依据的法律是否已经做出有利于被判刑人的变更,或者有无国防、外交等方面的特殊考虑,或者存在错判、误判之可能,有必要通过特别赦免渠道来救济的;最后,特别赦免一般还应考虑以下一些因素,如被判刑人的监内改造表现、人身危险性大小,被特别赦免后的就业等情况,原处理案件的法官、检察官的意见,被害方的意见,等等。

第四,赦免事务委员会的意见不具有直接约束赦免权的法律后果,但实际上会对赦免决定产生影响,如国家元首等赦免权行使主体在没有特别理由的情况下仍不顾赦免事务委员会的否定性意见,执意行赦,就会面临道义和政治上的责任和压力,这在当代民主社会,显然会对制约不当赦免产生积极影响。

### (三) 关于赦免令的颁布、执行与监督

如前所言,在完善我国的赦免类型后,一般赦免的决定权应由全国人

---

① 参见陈东升《赦免制度研究》,中国人民公安大学出版社,2004,第152~153页。
② 其中法官应占约1/3的比例,因为赦免本质上具有变更法院所做出的判决的效果,有必要让法官来考虑与其他判决之间的平衡问题;律师、法学教授以及其他民意代表也应占约1/3,以便能够比较准确地反映国民的意向。

民代表大会来行使,在全国人民代表大会通过一般赦免令之后,再由国家主席来颁布。一般赦免令的内容既可以是大赦,也可以是一般减刑,或者一般复权,或者大赦兼复权。需要指出的是,过去在中国的赦免实践中(虽名义上均为特赦,但有的特赦带有大赦的性质),立法机关通过的赦免决定往往比较简单,而国家主席据此发布的赦免令则详细规定了其实质内容和条件,这意味着国家主席对特赦的具体内容有实质决定权。笔者认为,这种做法应当改变,一般赦免令本身必须详细载明一般赦免的类型、罪种、刑期标准等内容,以及执行一般赦免令的环节和程序,全国人民代表大会通过后,国家主席不宜再另行发布包含其他实质内容的一般赦免令,只需履行《宪法》第 80 条规定的根据全国人民代表大会的决定而公布法律的职能(一般赦免令也是一种法律)。

至于特别赦免,按照前面笔者的设想,决定权一分为二之后,个案的特别赦免由国家主席直接决定并颁发特别赦免令(或特赦,或特别减刑,或特别复权,或特赦兼复权),多案的特别赦免则在全国人大常委会做出决定后再由国家主席以特别赦免令的形式颁行,同样,后者的具体内容应由全国人大常委会来决定,国家主席的特别赦免令不应再创制新的内容。

关于赦免令的执行,目前我国也缺乏明确的规定。从过去的赦免实践看,一般是在全国人大常委会通过"特赦"决定、国家主席颁布"特赦令"后,根据特赦令中要求的特赦条件,由罪犯管理机关在对罪犯进行严格审查后,经过最高人民法院批准并决定,由最高人民法院发给特赦通知书。[①]

就完善我国的赦免制度而言,对一般赦免令的执行可做如下构想。一般赦免令发布后,有关追诉、审判和刑罚执行机关应在第一时间告知被追诉人和被判刑人,要求其协助收集相关证明材料,由其本人或委托律师或其他人员拟定一份符合此次一般赦免条件的报告,然后将该报告和相关证明材料报送管辖法院初步审查后层报最高人民法院。最高人民法院对其进行审查后发放一般赦免通知书,载明:根据一般赦免令,被追诉人和被判刑人哪些具体情况符合一般赦免令的哪些具体规定,从而对其产生何种具体的赦免效力。一般赦免通知书应分别送达被追诉人和被判刑人的管辖法院、被追诉人和被判刑人本人,以及对被追诉人和被判刑人进行追诉或执

---

① 参见郭金霞、苗鸣宇《大赦·特赦——中外赦免制度概观》,群众出版社,2003,第 198~199 页。

行刑罚的机构。[1]

对特别赦免令的执行,我们要改变过去那种先颁发特赦令再审查犯罪人的有关情况,并根据审查意见由最高人民法院确定特赦的具体名单的做法,而应当根据提请或申请,先由赦免事务委员会初步审查,再视情况分别报国家主席或全国人大常委会决定,特别赦免令应直接写明被赦免人的姓名,并载明特别赦免的原因、具体类型、效力、附加条件等。

无论是一般赦免令还是特别赦免令的执行,都需要遵循公共政策执行领域的监督原理,[2] 加强对执行过程的监督,以确保实现政策的本来目的。特别是一般赦免令的执行,由于牵涉面广,加之一般赦免令本身并不直接确定具体的赦免名单,因而更需要在执行中采取听证等公开、透明的措施,以免出现腐败等现象。

## 五 死刑案件特别赦免程序之构想

在特别赦免中,有一类案件值得专门研究,这就是死刑案件。《公民权利与政治权利国际公约》第6条第4项规定:"任何被判处死刑的人应有权要求赦免或减刑。对一切判处死刑的案件,均得给予大赦、特赦或减刑的机会。"我国已经签署该公约,并正在为批准该公约做准备。鉴于我国短期内不可能废除死刑,因此需要在死刑案件中增设申请特别赦免的程序,以满足公约在这方面的最低人权标准。[3]

增设特别赦免的申请程序也是完善死刑案件刑事诉讼制度的需要。我国《刑事诉讼法》第251条规定:"下级人民法院接到最高人民法院执行死刑的命令后,应当在七日以内交付执行。但是发现有下列情形之一的,应当停止执行,并且立即报告最高人民法院,由最高人民法院作出裁定:(一)在执行前发现判决可能有错误的;(二)在执行前罪犯揭发重大犯罪事实或者有其他重大立功表现,可能需要改判的;(三)罪犯正在怀孕。"最高人民法院在1999年《关于对在执行死刑前发现重大情况需要改判的案件如何适用程序问题的批复》中指出:对上述需要改判的案件,由有死刑核准权的人民法院适用审判监督程序依法改判或者指令下级人民法院再审。

---

[1] 参见陈春勇《赦免及其程序问题研究》,中国人民公安大学出版社,2010,第246~249页。
[2] 参见刘仁文《论刑事政策的执行》,载《刑事法评论》第11卷,中国政法大学出版社,2002。
[3] 可以说,死刑犯申请特赦或减刑已经成为一项国际公认的权利:联合国《关于保护死刑犯权利的保障措施》第7条规定,任何被判死刑的人都"有权寻求赦免或减刑";《美洲人权公约》第4条也规定,任何一个被处死刑者"都有权请求赦免、特赦或者减刑"。

但问题是，根据我国《刑事诉讼法》的规定，刑事案件再审的理由是原生效判决"确有错误"，而《刑事诉讼法》第251条规定的第二种情形，即死刑犯在死刑执行前揭发重大犯罪事实或者有其他重大立功表现的，这种改判理由并不是因为原判决在认定事实和适用法律上有错误。第三种情形的改判理由也不一定是原判决在认定事实和适用法律上有错误，因为该妇女可能不是"审判时正在怀孕的"，而是在审判后才受孕，甚至是判决生效后才受孕，① 对在审判后受孕的女死刑犯进行改判，是基于人道主义和避免株连另一无辜生命的考虑，也是《公民权利与政治权利国际公约》第6条第5项规定的"怀胎妇女被判死刑，不得执行其刑"的要求。因此，笔者同意针对此两种情形构建一个新的程序即死刑赦免程序来加以解决。②

或许有人会说，我国的死刑案件已经有了一套普通刑事案件所没有的复核程序，已经体现了对死刑案件的特别重视，该复核程序可充当前述特别赦免程序的功能。对此，笔者的意见是否定的。首先，死刑复核程序是一套司法程序，而特别赦免程序是独立于司法机关之外的另一套程序。在死刑核准之前，死刑判决仍然是未生效的判决，但特别赦免程序则是在判决已经生效的情况下才提起的。其次，死刑复核并不能代行特别赦免的功能，如对于独生子女犯死罪的，在死刑复核环节必须坚持法律面前人人平等，但从国家施仁政的角度来看，也许在赦免上就可以找到理由。③ 又如，对被判死刑后患精神病或绝症的罪犯，可以赦免，但复核就不一定能从法律上找到免死的依据（除非在立法上明确规定此种情形下不可以核准死刑）。再次，在一审、二审和复核之外再加一套特别赦免程序，一点都不算多。许多教训表明，经过三级司法审查后仍然不能发现死刑案件的全部错误。即便像美国这样死刑案件诉讼程序时间漫长的国家，近年来仍不断爆

---

① 有人可能会说，审判后或判决生效后犯人被关在看守所里，怎么可能怀孕呢？但这种可能性在现实中确实存在，如有的女死刑犯勾引看守所的干警与其发生性关系致其怀孕，还有的女死刑犯被看守所所长等人强奸而致怀孕。例如，《江南时报》2000年7月15日以"谁令死刑无法执行"为题，报道了一名"血债累累、罪大恶极"的女囚，在看守所内被看守所所长等人多次强奸致其怀孕，结果本应处以死刑的她被改判无期徒刑。

② 参见竹怀军《论我国死刑赦免制度的构建》，《湖南师范大学社会科学学报》2004年第5期。

③ 法理学者苏力在反对废除死刑的同时，又主张对独生子女可以免死（参见苏力《从药家鑫案看刑罚的狭及效果和罪责自负》，《法学》2011年第6期），结果被刑法学者邱兴隆抓住了他逻辑上的软肋（参见邱兴隆《就独生子女免死对苏力教授说不》，《法学》2011年第10期）。其实，如果苏力不从法律层面而从政策层面，提出用赦免的方法来达到对独生子女免死的目的，也许从逻辑上就要顺畅得多了。

出无辜者被错误定罪、其中不少差点被错误执行死刑的消息。①

在具体设计死刑特别赦免程序时，有以下问题需要注意。

1. 死刑特别赦免的机关

有论者认为，赦免死刑的机关应是最高人民法院。② 这种意见值得商榷，因为在死刑核准权统一收回后，最高人民法院目前已经行使死刑核准权了，再将赦免权赋予它，在实际工作中核准权和赦免权就将由同一机构来行使，这样可能会带来机制上的不顺，导致效果不佳，例如，最高人民法院先核准死刑，再赦免死刑，即使是由不同的部门决定，也难免对最高人民法院决定的严肃性产生一定的冲击。因此，对于死刑案件的特别赦免程序，还是宜遵循前述笔者所构想的特别赦免程序，即个案的特别赦免由国家主席直接决定并颁布特别赦免令，多案的特别赦免则在全国人大常委会做出决定后再由国家主席以特别赦免令的形式颁行。③

2. 死刑特别赦免的类型

死刑犯申请的特别赦免类型以减刑为妥，不宜适用特赦和复权。特赦，即免除死刑犯的刑罚，走得太远，社会公众难以接受。相应地，由于赦免性复权以刑罚执行终了或刑罚执行免除为前提，而死刑案件还没有进展到这一步，所以也不存在赦免性复权。不仅如此，这里的赦免性减刑也应有所限制，即不应无限制地减刑，一般减刑为死刑缓期两年执行即可，因为毕竟经过了一审和二审以及复核程序，到减刑这一环节不宜步子迈得太大。

3. 死刑特别赦免的对象

赦免对象主要包括以下七种。一是前面所说的《刑事诉讼法》251 条规定的两种情形，即死刑犯在死刑执行前揭发重大犯罪事实或者有其他重大立功表现的，以及死刑犯在审判后怀孕的。二是被判死刑后患精神病或绝症的罪犯。三是年老或青少年罪犯。我国《刑法》虽然规定对犯罪的时候

---

① 需要指出的是，国内有媒体报道美国有许多无辜者被处死（参见王菊芳《二十七年全美近百人蒙冤而死 伊州死刑大赦引起强烈反响》，《检察日报》2003 年 1 月 14 日），但在一次国际会议上，有美国学者告诉我，这个消息是不准确的，正确的说法应当是："不可能确切知道，但也许有无辜者被执行了死刑。"（参见 DPIC 网站，DPIC 是 Death Peanalty Information Center 的简称，即"死刑信息中心"）根据这个信息，我们至少可以看出，美国尚无明确被证明是杀错了人的冤案，这说明它的死刑案件诉讼程序近乎漫长还是比较有效地保证了死刑案件的质量。

② 参见竹怀军《论我国死刑赦免制度的构建》，《湖南师范大学社会科学学报》2004 年第 5 期。

③ 如果需要对死刑案件进行一般赦免时，则遵循一般赦免的程序。

已满 18 周岁的人可以判处死刑，但如果被处死刑者仍然是青少年（特别是如果刚过 18 周岁），还是应当在其申请赦免时视其具体案情给予考虑。另外，《刑法修正案（八）》虽然规定了对审判的时候已满 75 周岁的人一般不适用死刑，但如果老年罪犯还没到 75 周岁（特别是马上就要到 75 周岁），因而被判处死刑的，仍然有根据案情需要通过特别赦免来减刑之必要。四是弱智罪犯和新生婴儿母亲罪犯。美国最高法院早些年曾有一个判决，该判决认为处决弱智罪犯违反了《美国宪法》第 8 条规定的"不得施加残忍的和异常的惩罚"，从此禁止对弱智犯执行死刑。① 罪犯的智商判定问题，现在科学上已经能够解决，因而笔者认为对弱智罪犯不执行死刑也是人道主义的体现。同样出于人道主义的考虑，对新生婴儿的母亲罪犯也不应执行死刑。如果这些人被判处死刑，应当尽量考虑通过特别赦免来减轻其刑罚。五是对于独生子女罪犯，特别是几代单传的，或者父母已经无法再生育的，如果被判处死刑，也应当尽量考虑通过特别赦免来免其一死。当然，并不是不加区别地对所有独生子女罪犯都可一律免死，还要看具体案情。六是出于外交等因素考虑的某些案件，如我国 2009 年判处英国毒贩阿克毛死刑并随后处决，不仅在英国，甚至在欧盟都引起强烈"地震"，因为包括英国在内的欧盟早已废除死刑，但依据我国法律，似乎不判其死刑又没有法律根据，类似案件如果有特别赦免程序，则可先由法院判处其死刑，然后再借助特别赦免这一渠道，将其减刑。七是出于其他国际、国内因素的考虑，或者案件本身的特殊情况需要用特别赦免来调节法律的刚性的。

4. 死刑执行的期限

与死刑特别赦免制度相关的一个问题是，按照目前我国《刑事诉讼法》的规定，死刑一旦核准，就将在 7 天内执行，这一间隔早已被学界批评为太短，若从构建死刑特别赦免制度而言，也必须延长死刑执行的期限，否则可能还没来得及启动特别赦免程序，死刑就已经执行了。笔者认为，把死刑执行期限由现在的 7 天改为 6 个月比较适宜，当然如果在这期间死刑犯提起特别赦免程序，则自当等该程序走完再执行，而不必局限于 6 个月。

## 结语　制定《中华人民共和国赦免法》的建议

从世界各国和地区的赦免立法模式看，在确立了赦免的宪法性基础的前提下，对赦免制度有分散型和法典化两种立法模式，前者体现为在刑法、

---

① 参见刘仁文《弱智罪犯不执行死刑之启示》，《检察日报》2003 年 1 月 17 日。

刑事诉讼法中分别规定赦免的实体和程序内容，后者则是制定专门的赦免法。通过本文前面的分析，我国赦免制度除了在宪法上需要加以完善外，还需要在实体和程序上予以具体化。对此，究竟是采分散型立法好还是法典化立法好？笔者的综合考量结果是，制定一部专门的赦免法对我国来说比较科学，也比较可行，理由如下。

首先，从1979年我国颁布《刑法》、《刑事诉讼法》以来，我国的赦免制度长期处于边缘状态。无论是《宪法》还是《刑法》和《刑事诉讼法》，对赦免制度的规定都"过于概括和原则，内容单薄、疏漏，缺乏可操作性……具体规定根本达不到'制度'的层次"[1]。实践中赦免制度被长期搁置，人们对建国后几次特赦的印象也还停留在政策性强、随意性大的记忆中，仿佛赦免是与法治相对立的产物。近年来关于国家特赦甚至大赦的建议此起彼伏，但由于该领域无法可依，因此各种建议也五花八门。为了激活赦免制度并规范其运行，在完善《宪法》关于赦免的基本类型的前提下，制定一部专门的赦免法，实有必要。

其次，现在很多国家或地区都将赦免扩大适用到行政性处罚和纪律性制裁上来，如韩国《赦免法》第4条规定："关于对违反行政法规规定行为的犯罪或惩罚，或者根据惩戒法规的惩戒（相当于纪律处分——作者注）或惩罚的免除，应准用赦免的规定。"由于在我国，行政处罚和行政处分的范围比较广，特别是还包括了治安处罚等诸多可以剥夺人身自由的处罚，赦免更应准用于这些领域，否则就不公平。实践中，有的事例也可以为我们提供进一步的思考，如2008年汶川地震时，广州市司法局"特赦"了29名川籍劳教人员，让其回去参与救灾。虽然"按照国家的政策，我们可以有给余期三个月以下的劳教人员减期的权限"，但"因为自然灾害而为劳教人员减期，这在国内还没有人尝试过"[2]。这其实是一种典型的"特赦"，它证明了在今后赦免制度的运行中，把劳教等考虑在内的合理性。把这种准用性赦免的内容放到《刑法》或《刑事诉讼法》中都不妥，最好是明文规定在专门的赦免法中。

再次，对赦免采分散型立法的国家和地区，赦免一般都早已成为习惯，且那些国家的赦免是通过长期的法治发展而形成的，对于我国这样一个需要重新在法治基础上激活赦免制度的成文法国家而言，专门立法是最有效

---

[1] 陈东升：《赦免制度研究》，中国人民公安大学出版社，2004，第204页。
[2] 廖杰华等：《广州29名川籍劳教人员获"特赦"赴灾区救赎》，《广州日报》2008年6月25日。

率、最能保证依法行赦、使赦免制度严格沿着法治的轨道运行的理想选择。尽管像大赦这类赦免，每次都需要立法机关单独出台法令，但那只是在大赦的具体内容上，如每次大赦的范围等。对于包括大赦在内的各种赦免，大至法律效力、一般程序，小至赦免状（减刑状、复权状）的颁布、送达，都需要详细加以规定。特别是我国正处于建设社会主义法治国家的进程中，社会的规范意识还亟待强化，公众对司法腐败极为关切，在这样一种情况下，通过专门立法，一方面可以重拾赦免这一重要的治国艺术，另一方面也能确保其有序运行。

曾有美国学者疑惑地发问：为什么现代社会在法院提供了如此精细的法律标准和诉讼程序后，还允许赦免的存在呢？其追问的结果是：法律并不是完美的，当法律制度自身不能实现正义时，有赖赦免来施以正义；当法律制度在个案中过于严厉时，有赖赦免来施以仁慈。① 其实，赦免的功能还不止于此。作为一项重要的刑事政策，它在对内赢得民心、凝聚民意、对外维护国家利益、树立国家形象等多方面均具有难以取代的作用。② 我国赦免制度的法律规范不健全和实践中的长期被搁置，不仅导致赦免的积极功能没有得到有效的发挥，而且助长了潜规则的流行，甚至带来法治上的困惑，如我国实践中对某些特殊罪犯采取"保外就医"的做法，其实这些人并不是因为身体健康的原因，只不过借这个制度来实现别的目的罢了。③

---

① 参见〔美〕琳达·E. 卡特等《美国死刑法精解》，王秀梅等译，北京大学出版社，2009，第260页。

② 还记得1999年国庆前夕，笔者到香港参加一个国际会议，当时有香港人士问我：你们国庆50周年，各行各业均要庆祝，有没有想过也要给那些犯人和他们的家人一个惊喜呢，比如特赦？这个提问我一直难忘（回来后还专门就此通过社科院的《要报》报送了一份关于在新中国成立50周年之际对那些确已悔改的犯人实行特赦的建议），它给我的启发是，国家在适当的时候，对符合条件的犯人实行赦免，给他们及其家人一种惊喜，不仅不会引起社会怨言，反而在某种意义上还能满足社会心理的期待。人类潜意识中其实是有一种天生的善和怜悯的感情，同时也有一种对惊喜的期盼，这可以用人在理性之外还有感性的一面来解释。据载，古代欧洲的囚犯在某些情况下会有机会给法官出谜语，法官若解不出谜底，就得开牢门放人，此之谓"赦豁之谜"。若真有某个令人同情的囚犯因此而获释（我相信这种概率一定是极低的），难道我们的本性不替他/她感到幸运吗？

③ 例如，曾为新疆首富的热比娅于2000年因向境外组织非法提供国家情报罪被判8年有期徒刑，2005年，在其允诺"出境后绝不参与危害中国国家安全的任何活动"后，司法部门同意其申请"保外就医"。又如，陈伯达于1980年被最高人民法院特别法庭判处有期徒刑后，1981年就获准"保外就医"。本来按照《刑事诉讼法》的规定，"保外就医"只能适用于"有严重疾病"的罪犯，但这两个例子都反映出，"保外就医"其实是"醉翁之意不在酒"，是为了实现更重要的政治目的。

又如，实践中对某些外国间谍判处有期徒刑，但并没有执行，仅将其驱逐出境，这显然有违我国法律，也是对法院判决的不尊重。① 如果对此类案件适用赦免措施，则能在维护法律权威的同时，妥善化解法律难题。

我国正处于社会和法律的转型期，恰当运用赦免制度，可以更好地实现社会正义。② 为此，借鉴其他国家和地区的经验，制定一部符合中国国情的《中华人民共和国赦免法》，明确赦免实施的各项实体和程序条件，使之真正成为国家在适当时机实现善治的一个选项，这应当可以作为本文的结论吧。

# On the Improvement of the Pardon System in China

*Liu Renwen*

【**Abstract**】Legal provisions on the pardon system in China are scattered among various parts of the Constitution, the Criminal Law and the Criminal Procedural Law. In a time of rapid development of Rule of Law, this legislative status quo has practically sealed the fate of the pardon system as an inoperable system. To make this system operable, China must first improve its substantive law and expand the scope of this system to include general pardon, special pardon, reduction of penalty through pardon and restoration of rights through pardon. Secondly, China must improve its Procedural law so as to ensure the standardized operation of the pardon system. Among various types of special pardon, the special pardon in

---

① 按照我国《外国人入境出境管理法》，驱逐出境可以作为一种行政处罚措施来适用。但一旦进入刑事程序，它就只能作为一种刑罚方法来适用。按照《刑法》第35条的规定，对于犯罪的外国人，可以独立适用或者附加适用驱逐出境。附加适用要在主刑执行完毕后才能执行，那种对外国间谍判处有期徒刑后又不执行就直接适用驱逐出境的做法，是说不通的。相比而言，曾经轰动一时的美国间谍波普一案，俄罗斯总统普京在法院对其定罪判刑后通过赦免来化解外交风波的做法，就显得更加名正言顺。

② 2010年12月1日，《法制晚报》报道了中国最后一个流氓犯在监狱服刑的消息，这使得消失已久的"流氓罪"再次进入舆论视野，引起很大的社会反响，许多人建议对其进行特赦，但至今未看到下文。

death penalty cases is worthy of special study. As for the legislative mode of pardon, China should adopt a special law on pardon in light of the actual situation in the country, so as to clearly define various subjective and procedural conditions for the application of the pardon system.

**【Key words】** Pardon; Procedure; Death Penalty Case; Legislative Mode

# Finnish Reforms of Procedural Law: A Success Story?

*Johanna Niemi*

【Abstract】 The Finnish law on court proceedings was totally reformed in the 1990s. The antiquated quasi-oral unstructured proceedings dating from 1734 were transformed into a modern trial model. Civil procedures at first instance were reformed first, with the slogan of orality, concentration and immediacy of trial. These three principles refer to the main hearing of the trial, which thus structures the whole process. The reform has in many ways been a success from which other countries may take lessons. However, reasonable time and costs still remain a challenge. The article reviews the Finnish reform process of civil procedureat first instance.

## 1. Introduction: Reforms of the 1990s

*The Finnish Code of Procedure* dates from 1734, the year of great Swedish codifications.[①] After the reforms of the 1990s, hardly a paragraph retains its original wording. The reforms of the 1990s had been in preparation for a long time. The first report to recommend a reform was presented by Professor R. A. Wrede in 1905 and that proposal already included many of the principles that were finally implemented in 1993. The reform process was delayed by the course of history in the 20th century. Court reform has generally not been a subject of political controversy but the 1970s saw a heated discussion on the position and recruitment of

---

[①] *The Code of Procedure*, like many other major Finnish Acts, is available in English at www. finlex. fi. Code of Procedure, http://www. finlex. fi/en/laki/kaannokset/1734/en17340004. pdf.

judges. The reforms of the 1990s saw the light in a calm political climate.

Of course, during the two and a half centuries that the 1734 Code remained in its original form, some partial reforms had been necessary. Most remarkably, the rules of evidence were reformed in 1948,[1] legal aid was introduced from the 1950s onwards, extraordinary review was reformed in 1960 and access to and procedures in the Supreme Court were reformed in 1978.

In the 1990s, the first reform package, consisting of four Bills, entered into force on Dec 1$^{st}$, 1993. Firsty, the organization of the district courts was reformed. The Parliament had already in 1987 confirmed the reform that abolished the historical difference between city courts and rural courts at first instance. Secondly, civil procedure in the first instance courts was completely reformed in 1991.[2] Thirdly and fourthly, an additional reform Act on legal expenses (Chapter 21 of the *Code of Procedure*) and the reform of injunctions (Chapter 7 of the Code) entered into force. All these reforms entered into force on Dec 1$^{st}$, 1993. With this reform, the civil procedure at first instance, which is the theme of this article, took on a new shape.

The reforms continued. The Finnish procedural system is divided into three distinctive procedural systems: civil procedure, criminal procedure and administrative (court) procedure. Both civil and criminal trials are processed in so called general courts: the district courts, the appeal courts and the Supreme Court. All cases are filed in the district courts (at first instance) and an appeal goes first to an appeal court. Administrative decisions can be appealed to the administrative courts, whose decisions in turn can be appealed to the Supreme Administrative Court. Under austerity constraints, the court system has been under intensive discussion at the beginning of the 21$^{st}$ century. In 2010, several district courts were merged and the original total of district courts reduced from over 50 to 27. Two appeal courts were merged in 2014 and there are now five of them. The structure of the court system has remained the same, however. The Finnish court system is illustrated in Figure 1.

---

[1] Ervo 1997 pp. 295 – 299, Pihlajamäki, 1997.
[2] Several new chapters were added to *the Code of Procedure*, e. g. Chapter 5 on summons and preparation for trial; Chapter 6 on the main hearing; Chapter 7 on injunctions; Chapter 9 on pleadings; Chapter 18 on joinder.

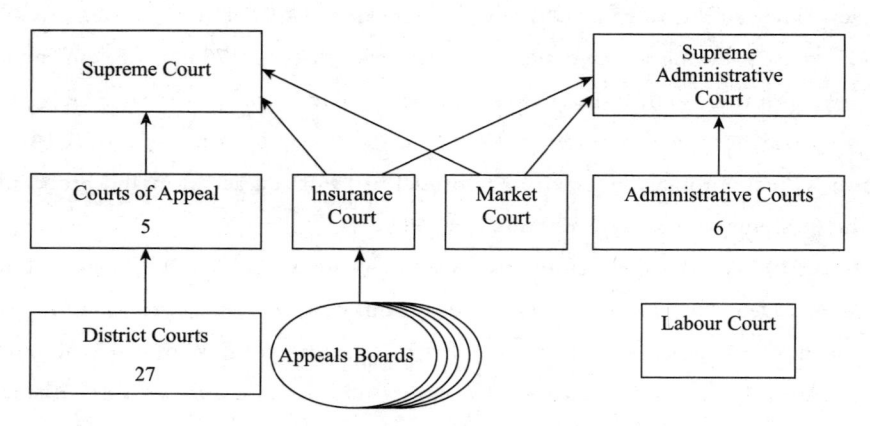

**Figure 1  The Finnish Court System**

Even if civil and criminal matters are processed in the same courts, the procedures are distinctly different. In a criminal trial, the claim always concerns a criminal sanction due to an offence prescribed by *the Penal Code* or some other law as a criminal offence. Civil matters are not defined, but they are all matters of a private law nature, such as commercial and consumer disputes, damages and torts, labour law cases, real estate and family matters. ①

While the focus of this article is on civil procedure, none the less it should be noted that civil claims based on or closely connected to a criminal offence can be processed in a criminal trial. Thus, a victim can claim compensation for damage caused by a criminal act at the same trial in which the prosecutor brings charges for an offence (principle of adhesion). In 1997, the criminal procedure was reformed and a separate *Criminal Procedure Act* (689/1998) was enacted. This reform followed the same principles of orality, concentration and immediacy as the civil procedure reform. However, as a criminal trial is preceded by investigation of the case, the structural changes were not as clear as in the civil procedure reform.

The third reform package was reform of the procedure in the appeal courts in 1998. ② The essence of the reform was to introduce oral hearings in the appeal courts, in which the procedure had been based on documents. Because of a lack of oral hearings in the appeal courts Finland had made a reservation to the ECHR

---

① Generally, Ervo 2009; Jokela 2002; Niemi-Kiesiläinen 2008; Niemi 2010.
② Reform of *the Code of Procedure*, Chapters 25 and 26, Law 615/1998.

but the reservation was removed after the reform. The reform has not been easy to implement[1] and appeal court reform has been amended several times since.

## 2. Reform of civil procedure at first instance

### Aims of the reform

Not surprisingly, the aim of the reform was to improve legal certainty[2] More specifically, the aim was to improve the possibilities of courts to handle cases in a thorough manner and to write a well-reasoned judgment.[3] In addition, the reform aimed at decreasing trial costs in terms of both time (in the shape of delays) and money, and thus to improve efficiency. We can already note that the last mentioned goal has not been achieved. The main ideas of the reform were often summarized in the slogan "orality, immediacy and concentration". Actually these three principles only apply to the main hearing of the trial but they also guide the whole structure of the trial, because the purpose of the preparatory stages is to guarantee that the main hearing can be held according to these principles.

### Trial structure

When we say that the pre-reform procedure (until 1993) was outdated and did not generally respect modern principles of fair trial, we mostly think about the uncoordinated structure of the proceedings. Trials at first instance were "semi-oral", that is, they consisted of a sequence of unstructured hearings. The intervals between hearings were usually one or two months. Many trials, however, needed only one hearing, because a number of simple cases were processed in the same way. In more complex cases, hearing witnesses could be spread out over a sequence of several hearings. Even if most trials were handled in one or two hearings, a complex case could be processed in over a year in the district court, which could mean up to ten hearings. At each hearing either the parties were heard, sometimes just so that the advocate of a party handed in a written pleading

---

[1] About the concerns and the discussion, see Niemi-Kiesiläinen 2007; Nylund 2006.
[2] Government Proposal for the reform of civil procedure in district courts (HE 15/1990 p. 5). About the reform, see Ervo 1995.
[3] Law Committee of the Parliament (LaVM 16/1990).

document, or one or two witnesses were heard. Since trials could take a long time, it was possible that the same judge did not preside over the whole trial. Sometimes the judge who wrote and gave the judgment had not in person heard all or indeed any of the witnesses. Therefore, what was said during the hearings was recorded and transcribed. The transcriptions often formed the basis of the judgment in the district court and proceedings in the appeal court.

In the 1993 reform, the structure of the trial was changed. A clear distinction was drawn between the preparatory stage and the main hearing. To allocate resources optimally, simple cases should be decided during the preparatory stage. The main hearing should be organized according to the principles of orality, immediacy and concentration, the slogan of the reform.

To achieve these aims and to realize these principles, two major structural reforms were made. Firsty, the procedure should be flexible and it should be suited to the demands of the nature of the individual case. Secondly, the process would be the structured in two phases, the preparatory phase and the main hearing. The main hearing would be uninterrupted (concentration) and oral and the judge (s) could not change during the trial (immediacy).

In the preparation for the 1993 reform, a funnel metaphor was frequently used to illustrate the flow of cases through the civil procedure. All cases would enter the procedure in the same way (by an application for summons), simple cases would be decided on documents, a number of cases would be decided after a preparatory hearing and only the most demanding cases would proceed to the main hearing. Thus, the flow of cases became narrower with each step in the procedure and an illustration of the procedure looked like a funnel. The funnel metaphor is illustrated in Figure 2:

Several civil procedural institutions were changed in order to facilitate these aims and principles.

Flexible process forms were developed. A separate process for the collection of undisputed monetary claims (*maksamismääräys* = payment order) was abolished. These kinds of collection claims are now decided under civil procedure on the basis of a summary action. Decisions are usually made on the basis of documents during the preparatory stage of the trial.[1] On the basis of the application for summons,

---

[1] Ervo 2001, pp. 121 – 129.

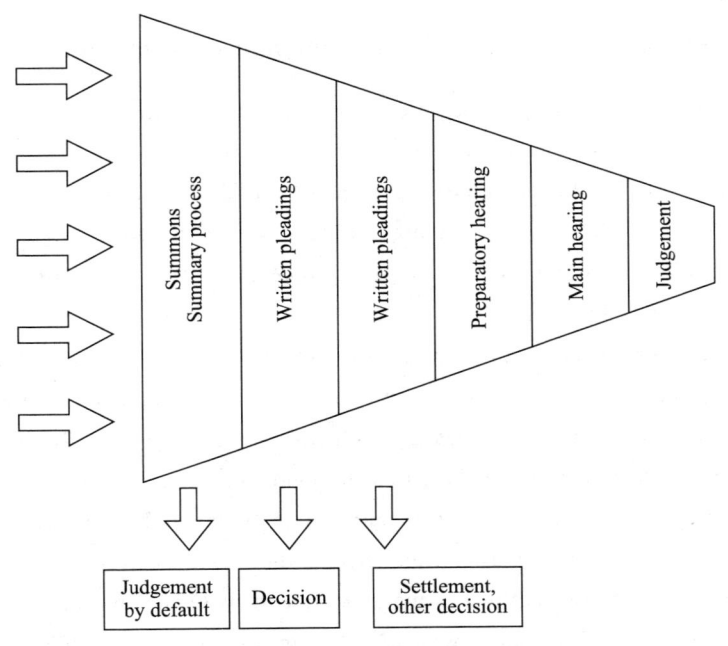

**Figure 2  The Funnel Metaphor**

the court issues a summons, which is served on the defendant. If the defendant does not send a written reply to the court, the court enters judgment by default. If the defendant admits the claim, judgment is given accordingly. The vast majority of cases in these summary proceedings are missed payment obligations, which the defendants do not dispute. Usually the claimants are represented by debt collection agencies, which today send applications to the district courts electronically.

Transfer of cases from these summary proceedings to ordinary civil proceedings, when the claim is disputed, is smooth. A separate procedure for family matters and *jurisdictio voluntaria* has remained[1] but the differences between application matters and ordinary proceedings have diminished. After amendments in 2002, disputed family matters are processed according to the normal rules of civil procedure. Some specific rules apply to trials over the custody of a child between the parents, but mostly the structure of the trial is the same as for other civil matters.

---

[1] Application as a form of action was first regulated in 1987 by the Law on application proceedings (306/1986). Regulation of applications was transferred to Chapter 8 ( "Procedure in Application Matters") of *the Code of Procedure* in 2002 (768/2002).

## Leading principles: Orality, immediacy and concentration

The main hearing should be organized according to the principles of immediacy, continuity and orality. According to the *principles of concentration and immediacy*, the material presented at the main hearing forms the basis of the judgment (*Code of Procedure* 24: 2). Thus, even though the claims and grounds are clarified and documentary evidence collected during the preparatory stage, they still have to be presented at the main hearing.

The judge (or a panel of three judges in complex cases) hears the claims and the evidence at the main hearing and the court bases its judgment on what it has received and heard at the main hearing. This principle means that the judges who decide the case have themselves heard all the evidence.

According to the principle of concentration, the main hearing must be held without a break. In relatively simple cases, the main hearing is held in one session. In complex cases, the hearing may extend to several working days but it must continue on at least three working days in any one week. There are very limited possibilities for extensions.

The principle of orality means that witnesses are heard at the main hearing and written witness affidavits are not allowed. ① After 2002, if neither witnesses nor the parties are heard, the main hearing can be replaced by exchange of documents.

The purpose of the preparatory stage is, besides deciding simple cases, to prepare for the main hearing so it can be carried out according to these principles (*Code of Procedure* 5: 17). While the aims of the reform of 1993 concerning the immediate, continuous and oral main hearing have been realized, the question sometimes arises whether distortion of these principles happened in the preparatory stage. ②

## Preparation for main hearing and mediation

During the preparatory stage, the court has the duty to ensure that the case is

---

① Some exceptions to this rule exist and in 2015 the reform of evidence rules added flexibility to the system. Under pressing circumstance a witness can be heard during the preparatory stage (*Code of Procedure* 17: 65). Also the possibility to hear witnesses through a digital connection or, if the witness is not a key witness, by telephone have been gradually added to the system.

② The purpose of the amendments to the *Code of Procedure* in 2002 was to make trial preparation more flexible.

ready for the main hearing. The parties must inform the court and each other in the application for summons and in the defence brief about their claims, grounds for the claims and the evidence they intend to present. The judge may give the parties additional instructions and deadlines for presenting their claims, grounds, documentary evidence and informing the court and the opposite party about the names of the witnesses and the evidentiary themes. A party that fails to follow the instructions may lose the right to introduce this material at the trial (preclusion).

A new function for the preparatory stage was the role that the judge should play in promoting amicable settlement between the parties. There was no obstacle to the activity of the judge in promoting settlements before the 1990s reform. However, after a specific paragraph mentioning this function was added, judges quickly increased their activity in this regard. After the reform, several books and treatises have been published on the role of the judge in promoting an amicable settlement. Normally, the judge takes up the possibility of amicable settlement at the preparatory hearing. Often this happens after the parties have stated their claims and listed their evidence. The judge may summarize the situation and point out that the evidence has not been heard, which means that the judge cannot predict the final decision. Not uncommonly, the parties reach a settlement at this point: if they want, the judge can confirm the settlement. The legal consequence of such confirmation is that the winning party can turn to the enforcement agency if the losing party does not comply with a confirmed settlement.

In addition, a specific procedure for court-led mediation is regulated in the *Act on mediation* in civil matters and confirmation settlements in general courts (CivMedAct 394/2011).[①] This court-led mediation was not particularly popular at first. In the early 2010s, an experimental project was started on mediation of child custody disputes between parents. After a trial period in some district courts,

---

[①] This procedure was introduced in 2005 by the CivMedAct (663/2005), which was replaced by the 2011 Act. More about mediation see Ervasti 2014. Another mediation procedure is regulated by the Act on conciliation in criminal and certain civil cases (*Conciliation Act* 1015/2005). Besides criminal matters and compensation claims related to crime, the scope of the Act also covers civil claims in which at least one of the parties is a natural person and which are of a minor nature (§ 1.2). According to this law, voluntary lay mediators help the parties to find an amicable solution to their disputes. In practice, this procedure is mostly used to mediate minor crime.

mediation of custody disputes has become a standard procedure according to changes to the CivMedAct in 2014 (316/2014).

The mediation procedure under the CivMedAct can be instigated either before a civil procedure has been started or during the preparatory stage and both parties must agree to mediation. The mediator in the CivMedAct procedure is a district court judge-but not the one in charge of the trial. An interesting difference from other court proceedings is that the parties may wish a named judge to become the mediator. That wish cannot always be fulfilled but even the possibility of expressing such a wish is exceptional. In child custody disputes, the judge is assisted by a psychological expert (the so called Follo-model).

## Structured main hearing

The main hearing is divided into three stages: the opening statement, presentation of evidence and the closing argument.

At the beginning of the main hearing, the judge presents a summary of the preparation (*Code of Procedure* 6: 2.1; 768/2002). Then the parties comment upon their claims, grounds and contestation as presented in the summary. Then both parties have an opportunity to present their case (opening argument). The presentation includes presentation of relevant law and the alleged facts on which the claim is based.

At the beginning of the proof taking, the parties are heard about the facts without taking an oath, first the plaintiff and then the defendant. Then the witnesses are heard under oath: first the witnesses for the plaintiff are heard and then those for the defendant. It is also possible to hear witnesses for each evidentiary theme separately. The party who has called a witness conducts the hearing first and the other party then cross-examines. Leading questions are allowed in cross-examination.

At the end of the hearing, the parties present their closing arguments, first the plaintiff and then the defendant. After the closing arguments, the parties have an opportunity to comment on each other's closingspeeches.

The presentation of the case and the closing arguments are not documented, taped or recorded in stenography. The oral evidence is taped (*Code of Procedure* 22: 6) and the tape is then stored until final judgment in the case is reached and in any case for at least a six-month period (*Code of Procedure* 22: 10).

## Preclusion

As already explained, several structures, rules and principles of the procedural law were reformed to realize the aims of the reform. One essential institution that was modeled to promote a concentrated and immediate main hearing was procedural preclusion. ① Procedural preclusion means that a party that does not follow the rules of procedural law and the instructions of the judge about the deadlines for presenting their case loses the right to present those claims, elements or evidence at all. Thus, preclusion is quite a harsh sanction for procedural omissions.

Preclusion has different effects depending on what element of action is involved. The elements of an action are divided into claims, grounds and evidentiary facts. Claims must be substantiated by legal grounds. Legal grounds are the foundation of the claim and of immediate relevance for approval of the claim. In the terminology of the Code of Procedure, the legal grounds are referred to as "grounds" (*perusteet*) or "circumstances" (*seikat*). Evidentiary facts may be alleged to support the grounds, but their function is to support the legal facts. Thus, evidentiary facts have only indirect relevance for approval of the claim. ②

The main principle is that the court is bound by the claims and the legal grounds invoked by the parties (*Code of Procedure* 24: 3; KKO: 1989: 105). As a main rule the claims and the grounds have to be presented as early as the summons. In addition, each party must explicitly present the claims and the grounds itself. It is not sufficient that a ground is mentioned by the other party or implied in the trial materials.

The claims and legal grounds as presented in the summons cannot be changed during the trial (*Code of Procedure* 14: 1.1). While the law allows important

---

① For a comprehensive discussion, see Männistö 2012.
② This doctrine is based on the writings of the P. O. Ekelöf, the grand old man of procedural law in Uppsala, Sweden. The doctrine was introduced in Finland in 1986 in a seminal article by Juha Lappalainen, later professor of procedural law at the University of Helsinki. Professor Jyrki Virolainen of the University of Lapland has been central in establishing the doctrine in Finland. Now it is generally accepted by scholars and it has influenced the reforms to the Code of Procedure.

exceptions to this principle, all amendments have to be made during the preparatory stage of the trial. Only if a party was not able to invoke a new ground during the preparation may it invoke that new ground at the main hearing.

This burden does not cover the evidentiary facts, which the court may rely on irrespective of who presented them at the trial. Nor is the court bound by the legal characterization of the case by the parties. The principle of *jura novit curia* is understood in such a way that the court may in its decision use another legal provision than the parties as long as the relevant grounds and the claimed outcome remain within the limits of the actions of the parties.

These rules may sound clear or obscure but the case law shows that application can be rather difficult in practice. First, the legal characterization of a ground may be difficult to distinguish from the legal fact itself. For example, in the following case the legal characterization of the situation changed, but we can question whether the interpretation would be the same today:

KKO: 1988: 37: The plaintiff had first invoked a breach of the by-laws of the association and later the equality of the members. This was not considered prohibited amendment of the grounds.

After the 1990s reforms the court might have held that the ground equal treatment—treatment according to the rules is different and thus not possible to change. In another case the same chain of events was first invoked as unjustified enrichment and later as a contractual guarantee obligation:

KKO: 2006: 54 The matter was characterized as a new ground for the claim. A bank as the plaintiff had based its claim on unjustified enrichment. In the appeal court it had changed its position and also invoked commitments as personal guarantors. The Supreme Court held that this was a new ground and dismissed it.

As the chain of events (the legal facts) remained the same, it is possible to argue that the case is more about legal characterization than about legal grounds. In this somewhat complicated situation, the bank had explicitly not invoked the guarantor contracts in the district court, which influenced the outcome. In any case this case shows that the borderline between legal characterization and (factual) grounds is not always clear-cut.

As long as the claimed outcome remains the same, the plaintiff may invoke new grounds. The Supreme Court seems to have adopted this theory even before the legislative reforms:

> KKO: 1990: 83 The plaintiff had claimed a share of a tax return on the basis of a sale contract, according to which she was entitled to the return before the real estate had been sold. The plaintiff invoked as an additional ground her status as one of the heirs of the original owner. The additional ground was allowed.

The difficulty in distinguishing between legal facts, for which preclusion is relevant, and evidentiary facts, with no risk of preclusion, is illustrated in the next case:

> KKO: 2003: 4 Defendant Company C had fired employee E. In the district court E claimed compensation for overtime work. The defendant C rejected the claim that the original written employment contract had been modified by an oral contract which changed the rules for compensation for overtime work. The district court judgment was in favour of E. C appealed the verdict. In the appeal court C argued that the employment contract was modified by an implicit agreement because C and E had for a long time calculated pay in a way that was incongruent with the written contract. The Supreme Court held that the defendant C had not shown that she had a valid reason not to invoke the new ground in the district court and, thus, was not allowed to invoke that ground in the appeal court either.

Analyzing this case, we can identify two different factual events: an orally made explicit contract and a practice that formed the basis of an implicit informal agreement. The Supreme Court held that these factual events constituted two different legal facts (which would have led to the same result). Arguably, we could formulate the legal fact as a mutual understanding that the written contract was modified. In this alternative formulation the form of modification of the contract would be an evidentiary fact that could be invoked without the risk of preclusion. This example shows that the concepts of legal fact and evidentiary fact are subject to interpretation and that the borderlines can be rather difficult.

The case law examples have already indicated that the doctrine of preclusion is also relevant in the appeal procedure. In general, new claims and grounds cannot be invoked in the higher instance courts. Two examples illustrate that the borderlines are not quite self-evident here either:

> In KKO: 2000: 41 the SC held that the claimant, the victim of a crime, could not make additional claims in the appeal court on the basis of new symptoms after the district court decision.

A rather liberal view of allowing a new ground for denial of a claim was taken in KKO: 2010: 9:

> In this case the plaintiff had requested that a contract condition of life-long occupancy in a sale of half of a piece of real estate should be cancelled as the intimate partnership had ended. The district court ruled for the plaintiff. The defendant claimed in the appeal court that the conditions of the sale of the real estate should be moderated as the outcome was unfair. The Supreme Court agreed with the defendant and submitted the case to the appeal court for reconsideration. Two justices, however, disagreed. They found that the new claim should already have been presented in the district court.

## Judgment

Judgment is either declared after the main hearing or is given in chambers. As a rule, the law requires that judgment should be declared after the hearing. If the matter was complicated, judgment can be given in chambers fourteen days after the hearing and, for special reasons, even later. This possibility is probably used more often than intended.

A judgment of the district court can be appealed (*Code of Procedure* Chapters 25 and 26). Notice of intention to appeal must be given within seven days and the time for appeal is 30 days. Thereafter, the other party can lodge a counter appeal within 14 days. Counter appeal is dependent on the main appeal, so that if the main appeal is withdrawn the counter appeal becomes void as well. An appeal requires leave if the disputed value in the appeal is less than 10000 euros. If the appeal court refuses leave, its decision may be appealed to the Supreme Court.

If there is no notice of appeal, the judgment obtains the effect of res judicata after seven days. The limits of the res judicata effect are congruent with the doctrine of preclusion, that is, grounds that could have been invoked in the first trial cannot form the basis of a new case.

## Responsibility for legal costs

The rules on compensation of costs were also reformed in 1993. There was a strong rhetoric in the bill that unnecessary or even frivolous trials must be prevented. Therefore, the rule that the losing party compensate the costs of the winning party was reinforced. By 1999 it was clear that this rule is prohibitive. The costs risk is so high that it probably discourages most middle class persons from going to court with their disputes. While legal aid and insurance may cover the costs of a party in some civil cases, the obligation to compensate the costs of the winning party is not covered by any compensation system.

In 1999 the rule was modified. The obligation to compensate the costs of the winning party can be adjusted if the matter was so unclear that there was a justifiable reason to start the process or if the "winner takes all" approach to costs would be manifestly unreasonable (*Code of Procedure* 21: 8a-b). In case law, however, the adjustment has been rare. Even in child custody cases, in which the "winner takes all" rule is not the basic line, the Supreme Court has underlined that the losing party compensates the costs of the winner, that is, the mother or the father of the children who loses a custody dispute has to compensate the costs of the other parent (KKO: 2014: 96).

## 3. Experiences-evaluations

### Success

As an overall assessment, the reform has been a success. The time was ripe for reform in the 1990s. The reform had been prepared long before but its implementation coincided with joining and adjusting to the European Convention of Human Rights in and after 1990. The antique process forms of 1734 were ready to be abandoned. Some unexpected features, such as enthusiasm about mediation and amicable settlements, promoted the overall reform.

The quality of reasoning in judgments has clearly improved. If the judgments of district courts could be rather laconic before the reform, the critique today would be that they are too detailed and lengthy. Indeed, in many cases the district court feels obliged to give a resume of the oral testimonies in its decision. This is understandable as the testimony is not recorded in the protocols as it used to be before the reform. Testimony is recorded in electronic form but is rarely transcribed- indeed, never at the district court level. The Supreme Court has revised its writing style and uses a clear structure in its verdicts. This is clearly a field in which continuous development is under way.

Reform of the trial structure has been successfully implemented. The preparatory stage and the main trial have fulfilled their functions. Main hearings are held in a structured manner according to the three principles of immediacy, concentration and orality. The strict preclusion rules have probably been necessary to put the reforms into practice.

Implementation of the reforms was so successful that in subsequent reforms some of the darlings of the reform could be, if not killed, at least modified. The principles of orality and concentration have been slightly modified but far from abandoned. The preclusion rules are not as strict as they used to be but the theory of preclusion has been accepted. As the examples from case law show, there will be continuous discussion in case law and jurisprudence on the legal elements and legal facts, which can be taken as a sign of a healthy legal culture.

## Challenges

The overall success does not mean that there have been no problems. The main problems of the reform can be identified as the length of trials and the increase in legal costs.

The European Court of Human Rights has given all too many judgments against Finland in which it has, today with standard reasoning, stated that the length of the trial has exceeded what is acceptable according to the principle of fair trial. Most judgments have concerned criminal trials but there are cases in which the same has been said about civil trials as well (e. g. *Nuutinen v. Finland* 27. 6. 2000). To some extent the pre-reform delays in more complex cases are repeated in the preparatory stage of the trial. The strict preclusion rules have emphasized the duty of the advocate to prepare diligently before a case is filed and especially before the main hearing, which may contribute to delays during the preparatory stage.

Since 2010, there has been an attempt to deal with the problem of over-long trials at national level. A party can claim compensation for unreasonable delay in the district court before judgment is delivered. Compensation was set at 1500 for each year of delay, with a maximum of 10000.

The increase in legal costs seems to discourage middle class people from bringing their disputes to the courts. Finland has a relatively advanced legal aid system but its compensation level is modest in relation to the fees of private lawyers. [1] Thus, many middle class households are excluded from the scope of legal aid because of their income level. At the end of the day, legal aid or legal costs insurance does not cover the risk that a party can be liable to compensate the costs of the other party upon losing the case.

## Conclusion

The reforms in the 1990s did not increase the amount of oral hearings in the district courts, but the nature of the hearings and the trial have changed fundamentally. This has been a profound change in legal culture. The reform has

---

[1] Rosti et al. 2009.

not been without its bottlenecks and growing pains. However, the profile of the courts in producing legal protection, legal security and dispute resolution has been strengthened.

# 芬兰程序法的改革：一个成功的故事？

约翰娜·尼厄米

【摘要】芬兰于 20 世纪 90 年代彻底改革了有关法庭程序的法律，从而将一个可以追溯到 1734 年的已过时的准口头、非结构性诉讼模式转化成为一个现代的审判模式。芬兰首先按照审判的口头性、集中性和直接性原则对一审民事程序进行了改革。这三项原则适用于在整个审判程序中起到决定性作用的听证。这一改革在很多方面都是成功的，值得其他国家借鉴的。但是如何将诉讼时间和诉讼费用控制在合理的范围内仍然是芬兰诉讼程序所面临的挑战。本文回顾了芬兰改革一审民事诉讼程序的过程。

# 公益诉讼与中国的司法体制改革

贺海仁*

**【摘要】** 公益诉讼入法标志着公益诉讼获得了法律上的正当性和规范性。《民事诉讼法》第55条确立了具有中国特色的公益诉讼制度,这为通过司法方法维护公共利益开辟了认识和确立公共利益的新范式,成就了公益诉讼规范、理性解决社会冲突的内在价值。公益诉讼是司法体制改革实践的成果,也给司法体制提出了挑战和要求。

**【关键词】** 公益诉讼　公共利益　试验性价值　司法体制改革

公益诉讼入法标志着公益诉讼在法律和司法制度中获得了正当性,这既是对十几年来中国公益法实践的总结,也是规范公益诉讼的行为。着眼于公共利益的公益诉讼为非政府组织依法维护公共利益提供了依据,开辟了新的诉讼类型。解读公益诉讼入法有助于理解公益诉讼在中国发展的意义,强化司法职责,为新一轮司法改革提供源于实践的正能量。

## 一　公益诉讼入法与公共利益

2013年1月,修订之后的《中华人民共和国民事诉讼法》正式实施。修订后的该法第55条规定,对污染环境、侵害众多消费者合法权益等损害社会公共利益的行为,法律规定的机关和有关组织可以向人民法院提起诉讼。随后,经过修订并于2014年3月15日实施的《中华人民共和国消费者权益保护法》第47条规定,对侵害众多消费者合法权益的行为,中国消费者协会以及在省、自治区、直辖市设立的消费者协会,可以向人民法院提起诉讼。2014年4月24日修订后的《中华人民共和国环境保护法》第58

---

\* 中国社会科学院法学研究所研究员。

条规定，对污染环境、破坏生态，损害社会公共利益的行为，依法在设区的市级以上人民政府民政部门登记并且专门从事环境保护公益活动连续5年以上且无违法记录的社会组织可以向人民法院提起诉讼。《民事诉讼法》第55条、《消费者权益保护法》第47条和《环境保护法》第58条分别是所属法律修订时新增的条款，统称为公益诉讼条款。从立法技术上看，《民事诉讼法》第55条是对中国特色公益诉讼的原则性规定，它开启了公益诉讼入法的先河，为消费者权益公益诉讼和环保公益诉讼制度提供了依据，而消费者权益公益诉讼和环保公益诉讼制度则是对《民事诉讼法》中的公益诉讼条款的细化和补充。[①]

以成文法规定公益诉讼制度在当今世界上是颇为罕见的。美国、印度和南非的公益法律实践并无明确的法律规定，这些国家的公益法律活动更多的是通过法官的释法行为而得以有序地展开的，立法机关对其采取不干预的政策。在美国，公益诉讼主要是职业法律人的法律援助行为。Pro bono意指法律人为了公共的善而从事的法律援助行为，这种通过职业而体现出来的善针对的是社会上的弱势群体以及无力支付诉讼费用的穷人。[②] 律师在诉讼或非诉讼过程中为穷人提供法律援助就可以被视为从事Pro bono活动，因此，广义上的公益诉讼包含了法律援助实践。2003年9月1日实施的《法律援助条例》确立了中国的法律援助制度，律师有义务为特定的当事人提供免费的法律服务。但是，《民事诉讼法》第55条规定的行为是有别于一般法律援助的特定行为，它专指法律规定的机构以自身作为原告为了公共利益而提起的诉讼。在法律援助中，诉讼中的原告往往是受援助的对象，而不是提供法律援助的律师或其他法律人，通过法律援助所获得的法益也可能是私人利益。专门的公益诉讼是为了公共利益的诉讼，它创造了通过诉讼实现公共利益的方法，开辟了公众参与公共领域的新视角。

密集地对公益诉讼给予法律认可显示了中国社会对公共利益的重视和保护。虽然立法对何为"社会公共利益"缺乏定义，学术界对什么是公益诉讼也存在较大的分歧，但公共利益或社会公共利益是有别于私人利益和国家利益的概念却逐渐形成了共识，这个共同的利益超越了一般的私人利益，也与国家利益不同。以污染环境而损害社会公共利益的立法表达为例，

---

① 新增的公益诉讼条款有别于早已存在的共同诉讼或代表人诉讼，《民事诉讼法》在其他条款中对此有特别的规定，参见《民事诉讼法》第54条的规定。
② 美国律师协会：《支持正义：美国律师公益工作报告》，廖凡译，载北京东方公益法律援助律师事务所编《公益诉讼》第3辑，中国检察出版社，2008。

如果一个严重的污染环境事件发生了，受到损害的不仅是一个地区的居民，也有可能是事件发生地以外的其他居民，乃至相邻国家的人。那种把国家利益等同于公共利益的认识是错误的。国家利益是特殊的公共利益，但国家利益只在国家主权范围内才能成立。无论是立法机关、行政机关还是司法机关，法律都赋予其保护合法的私人利益、集体利益和国家利益的特殊职责。倘若把国家机构履行其职责的行为都视为维护公共利益的行为，公益诉讼入法就有多余之嫌。

虽然公共利益不可定义，但并非不能分析。公共利益是共同共有并共同享有的众益。在《现代汉语词典》中，对"共"的基本解释是"相同的"、"在一起"，对"共同"的基本解释是"属于大家的，彼此都具有的"。共同利益就是有别于"个别的"、"特殊的"的利益，就是"大家的利益"而不是"小家的利益"。大家的利益具有不可分割性，公共利益不像私人利益那样可以被划分，也不能由个人按照他们的偏爱多要一点或少要一点。公共利益的这一特点提醒人们注意区分偶然的公益和内在的公益，它们因分别体现了工具价值和内在价值而有所不同。莱兹指出："如果某物的价值来自它的后果的价值，或者来自这样的事实，即它使得某些后果更有可能，或者它有助于某些后果的出现，该物就具有工具意义上的价值。某物是内在的善或者具有内在意义的价值是指，它的价值对立于它的实际的或可能的后果，而且决不依赖它被可以用来促进或它可以帮助产生的任何后果。"① 在民法理论中，共同共有与按份共有相区别。在按份共有中，利益是可以被区分而且可以被分割的，利益共同体不会因分割而分裂。共同共有是权利人对某物的共同占有、使用、收益和处分的权利。在共同共有中，无法区分出每一个具体的人的利益，每一个人的利益就融合在这一利益共同体当中，一旦分割出单独的利益，利益共同体就不复存在，从这个意义上讲，公共利益是连带的利益、共享的利益。

共同体就是人们在一定条件下形成的特定组织。人类的组织有大有小，但所有的组织都承担了为其成员谋求集体产品的义务，这是所有组织存在的合法性基础。② 需要注意的是，共同利益可以是公共利益，但在很多情况下，共同利益也可能指由特定的少数人或多数人所享有的私的共同利益。

---

① 〔英〕莱兹：《以权利为基础的道德》，吴玉章译，载夏勇主编《公法》第2卷，法律出版社，2000，第412~413页。
② 有关组织的目的的论述，参见〔美〕曼瑟尔·奥尔森《集体行动的逻辑》，陈郁等译，上海人民出版社，1995。

工会会员对更高的工资有共同利益，农场主对对其有利的法律有共同利益，卡特尔成员对追求更高的价格有共同利益，股东对享受更高的分红有共同利益，公民对建立出色的政府有共同利益。许多证据显示，国家往往有自己的独立利益。不仅私的共同利益大量存在，而且它们也会相冲突。因此，笼统地说公共利益就是共同利益是有局限性的，这个局限性需要用"公的利益"这个词加以弥补。如果说"共同利益"与"特殊利益"相对，"公的利益"和"私的利益"相对，那么公共利益就是"公的共同利益"的总称。按照中国传统文化的术语表述，公的基本含义是"天下"，它是有别于家和国家的相对独立的概念。天下的主体是具有道德资格的所有人，而不是家人或国人。天下的利益既不是少数人的利益，也不是大多数人的利益，而是全体人的利益。[①]

## 二 公益诉讼的内在价值

将公共利益从私人利益和国家利益的二元框架中解放出来为公共利益提供了相对独立的领域。这个认识对中国社会之所以重要，乃在于处于现代化和全球化进程中的中国面临着既要克服市场经济理性人假定带来的偏激的个人主义倾向，也要在逐渐形成的全球社会中承担有关人类公共利益的任务。在利益多元化和全球化的时代，个人利益、集体利益和国家利益仍然需要加强和保障，但维护涉及所有人的公共利益的客观需求也不容忽视。《民事诉讼法》第 55 条规定的社会公共利益不限于环境公共利益和众多消费者的公共利益，立法使用了"等"这一可以扩展的用语，为更多不同表现形式的公共利益进入立法的视野提供了空间。不过，确立一个相对独立的公共利益固然重要，但维护和救济公共利益更为重要。在众多维护公共利益的方法中，通过诉讼维护公共利益是当代中国社会的新方法，这一方法对一个有着厌诉传统的国家显得格外重要。

美国是最早发起公益诉讼的国家，公益诉讼的出现是美国民权运动的一个重大转折点，它把民权运动从大街上引入法庭，用多数人（包括反对者）更愿意看到的方式解决社会矛盾。[②] 公益诉讼在中国起步晚，但发展迅速，这与民众希望建立一个公平正义的社会制度的大气候有关。20 世纪 70

---

[①] 关于中国传统资源与公益法的关系，参见梁治平《再续传统，重拾法的公共性：以中国当代公益法运动的兴起为例》，载梁治平《法律何为：梁治平自选集》，广西师范大学出版社，2013。

[②] 参见贺海仁《域外公益诉讼的缘起与启示》，《环球法律评论》2010 年第 4 期。

年代末，中国开启了改革开放的新纪元，经过 30 多年的高速发展，中国的面貌发生了巨大变化，人民的生活水平得到了显著提高，在全国范围内基本解决了温饱问题，总体上实现了小康社会的发展目标。然而，在社会进步和发展的同时，也出现了一些问题，有些问题愈演愈烈，以致成为妨碍社会团结的巨大障碍。择其要者，这些问题包括贫富差距加大、环境污染严重、食品安全堪忧、权力腐败现象加剧等。改革开放的总体收益没有在全体成员中获得公平的分配，这加剧了人与人之间、不同阶层和地区之间的不平等状况。机会平等和资格平等、能力平等以及实质平等成为当代中国民众的基本需要。以往人们对一个平等的社会制度的追求要么诉之于急风暴雨式的革命，要么求助于游行、示威等对抗性较强的街上运动或群体性事件以及大众文化式的抵制行动，这些方法虽然都具有一定的合理性，却破坏性有余而建构性不足。公益诉讼在化解社会矛盾和纠纷方面发挥了其独特的价值，即把政治法律化、把事件案件化和把对抗理性化。

第一，政治法律化。公益诉讼具有很强的道德色彩，公益诉讼追求的公益超出了私人利益和国家利益的范围，促进公益就是促进人的全面发展。如果说政治是治理人的行为的事业，公益事业就是最大的政治和最需要加强治理的对象。但公益诉讼作为一项治理事业在方法上是独特的。公益诉讼遵循的是规则之治，它通过司法的力量把道德权利转化为法律权利。政治是关于权力分配及其制约的规范、策略和技术，在某种程度上，它就是控制与反控制他人的力量规则。就保卫公共利益而言，公益诉讼是对有损于它的一切权力，尤其是政治权力和经济权力展开反控制的司法路径。政治法律化要求把一切权力行为都纳入到法律的框架范围之内，这使得一切权力的配置和运行都服膺于法律的最高准则，与此同时，权力之间、权力与权利之间、权利与权利之间的斗争需要在法律和司法的框架内进行。美国的政治制度体现了美国的本土特色，但美国将政治法律化、司法化的治国经验却能够成为多元化社会的有效治理模式，这对克服现代民主的弊端——多数人的暴政也是有益的。[1]

第二，事件案件化。近年来，中国各地发生的群体性事件越来越与公共利益相关，它们程度不等地显现了人与人、人与公权力之间的紧张关系。

---

[1] 托克维尔通过对美国社会的考察，得出了这样一条观察结论："在美国，几乎所有的政治问题迟早都要变成司法问题。因此，所有的党派在它们的日常论战中，都要借用司法的概念和语言。"〔法〕托克维尔：《论美国的民主》上卷，董国良译，商务印书馆，1988，第 310 页。

群体性行为一开始总是以事件的形式出现的,事件遵循其自身的规律,往往具有不确定性和不规范的特点,有的群体性事件则带有偶发性。为了避免发生新的群体性事件或解决已经发生的群体性事件,就需要包括公益诉讼在内的新的纠纷解决机制。公益诉讼的优点之一就是能够为公益纠纷引入一些可以遵循和明确的规则,用言辞和逻辑的力量代替暴力的逻辑。

第三,博弈理性化。把事情闹大因而形成"大乱大治"的局面正是对抗非理性化的表现。现实中存在多种对抗的形态,如游戏、赌博、竞争、竞技、诉讼、抗议、战争等,这些抗争的方法或是和平的或是暴力的。理性的抗争是非暴力的,它要求在一个所有对抗者都认可的法律框架内实现利益的最大化,倘若对抗行为离开了法律框架,对抗本身就随时会变得不可控制。公益诉讼借助于诉讼的形式确立了其理性抗争的品性,它把涉及公众的利益带进了一个可以公开讨论的场域,给每一个关心公共利益的人提供了认识和维护公共利益的新方法。

政治法律化、事件案件化和博弈理性化为公益诉讼提供了原则性的方法。然而,公益诉讼要求维护的公共利益不是静止、不变的利益,对公共利益的体认和把握需要在具体的个案中予以展示。公益诉讼就如同一块试金石,具有测试制度的良性程度的作用。公益诉讼的试验价值体现在三个方面:试错价值、试对价值和试新价值。

第一,试错价值。试错针对的是明显不合理、不公正的社会制度,比如孙志刚案件挑战的是不合时宜的收容审查制度。由于当代中国的法院不具有司法审查的权力,一些公益诉讼采取了公益上书的形式。公益上书的内容涉及消费者保护、环境保护、出版自由、社会歧视、性别平等、城乡差异、劳动保护、农民负担、农村义务教育、物业管理、动物保护等。[①] 在很多情况下,制度不合理是由于政治惯例形成了自身难以克服的惰性,以致制度不能与时俱进,使原本合理的变得不合理,原本正义的变得不正义。此外,现代社会的议事程序和官僚主义也使得某些当权者在需要改变时无力或不便改变,这也是为什么美国有些公共服务机构鼓励权利受到侵害的人起诉自己的原因之一。

第二,试对价值。由于种种原因,制度体系中有一些相对不错的规定不能得到具体落实。《中华人民共和国义务教育法》第 4 条规定:"凡具有

---

① 参见北京东方公益法律援助事务所编《公益诉讼》公益上书专辑,中国检察出版社,2009。

中华人民共和国国籍的适龄儿童、少年,不分性别、民族、种族、家庭财产状况、宗教信仰等,依法享有平等接受教育的权利,并履行接受义务教育的义务。"为了保障农村义务教育的发展,国务院发布了《国务院关于深化农村义务教育经费保障机制改革的通知》,规定全部免除农村义务教育阶段学生的学杂费,对贫困家庭学生免费提供教科书并补助寄宿生的生活费。然而,2006年前后,一些省份通过红头文件剥夺了农村民办学校义务教育阶段学生的"两免一补"的权利。"小箐诉教育部、财政部等民办学校学生歧视案"要求平等落实教育权,[①] 公益诉讼的目的之一就是让这些条款活起来、用起来,达到当初制定它们的目的,把政治家的法律变为法律人的法律,把死的法律变为活的法律,确保宪法和法律在全国范围内有效实施。

第三,试新价值。权利是发展的。以权利来界定和衡量那些随着社会进步而产生的新的法律关系需要人们有探索新领域的功夫和勇气。这种情况通常是指法律既未禁止也未明确肯定的模糊事项和领域,例如关于动物福利的问题,随着社会的进步,对动物权利的探讨和实践逐渐出现在公共领域的话语之中。2009年陕西省汉中市被爆杀狗2万余只,引起全社会的关注。法律援助律师通过中国小动物保护协会向汉中市人民政府提出信息公开申请,要求依法说明被杀的狗的数量、原因、依据、尸体处理情况等,汉中市人民政府在法定期限内做了披露和回答。近几年来,活熊取胆事件进入公众的视野,动物保护组织、环境保护机构和一些公益律师通过诉讼和非诉讼的方法向从事活熊取胆的企业施压,要求取缔残忍的取胆行为,最大限度地保护动物的福利。

公益诉讼假设某种制度上的原因给人们造成了损害,且这种损害剥夺了潜在的不特定多数人的利益。只要有足够的理由认为,提起公益诉讼的人不是单纯地为了自己的利益,那么这种类型的诉讼就是公益诉讼。即使法庭经过审理最终认为原告的请求是不成立的,也不能否定公益诉讼的价值。公益诉讼呈现给世人的是不同于议会场景下的公共领域,它通过将一个吸引公众注意力的事件法律化,开辟了一个特殊的公共领域。在这个特殊的公共领域中,在场的原告与不在场的原告以及相关的利益人产生了共鸣,在场的法官与不在场的法官同时或分别地对案件做出判决。形式上的判决是在场的法官做出的,他们主要根据形式主义的法律并且兼顾实质正义原则对公益诉讼原告的请求做出肯定或否定的裁定,相应地,实质意义

---

[①] 参见北京东方公益法律援助事务所编《公益诉讼》第3辑,中国检察出版社,2008。

上的判决乃是由不在场的法官做出的，他们或许不具备形式法律的知识或者忽视了形式法律的要求，但是可以根据情感、常理和天理为公益诉讼的案件做出裁决。公益诉讼的审判场景如同是一个人人参与的陪审团审判，人人皆是原告，人人都是法官，其目的在于通过审判确认和维护与每一个相关的公共利益。

### 三　公益诉讼与司法体制改革

公益诉讼不是单纯的慈善行为，它的特点决定了公益诉讼必然与司法体制具有千丝万缕的联系。公益诉讼在中国的产生和发展既是司法体制改革的结果，也给司法体制提出了挑战和要求。

首先，律师成为公益诉讼的主体。在中国当前的公益法实践中，律师是公益诉讼的主要践行者，这既体现了律师的职业之善，也表达了中国改革开放后司法体制改革的成果。[①] 20世纪90年代，司法制度中的律师制度率先开始改革，经过改革，律师完成了从国家干部到社会法律工作者的身份转换。律师依法独立办案，忠实于法律和当事人，负有维护社会公平正义的职责。法律援助不仅符合每一个职业律师的职业伦理，也是他们的法律义务。公益诉讼虽然不是一般的法律援助行为，但公益诉讼体现了律师无偿为社会服务的奉献精神。律师自觉的公益行为极大地促进了公益诉讼在中国的发展，如果没有律师体制改革，公益诉讼就不会获得今天的成就。

每一种职业都是社会分工的产物，每一种职业都体现了内在的本分之善。对于公益诉讼而言，只有公益精神和热情是不够的。无论公益诉讼有什么价值，它都要遵循诉讼的规律，需要较为成熟的诉讼技巧和专业知识。在司法体制改革中，律师早于法官和检察官成为规范的法律职业工作者。早在1986年，中国就开始了全国律师资格考试，确立了律师职业化的发展方向。2001年6月30日，第九届全国人大常委会第22次会议通过了《关于修改〈中华人民共和国法官法〉的决定》和《关于修改〈中华人民共和国检察官法〉的决定》，规定初任法官、检察官必须从通过国家统一司法考试的人员中择优选取。随后，最高人民法院、最高人民检察院、司法部联合发布公告，决定当年的初任法官考试、初任检察官考试和律师资格考试不再单独组织，纳入2002年的首次国家统一司法考试。司法资格考试制度

---

[①] 参见贺海仁、黄金荣、朱晓飞《天下的法：公益法的实践理性与社会正义》，社会科学文献出版社，2012。

的确立为中国律师、法官和检察官的职业统一化发展奠定了基础，从而终结了"复转军人进法院"的公共讨论。①

其次，公益诉讼的发展促进了法院内部的改革。越来越多的公益诉讼走向法院，面对这一新的诉讼类型，一些地方法院开始尝试对公益诉讼的受理和审判。2008年11月，江苏省无锡市中级人民法院和无锡市人民检察院共同出台了《关于办理环境民事公益诉讼案件的试行规定》，虽然这份地方司法文件原则上只认可人民检察院是环境公益诉讼的合格原告，但其在地方司法制度中开启了公益诉讼的规范实践，明确将公益诉讼作为新的诉讼类型予以规定。2009年7月，江苏省无锡市中级人民法院受理了一起粉尘污染案。被告江阴港集装箱有限公司在铁矿石作业过程中，露天作业，造成了粉尘直接侵入周边民居，同时企业对散落的红色粉尘用水冲，直接排入周边河道和长江水域，形成大气和水质双重污染。中华环保联合会通过实地调查，确认污染事实，遂向法院起诉。中华环保联合会是在北京注册的非政府组织，在该案中，人民法院认可中华环保联合会以原告的资格起诉位于江苏的污染企业。

《民事诉讼法》第119条规定，原告是应当与案件具有直接利害关系的公民、法人和其他组织。在江阴港集装箱有限公司铁矿石作业污染案之前的许多公益诉讼案件，因原告与案件无直接利害关系而不被受理。中华环保联合会与该案同样没有直接的利害关系，而仅有间接的利害关系，但无锡市中级人民法院对《民事诉讼法》第119条做出了扩大解释，裁定认可中华环保联合会的原告主体资格。该案在不修改法律的情况下，由地方人民法院通过司法解释的方法完成了对公共利益的司法保护，这体现了地方司法机关先于制度设计而为的首创精神。值得重视的是，新修订的《民事诉讼法》把"有关机关和有关组织"作为公益诉讼的原告，但关于起诉的当事人需要与案件具有直接利害关系的规定却没有变化。这或许不是立法技术上的失误，一个合理的解释是，对于危害公共利益的案件，任何人都不是间接的受害人，而不是程度不等的直接受害人。也就是说，符合条件的公益诉讼的原告就是与公益案件有直接利害关系的主体。如果说"任何人都不能从其过错行为中获益"是一个基本的民事原则，对于公益诉讼案件而言，任何人都与公益案件具有直接的利害关系应当是有待进一步发展

---

① 参见贺卫方《复转军人进法院》，《南方周末》1998年1月2日；曹瑞林：《复转军人缘何不能进法院》，《中国国防报》1998年2月10日。

的新的民事原则。

最后，先行一步的公益诉讼实践为新一轮司法体制改革提供了经验。2007年中国第一个专属管辖环境案件的法庭——清镇市人民法院生态保护法庭成立，贵州省高级人民法院根据贵州实际情况实行划片区集中专属管辖，将贵阳、安顺、贵安三地的环境民事、行政案件集中交由清镇市人民法院生态保护法庭管辖，打破了涉及公共利益的案件因地方保护主义而无法立案、审理和公正判决的制度障碍。2010年11月，云南省昆明市中院与该市检察院联合制定的《关于办理环境民事公益诉讼案件若干问题的意见》创造性地规定了环境公益诉讼的胜诉利益归属社会的原则，创设环境公益诉讼救济基金，鼓励更多的环保组织和有关机关从事公益诉讼。

党的十八大报告提出，要"进一步深化司法体制改革，坚持和完善中国特色社会主义司法制度，确保审判机关、检察机关依法独立公正行使审判权、检察权"，这揭开了中国新一轮司法改革的序幕。新的司法体制改革的一个重大目标是要求司法去地方化和去行政化，避免司法受到地方保护主义的干扰，树立司法的权威和法律的权威。地方保护主义强化了部门利益和地方利益，损害了普遍利益和国家利益，进而也损害了公共利益。不断发展的公益诉讼案件亟待破除地方保护主义，这需要公益诉讼的审判法院通过提级管辖、集中管辖来审理跨地区的公益诉讼案件，保障公共利益在不同地方都能获得平等的保护。贵州等地的环境公益诉讼实践在法律范围内灵活运用了提级管辖和指定管辖，以达到集中管辖的目的。正在探索和谋划的司法体制改革走得更远，它试图建立与行政区划适当分离的司法管辖制度，这就意味着不是在所有的行政管辖区域都按照地域管辖原则建立相应的司法机构，而是超越行政区分设立长久、集中的司法制度。

以上我们边叙边议地讨论了公益诉讼入法的制度性规定、公益诉讼的内在价值以及公益诉讼对司法体制改革的促进作用。不过，公益诉讼所面临的问题远不止这些，以下的问题仍旧是未来一段时间讨论的重点。谁能代表公共利益？公民和法律未规定的非政府组织能不能成为公益诉讼的原告？在理论层面，人民检察院是否可以作为公益诉讼的原告？公益诉讼入法是否有垄断公益诉讼之嫌？在新一轮司法体制改革中是否有必要建立专门的公益诉讼法庭？事关公益诉讼的案件是否需要普遍采取陪审制度？如何防止恶意的公益诉讼？作为一个新生事物，公益诉讼在中国的成长还有很长的一段路要走。

# Public Interest Litigation and Judicial Reform in China

*He Hairen*

【Abstract】 The adoption of legal provisions on public interest litigation is an indication that public interest litigation has acquired the legitimacy and formalization in law in China. Article 55 of the Chinese Civil Procedural Law established a public interest litigation system with Chinese characteristics. The upholding of public interest through judicial means represents a new paradigm for the recognition and confirmation of public interest and highlights the intrinsic value of public interest litigation as a mechanism for the rational resolution of social conflicts. Public interest litigation is one of the results of judicial reform. At the same time, it also poses new challenges and raises new demands to the judicial system.

【Key words】 Public Interest Litigation; Public Interest; Experimental Value; Judicial Reform

# Nordic Supreme Courts—Differences and Similarities

*Ditlev Tamm, Copenhagen*

**【Abstract】** This paper deals with the Nordic Courts' system. The point is to explain how the judicial systems in the Nordic countries are quite different even if they may appear similar. Thus Finland and Sweden have a system of two apex courts-a supreme ordinary and a supreme administrative court-whereas you only find one ordinary Supreme court in Denmark and Norway. The historical reasons for this difference are given. Common for the Nordic countries is the lack of a constitutional court which is not felt as a relevant institution in countries with a continuous legal history without ruptures or transition from a totalitarian to a democratic system.

To the outsider, the Nordic countries may appear rather similar. However, basic institutions are often organized in different ways. This will be clear if we draw a comparison between the Nordic countries as to the way in which especially Supreme Justice is organized.

It is common to talk of a Nordic legal family[①] but even if there is agreement that such a family exists, which implies that one can accept the idea of such families, Nordic law has no unity. Moreover, even legislation introduced as part of international collaboration in the field of law is not applied in the same way in all the Nordic countries. You may hear decisions from one Nordic country being quoted in others, although this is not a common occurrence, but Danish law is

---

[①] For discussion of the concept of a Nordic legal family, see e. g. Zweigert and Kötz: *Introduction to Comparative Law*, 3. ed. 1998, p. 277, and now esp. Husa, Pihjamäki and Nuotio (eds): *Nordic Law between Tradition and Dynamism*, Antwerp-Oxf. 2007, p. 5.

still Danish, as indeed is Finnish law, Icelandic law, Norwegian law and Swedish law each a law in its own right. Each country has its own legal institutions that work in very different ways. University teaching and law professors may be more or less internationally oriented, but legislators and courts are national and produce or judge according to national law even if international conventions and international courts play an important role. Even if to some the national approach may seem obsolete, we are still living in a world of nation states where the law is made and applied by national institutions. One of these institutions, and a very important one, is the law court and court system.

The following reflections on the role of courts and judges are related to a research project on supreme justice which was originally inspired by studies of the history of the Supreme Court of Denmark. Comparisons of courts have been carried out before. The style and way of presenting judgments has been a topic of research interest[1]. My aim is different. I look at the position of the Supreme Court in society, its role, its understanding of itself, its possibilities and ambitions. As a legal historian my natural inclination is to look at the courts in a historical perspective and to combine legal history and legal comparison.

Today courts, like other institutions, live in a time of internationalisation, but as already stressed their work is still *local*. Many courts around the world live a secluded life, being only rarely if ever confronted with cases that include elements of foreign origin. Even if discussions of the role of the courts are international and often take their starting point in the role of well-known courts such as the US Supreme Court or in discussions of international courts like the European and the Inter-American Court of Human Rights established in 1979 or supranational courts such as the ECJ,[2] the nation-state still plays a decisive role in the understanding of

---

[1] See Mitchel de S-O-L'E Lasser, *Judicial Liberations—A comparative Analysis of Judicial Transparency and Legitimacy*, Oxf. 2004 for a comparison of the French Cour de Cassation, The US Supreme Court and the ECJ.

[2] Other examples are the courts of the EFTA, the court of the South American Communidad Andina (CAN), the Southeast African COMESA. It is important to stress in this connection how the existence of supranational courts and international courts is changing the idea of justice being local. Danish courts or other courts in the EU have an obligation to place preliminary questions regarding community law before the ECJ. The possibility of having national decisions tried by an international court of human rights is another example of how courts cannot isolate themselves.

the way in which *local justice* functions. In that respect every country has its own way of looking at justice, legal education and the way the courts function.

I think one can safely say that courts in general—and this also applies to Danish courts—have for many years understood and still basically understand their role not in an international context but as national institutions with a specific professional task to fulfil. This is changing, especially in the higher courts, and even if most cases are still local and decided according to local rules, there is a growing understanding of courts and judges as fulfilling a function that implies an outlook towards the world beyond the courtroom. European courts in particular must be aware, and are increasingly, so, of the diversity of legal sources often of supranational or international origin and of their being assessed and measured themselves by an international standard as part of modern legal culture.

Several features are common to today's discussion of the role of courts. Especially at Supreme Court level judges have more international contact and learn from each other.[1] We talk of a dialogue between courts. Another important question is that of judicial activism. Should courts anticipate a political decision and make new law or should they rather be reluctant to transgress the border between law and politics, respecting their position as courts and not a political organ? The concept of there being a "universal epistemology" among judges has been used of the phenomenon that despite national differences judges in different countries have a common understanding of their role[2].

"Judicialization" means that courts increasingly take a stand in conflicts that used to be considered political or administrative or in general in fields formerly not normally considered by courts. The American phenomenon is now also seen in England, Germany and Southern Europe. The question is important and has ramifications for our understanding of how democracy should function and the role

---

[1] Julie Allard and Antoine Garapon, in *Les juges dans la mondialisation. La nouvelle revolution du droit*, Paris, 2005, discuss a specific "commerce des juges". The idea that judges are part of an international network that will create a new form of "global governance" was introduced by A-M Slaughter, *The New World Order*, Princeton, 2004.

[2] The expression was used by Italian professor and judge of the Italian Corte Costituzionale, Sabino Cassese, in a paper at the XVIII *International Conference of Comparative Law*, Washington DC, July 2010.

of judges within it.[1] Another question connected to the function of supreme justice has to do with the legitimacy connected to the appearance of a final judgment as unanimous. Since 1938 the Danish Supreme Court has published both majority and minority votes, whereas e. g. the French Cour de Cassation or the ECJ do not. The disclosure of dissenting opinions is seen from a Danish point of view as being important for the legitimacy of the decision, but this question is seen differently in systems based on the French tradition. A judgment is seen as stronger when it appears as unanimous and also avoids speculation as to why some judges may have different views. In the Danish Supreme Court the unwritten rule is that judges do not publish individual votes but tend to find a common solution, in most cases unanimously, but otherwise as a majority and a minority, or sometimes several minorities. A dissenting judge is not the ideal. In the Danish tradition judgments are also rather brief, a consequence of the quest for a common denominator, without however competing in this respect with the style of the French courts.

The way a supreme court is perceived in society is dependent on a series of features apart from those already mentioned. The independence of the court and its ability to reach judgments without influence from other state powers is essential. Delay is a serious problem in many court systems. The absence of corruption and the quality of judgments are other features, and differences from one country to another are obvious in a picture of "global justice" that does not always offer justice the best conditions.

Many themes may be compared regarding supreme courts. There may be one apex court or there may be a system of several supreme courts dealing with ordinary cases, constitutional matters or administrative matters. Denmark is an example of a country in which the Supreme Court is traditionally competent in all matters. There is only one apex court, as is the case in Norway, whereas the structure is different in Sweden and Finland.

Another important question as to the role of courts has to do with the way in

---

[1] See e. g. C. Guarnieri and P. Pederzoli, *The Power of Judges*, A comparative Study of Courts and Democracy, Oxford, 2002.

which judges are nominated[①]. An important issue today is how to determine the balance between those decisions made by politically chosen organs and decisions made by judges who are nominated and not democratically elected. In some countries judges or at least higher judges are nominated by the government; this was also the case in Denmark until a specific Board of Courts and a Committee for the Selection of Judges was established in 1999 in order to keep these nominations outside the political system and with a view—only partly achieved—to recruiting future judges from among lawyers without a previous career as a judge rather than solely from the ranks of professional judges, another important feature in the picture of modern courts. The Danish Supreme Court has more recently recruited judges with a background as practical lawyers, as professors or in other areas of professional experience, even if most judges still make their career as judges.

The political role of courts and judges is a theme which is becoming increasingly important. In a legal culture like the Danish one there has been a marked reluctance to touch upon the idea that judges may be political actors. Denmark has a tradition of considering the courts in general, including the Supreme Court, as being outside the political sphere, whereas in other countries the courts and the political views of judges are the object of public interest.[②]

A look at the Supreme Courts of the Nordic countries will reveal extreme variations in traditions and ways of organisation. The Danish Supreme Court belongs to the minority of single apex courts and is in many ways unique. As a still functioning institution it can trace its history back to its foundation in 1661 as part of a series of administrative reforms introduced by a newly installed absolutist

---

[①] See Malleson and Russell (ed.), *Appointing Judges in an Age of Judicial Power*, Critical Perspectives from around the World, Toronto, 2006.

[②] Se e. g. Robert A. Dahl, Decision-making in a Democracy: The Supreme Court as a national policy-maker, *Journal of Public Law* 6 (1957), pp. 279 – 95. (Quoted from Lee Epstein (ed.), *Courts and Judges*, 2005, p. 485): "To consider the Supreme Court of the United States strictly as a legal institution is to underestimate its significance in the American political system. For it is also a political institution, an institution, that is to say, for arriving at decisions on controversial questions of national policy. As a political institution, the Court is highly unusual, not least because Americans are not quite willing to accept the fact that it is a political institution and not quite capable of denying it...". See also Sunstien et al.., *Are Judges Political?* An Empirical Analysis of the Federal Judiciary, Washington, 2006.

government. Whereas many supreme courts have their legal basis in a constitution, the Danish Supreme Court is older than the Danish Constitution of 1849. It thus has had to carry the burden of history to find its place as an absolutist institution in a constitutional system, which has not always been easy. However, frictions have been few, and one may see the reluctance of the Danish Supreme Court to accept "judicial review" and to actually consider a statute unconstitutional as a remnant of a past in which the court had close ties to the government. ①

The closest cousin of the Danish Supreme Court is the Norwegian Supreme Court, which was founded in 1814 when Denmark and Norway were separated. The Norwegian Supreme Court was part of a new constitutional system set up in 1814 when Norway acquired a new constitution that created institutions which secured for the country a new and much more independent position in its union with Sweden-lasting from 1814 – 1905-following more than four centuries of Danish-Norwegian union. ② A separate Norwegian Supreme Court was part of Norwegian nation building after 1814. Even if there are institutional similarities with the Danish Supreme Court, the constitutional position is different, and this may also explain some of the most marked differences as to the way in which the Norwegian Supreme Court has acted in certain situations③. The Danish Supreme

---

① Until now there has only been one case, in 1999, in which the Danish Supreme Court has considered a statute unconstitutional. The case concerned an Act adopted by the Danish parliament to stop public aid to certain listed private schools, all part of the same corporation (Tvind). In its 1999 ruling the Supreme Court annulled the Act as unconstitutional because it was seen as a violation of the division of power between legislators and courts as it deprived the schools of the right to have their status brought before the courts.

② The history of the Norwegian Supreme Court from 1814 – 1965 has appeared in two volumes as Nils Rune Langeland: *Siste ord. Høgsterett i norsk historie 1814 – 1905*, Oslo 2005 and Erling Sandmo, *Siste ord. Høgsterett i norsk historie 1905 – 1965*, Oslo 2006 and Jørn Sunde, *Høgsteretts historie 1965 – 2015*, Oslo 2015.

③ Special mention should be made of the fact that judicial review was already known and practised in Norway in the middle of the 19th century. Rune Slagstad, Rettens ironi, p. 27, (in*Forhandlingene ved det 35. nordiske juristmøtet i Oslo 18. – 20. August 1999. Del 1.* 2000, pp. 23 – 31) stresses how Norway had established a constitutional court even at the time of the Union with Sweden (1814 – 1905). Also during the Second World War and the German occupation of both countries the Danish and the Norwegian Supreme Courts took different stands. The Norwegian Supreme court resigned because it would not accept Nazi legislation, whereas the Danish Supreme Court continued its function even if that implied acceptance of legislation against German interests.

Court was also the Supreme Court of Iceland① until a separate Supreme Court for Iceland was established in 1919 to act as second instance for all Iceland.

The way the two supreme courts, the Danish and the Norwegian, work are similar. In both courts oral proceedings are the rule. Judges vote orally when proceedings are over. Danish Supreme Court judges start with the youngest judge whereas in Norway the president of the court decides the order. Norwegian decisions are formed as personal opinions. Danish judgments, as already mentioned, are the result of intense work to agree on a common text.

A peculiarity of the Danish system is that the Supreme Court does not itself decide which cases to hear on appeal. This is the task of a specific board composed of judges and other lawyers to grant permission to have a case brought before the Supreme Court if it has already been heard twice. In Norway as in the other Nordic countries the Court itself decides whether a case has sufficient interest as a precedent for it to be tried by the Supreme Court.

The Danish, the Norwegian and the Icelandic Supreme Courts belong to what we can call the West—Nordic part of the Nordic legal family and they are institutions stemming from a common past. The court system of Sweden and Finland is quite different, as is the approach to public law and public institutions there in general. Common to the Nordic countries, however, is the absence of a constitutional court.

The organisation of the Swedish-Finnish system stems from the establishment of so called "*hovrätter*" or royal courts in the 17$^{th}$ century. The first royal court was established in Stockholm in 1614, next came Åbo (now Turku) in Finland in 1623, then Dorpat (today's Tartu) in Livonia (at that time a Swedish possession) in 1630 and Jönköping in Sweden in 1634. Later more courts were added both in Sweden and in Finland after the separation in 1809.

The Swedish Supreme Court was established by King Gustav Ⅲ in 1789, and like the Danish Supreme Court it has an authoritarian past without a constitutional foundation. The King originally had two votes. It was only in 1809, with the introduction of a new constitutional order, that the Court came to have a

---

① Iceland belonged to Norway but in 1814 remained with Denmark. In 1918 Iceland was granted autonomy and the Supreme Court was part of the new order. In 1944 Iceland became independent.

constitutional basis. It became the administrative Supreme Court in 1909. Until 1974 the decisions of the court were issued in the name of the King. The Swedish Supreme Court is not a constitutional court; however in later times it has changed its attitude and even does some "judicial review".

The court systems of Sweden and Finland are based on a distinction between ordinary and administrative procedure, as in the French system. The highest administrative court in Sweden, corresponding to the French Conseil d'État, has since its foundation in 1909[1] been known as the Government Court (*Regeringsrätten*) and the highest Finnish administrative court is the Highest Government Court (*Korkein hallinto-oikeus*). The Finnish Supreme Court dates back to 1809, whereas the Supreme Administrative Court was established in 1918 and thus is contemporary with Finnish independence and the new Finnish constitution.

There are notable differences also in the function of the Swedish and the Finnish ordinary and administrative courts.[2] A common factor is written procedure at the supreme level, which differentiates these courts from the Danish, Norwegian and Icelandic Supreme Courts. The Swedish Administrative Court system is three-tiered and thus the highest Administrative Court, like the ordinary Supreme Court, only hears cases of general interest as precedents. The highest Finnish Administrative Court is second instance and deals with a much greater number of cases.

The Danish system is different with regard to administrative procedure. There are a few specialized administrative courts, such as the National Tax Court and the Social Appeal Court, which function as courts under appeal to the Supreme Court (when granted). Apart from those institutions there are no administrative courts but specialized boards fulfil the function of hearing complaints about administrative decisions in the various fields.

In the Nordic countries are found fewer detailed studies of individual judges,

---

[1] The centenary was celebrated by the book *Regeringsrätten 100 år*, Uppsala 2009. See e. g. about differences between the procedure in the Supreme Court and the Highest Administrative Court, Johan Munck, l. c., pp. 365 – 370.

[2] See Pekka Hallberg, Regeringsrätten som samarbejdspartner, in *Regeringsrätten 100 år* (Note 15), pp. 175 – 180.

the role of the court and its political role as one might find in the United States or other countries. The courts are generally highly respected as important legal actors but not seen as institutions over which openly to debate or disagree. This impression is reflected in the books that have come out in later years to commemorate anniversaries of the different Nordic Supreme Courts. The 350$^{th}$ year of the foundation of the Danish Supreme Court was marked in 2011. The Swedish Svea Hovrätt, which in 2014 had existed for 400 years, is not the Swedish Supreme Court but within the Swedish hierarchy of Courts in many ways is considered the most prestigious court. Court history and the way courts are organized tell an important story of the society in which it functions. Courts are local in their function but at the same time it is important to recognize that to grasp what is unique in the legal system of each country one must look across borders and make comparisons. The way the court system is organized tells an important history of differences and similarities.

# 北欧国家最高法院的异同

迪特列夫·塔姆

【摘要】本文介绍北欧法院系统,其目的在于说明为什么北欧各国的司法制度虽然表面上看上去相似,但实际上却非常不同。芬兰和瑞典都有两个最高法院——一个最高普通法院和一个最高行政法院;而丹麦和挪威则只有一个最高普通法院。本文分析了这些差异的历史原因。北欧国家的一个共同之处就是它们都没有一个宪法法院。这是因为这些国家都拥有一部没有遭到破坏的连续的法律历史,并且都没有经历过从专制制度向民主制度的过渡,因此它们都感到没有必要建立此类机构。

# 审判中心：以人民陪审员制度改革为突破口

施鹏鹏[*]

**【摘要】** 人民陪审员制度改革，对于推进司法民主、保障司法公正以及推进以审判为中心的诉讼制度改革具有重要意义。合理地发挥人民陪审员在审判中的作用，有助于充分发挥庭审的功能，推动建立新的审判秩序。

**【关键词】** 审判中心　人民陪审员　司法民主　司法公正　审判秩序

中国共产党第十八届中央委员会第四次全体会议审议通过了《中共中央关于全面推进依法治国若干重大问题的决定》，该《决定》以"依法治国"为主题，提出"推进以审判为中心的诉讼制度改革，确保侦查、审查起诉的案件事实证据经得起法律的检验"。在当前深化司法改革的大背景下，"审判中心"的提出，既涉及公、检、法三机关在刑事司法体系运行过程中的职权配置，也涵盖了决策者对庭审在事实认定、证据裁判以及法律适用等方面的功能定位，具有极为重大的理论价值及实践意义。

从制度内涵上看，"审判中心"是司法架构及诉讼规则的综合体，主要包括四项内容：其一，在刑事诉讼的各个环节中，审判应是事实认定最为重要也是最为权威的阶段；其二，在庭审过程中，裁判者应秉承直接言辞原则，直面各项证据及待证事实，并最终形成内心确信以做出判决；其三，在审级体制中，一审应是事实认定最基本也是最核心的阶段；其四，在刑事司法结构上，侦、控、审应分权制衡，法庭具有终局裁判权。"审判中心"的诸项内容相互联系，是一项系统工程，故所面临的困难与挑战也是

---

[*] 中国政法大学教授。

全方位的，包括：公、检、法三机关分工配合的刑事司法结构，高度行政化、官僚化的司法层级体系，以侦查为中心的传统犯罪打击模式，卷宗发挥主导作用的庭审调查程序以及受各方力量制约并深负司法重责的裁判官的地位设置问题。可见，审判中心主义的落实，绝非一纸文件可轻易推动，其势必涉及诸多司法传统以及背后各部门利益的综合考量。从刑事司法体系的内部进行观察，司法改革已逼近瓶颈，体制内外的各种功能衔接及各主要政法机关在利益及资源分配方面的矛盾日趋尖锐，倘若改革不能在时下的制度框架下寻求合理的突破口以确立共识，则新旧理念之间的摩擦乃至冲突可能被无限放大，并最终使既定的目标无疾而终。依拙见，推进人民陪审员制度改革、确立真正意义上的陪审团制度，这不失为时下突破审判中心主义之种种障碍的良策。

## 一 人民陪审员制度改革之于"审判中心"的重要司法价值

托克维尔在论及陪审制时曾精辟地指出，"在讲述陪审制度时，必须把这个制度的两种作用区别开来：第一，它是作为司法制度而存在的；第二，它是作为政治制度而起作用的"①。中国时下在推行人民陪审员制度改革时更强调的是该制度的政治价值，即"拓宽人民群众有序参与司法渠道"②，殊不知人民陪审员制度对于实现裁判权的主体回归、催化庭审结构的改革以及确立现代庭审原则等亦有重要作用，而这三者恰恰是"审判中心"制度的重要内容。

### （一）人民陪审员制度改革与裁判权的主体回归

一如前述，"审判中心"势必要求裁判权的主体回归，让法庭成为事实判断及定罪量刑的最终决定者。但时下，无论是在立法层面还是在实践层面，程度不一的裁判权虚置问题已成为危及审判中心制度乃至司法公信力的重要因素。这突出地体现在三个方面：其一，在重大疑难案件中，审判权被割裂，合议庭"审而不判"，审判委员会"判而不审"；其二，在涉及敏感事项的案件中，审判权被干预，源自司法系统内外的各种权力以及源自网络舆论的各种压力，时常令合议庭无法严格按事实和法律进行裁断；

---

① Alexis de Tocqueville, De la démocratie en Amérique, vol. I, in œuvres, Paris, Garnier-Flammarion, 1981, pp. 311 – 317.
② 中国共产党十八届三中全会议通过的《中共中央关于全面深化改革若干重大问题的决定》。

其三，在一般性的案件中，审判权被放弃，时下人民陪审员"陪而不审，合而不议"的现象极为突出。决策者已意识到这些问题，并确立了相应的改革措施，如最高人民法院《四五改革纲要（2014—2018）》便提出了"合理定位审判委员会职能，强化审判委员会总结审判经验、讨论决定审判工作重大事项的宏观指导职能……除法律规定的情形和涉及国家外交、安全和社会稳定的重大复杂案件外，审判委员会主要讨论案件的法律适用问题"，"建立法院内部人员过问案件的记录制度和责任追究制度"以及"配合中央有关部门，推动建立领导干部干预审判执行活动、插手具体案件处理的记录、通报和责任追究制度。按照案件全程留痕要求，明确审判组织的记录义务和责任，对于领导干部干预司法活动、插手具体案件的批示、函文、记录等信息，建立依法提取、介质存储、专库录入、入卷存查机制，相关信息均应当存入案件正卷，供当事人及其代理人查询"等。但前述措施在时下国家权力配置的大背景下很难在短期内得到全面落实，尤其是"过问案件的记录制度"。可以想象，在法官独立的身份保障尚未完全确立前，审判人员在实施"过问案件的记录制度"时将面临严重的职业风险，甚至可能影响今后的晋升及去留。

而"推进人民陪审员制度改革、确立真正意义上的陪审团制度"可一劳永逸地解决前述问题。其一，陪审员在公众中临时随机遴选产生。在这种情况下，没有任何外部机构或法庭内部人员可以控制合议庭的人员组成，并进而干预审判或影响诉讼结果。其二，陪审团的裁决具有终局性、权威性的特点，这是"人民主权"理念的必然延伸，不仅职业法官应遵守这一判决，审判委员会也必须遵守之。考虑到重大刑事案件一般采用陪审团审判，因此，陪审制的落实必然导致审判委员会的职能最终转向法律适用问题。其三，陪审员源自社会大众，其所做出的判决是"人民的判决"，因此具有抵抗公众舆论的天然能力。如此可见，陪审制的推行，将"自然而然"地保障裁判权的主体回归。

## （二）人民陪审员制度改革与现代庭审结构的设立

在现代刑事诉讼中，庭审结构可理解为是"对抗"与"判定"的综合体，控、辩、审三方的诉讼活动构成了刑事庭审的基本支点。在审判中心模式下，法庭在刑事庭审结构中应处于居中的主导地位，控制诉讼进程，决定程序性事项及实体事项，并最终做出具有既判力的刑事判决。但诚如龙宗智教授所言，"我国目前的庭审方式是一种具有中国特色的混合式庭审方法。它是中国传统和固有的制度因素、现代职权主义以及当事人主义三大要素的糅合"①。因此，庭审结构的定位并不明确，存在较为明显的职能角色的重叠和冲突，这主要体现为以下几方面。其一，侦查机关在国家权力格局中处于优势地位，这决定了其在刑事诉讼中的强势地位；与之相比，孱弱的刑事辩护权一直饱受理论界及实务界的诟病。其二，检察机关除享有公诉权外，还享有侦查权和法律监督权。检察权与裁判权在庭审中处于微妙关系，并未严格遵循裁判至上的诉讼理念。其三，公、检、法三机关的相互配合多于相互制约。在司法实践中，三机关在长期的业务合作中形成较为默契的配合，庭审很难形成控辩"平等对抗"的合理结构。其四，极为严苛的司法责任追究制度进一步加强了公、检、法三机关的合作关系。"捕得准、诉得出、判得下"的业务标准使追责压力逆推，法院很难顶受源自侦、检机关的定罪压力。

相比时下的职业法官裁判制度，陪审团制度无疑更有利于实现庭审结构的合理化。首先，陪审制有助于强化裁判者的中立地位。陪审员来自社会的普通大众，他们绝大部分与检察官素昧平生，既未有工作业务往来，也不会考虑检察官的特殊地位，因此，他们更容易充当中立裁判者的角色。其次，陪审制也有助于强化控辩双方的平等对抗。在陪审团主导的庭审结构中，控方并不因为是国家的代言人而取得优势地位，而辩方也不因为是追诉对象而处于弱势地位。因此，裁判者作为"忠实听众"的职能定位更容易为控辩双方提供平等辩论的"表演舞台"。

### （三）人民陪审员制度改革与现代庭审原则的确立

审判中心还意味着应确立一系列现代的庭审原则，尤其是集中审理原则、言辞原则和对席审判原则等。集中审理原则又称为连续审理原则，指法庭对案件的审判应当持续不断地进行，一气呵成，至审结为止。该审理原则主要是为了实现迅速审判，保证裁判人员心证的准确性，以避免裁判人员因时间拖延而记忆模糊，从而加大心证的难度。言辞原则指法庭审理应通过诉讼参与人员的言辞进行，而不应以书面陈述代替出庭陈述和质证。裁判者通过对各诉讼参与人的"现实状况"进行亲身体验，并通过双方的质证获得全面的认识和评价，唯有如此方可准确地形成心证。对席审判原则则指控辩双方地位平等，可以对案件中的所有证据材料进行质证，也指双方当事人权利平等，尤其是平等地享有对证人进行提问的权利。在审判

---

① 龙宗智：《论我国刑事庭审方式改革》，《中国法学》1998年第4期。

中心模式之下，集中审理原则、言辞原则以及对席审判原则是确保裁判者准确、及时、客观地形成心证的重要保障。

中国的《刑事诉讼法》虽也确立了一系列庭审原则，但大抵不全面或无法落实到位，例如：《刑事诉讼法》中也有证人出庭作证制度，但在司法实践中，证人不出庭的现象却广泛存在；庭审也要求辩论，但却往往流于形式。诸多庭审原则的缺失或虚置已严重损及庭审功能的实现，架空了"审判中心"的制度支撑，损害了司法公正及司法公信力。然而，如何弥补这一制度性缺陷、确立符合刑事司法规律的现代庭审原则？依拙见，只要对现有的人民陪审员制度进行实质性的改造，则前述问题可迎刃而解：陪审制必然要求适用集中审理原则，因为陪审员非常设，需尽快完成裁判以回归日常生活，且集中审理原则方可保证陪审员在尽可能短的庭审时间内形成准确心证；陪审制必然要求言辞原则，因为陪审员在庭审前不能接触卷宗，故所有证据均必须提交法庭，而不能以书面材料代替证人作证；陪审制必然要求对席审判原则，因为陪审员并非专业人士，唯有通过对席审判形成的"二选一"判断模式减少心证难度，才能使非专业人士的裁判成为可能。

一言以蔽之，人民陪审员制度对中国诉讼制度尤其是庭审程序的改革具有十分独特的意义，而非一项孤立的技术设计。这应引起决策者的高度重视。

## 二　人民陪审员制度的现状及改革思路

如前所述，人民陪审员制度改革完全可以作为时下中国确立审判中心模式的突破口。但现有的人民陪审员制度究竟存在怎样的缺陷，以及如何改革人民陪审员制度以使其承载确立审判中心模式的重责，需要我们做出更进一步的解读。

### （一）人民陪审员制度的现状

中国的人民陪审员制度最早规定于《人民法院组织法》和诉讼法中。但在早期的司法实践中，由于相关法律规定过于粗疏，可操作性不强，人民陪审员制度在各地法院形同虚设，未引起过多的重视。2000年10月，最高人民法院曾将《关于完善人民陪审员制度的决定（草案）》提请第九届全国人民代表大会审议。该草案对人民陪审员制度的适用范围、人民陪审员的资格条件、产生方式、权利和义务及执行职务的待遇等内容均做了具体的规定，力图使我国的人民陪审员制度趋于规范。此后，最高人民法院又根据九届全国人大法律委员会提出的修改意见，在全国法院范围内经全面、深入的调查研究和论证后对草案进行相应修改，将其作为新的立法建议报送十届人大常委会。2004年8月28日，第十届全国人大常委会第十一次会议通过了《关于完善人民陪审员制度的决定》（以下简称《决定》），并定于2005年5月1日正式施行。据官方统计，《决定》实施8年来，全国人民陪审员参加审理案件共计803.4万人次，其中2012年参加审理案件人次是2006年的3.8倍。全国人民陪审员参加审理案件的总数为628.9万件，其中刑事案件176.4万件、民事案件429.8万件、行政案件22.7万件。人民陪审员参加审理的案件比例逐年提高，2013年上半年全国法院审理的一审普通程序案件陪审率已达71.7%，比2006年提高了52%。①

但也应看到，人民陪审员工作在取得较大成效的同时，仍凸显了一些极为严重的问题，有些问题已成为制约该制度进一步深化拓展的瓶颈。首先，在制度观念上，许多法官仅将人民陪审员制度作为司法民主化的"象征"，忽视了该制度在推进独立司法、优化诉讼构造、彰显"大众理性"方面的重要作用。这一认知也导致了司法实践中陪而不审、陪审工作形式化的现象普遍存在。其次，在制度设计上，时下的人民陪审员制度也存在诸多缺陷，如适用范围不确定、遴选程序不民主、职务任期不合理、裁判权责不清晰、经费保障不充分等。面对以上种种弊端，不少理论及实务工作者提出了一个尖锐的问题：在倡导司法职业化、专业化的今天，公众参与司法是否还有必要以及如何成为可能？

**（二）改革思路**

对于人民陪审员制度，中国决策层的态度是十分明朗的，其认为"人民陪审员制度是中国特色社会主义司法制度的重要组成部分。要通过改革人民陪审员制度，推进司法民主，促进司法公正，保障人民群众有序参与司法，提升人民陪审员制度公信度和司法公信力，让人民群众在每一个司法案件中感受到公平正义"。党的十八届三中全会明确提出，广泛实行人民陪审员制度、人民监督员制度，拓宽人民群众有序参与司法的渠道。十八届四中全会进一步提出，"完善人民陪审员制度，保障公民陪审权利，扩大参审范围，完善随机抽选方式，提高人民陪审制度公信度。逐步实行人民陪审员不再审理法律适用问题，只参与审理事实认定问题"。

---

① 《最高法向全国人大常委会报告人民陪审员工作情况》，《人民日报》2013年10月23日。

2015 年 4 月 24 日，全国人民代表大会常务委员会授权最高人民法院在北京等 10 个省（自治区、直辖市）各选择 5 个法院开展人民陪审员制度改革试点工作，对人民陪审员的选任条件、选任程序、参审范围、参审机制、退出和惩戒机制、履职保障等制度进行改革。改革的基本思路是清晰的：其一，扩大人民陪审员制度的适用范围，对于涉及群体利益、社会公共利益的，人民群众广泛关注或者其他社会影响较大的刑事、民事、行政案件，涉及征地拆迁、环境保护、食品药品安全的案件，以及可能判处 10 年以上有期徒刑、无期徒刑的刑事案件，原则上实行人民陪审制审理；其二，大幅增加人民陪审员的人数，强化陪审员遴选的随机性及民主性，试点法院每 5 年从当地年满 28 周岁、无犯罪记录的选民或者常住居民名单中，随机抽选本院法官员额数 5 倍以上的人员作为人民陪审员候选人，建立人民陪审员候选人信息库，制作人民陪审员候选人名册；其三，强化人民陪审员的诉讼职权，人民陪审员应当全程参与合议庭评议，在集体评议过程中独立就案件事实认定问题发表意见，不再对法律适用问题进行表决，但可以对法律适用问题发表意见；其四，确立人民陪审员在合议庭中的优势地位，原则上合议庭中人民陪审员在数量上应多于职业法官。

可见，改革后的人民陪审员制度已极其类似于域外的陪审制或参审制，但仍有若干明显的差异。首先，陪审员遴选的民主性及随机性已极大加强，但任期仍较长（5 年），依然有常设化的趋势。其次，陪审员的职权设定仍具有一定的模糊性。如果法官与人民陪审员的多数意见存在重大分歧，且认为人民陪审员的多数意见对事实的认定可能导致裁判结果错误的，可以将案件提交专业法官会议讨论并由其提供咨询意见。合议庭根据专业法官会议的咨询意见再次评议。再次评议后，法官与人民陪审员的多数意见仍存在重大分歧的，可以将案件报院长决定是否提交审委会讨论，这一规定有悖于"人民主权"的基本原则。再次，陪审员的合议及表决机制仍相当粗糙，未引入欧陆通行的"问题列表"制度，这将给陪审员的事实认定带来极大的困扰。最后，在刑事、民事及行政诉讼中均适用陪审团制度，可能导致陪审团在后两者中无法准确厘清事实和法律的界限，进而无法准确做出裁断。

但无论如何，深化人民陪审员制度改革已经提上日程，改革成果将在不久的将来接受公众的考验。新人民陪审员制度下的新"审判秩序"尤其值得期待。

## 三 新人民陪审员制度下的新"审判秩序"

可见,人民陪审员制度改革对于审判中心模式的确立具有极其重要的司法价值,这在比较法上也有范例。在欧陆法史中,刑事诉讼的重大变革经常以陪审制的改革为主轴和突破口,① 如 1789 年的法国陪审制改革、1864 年和 1993 年的俄罗斯陪审制改革以及 1995 年的西班牙陪审制改革。沙曼教授曾对这一现象进行了精辟的分析,"现代刑事诉讼中的程序公正理念已经在各国的宪法及国际人权公约中获得一般的共识。作为程序公正之载体的诸多刑事诉讼原则往往源自英美法中的陪审制及对抗制或在陪审制及对抗制的环境下发扬光大,如无罪推定原则、反对自我归罪原则、平等武装原则、公开审判原则、直接言辞原则、控诉分离原则等……尽管以纠问式职权主义为传统的大陆法系国家往往也承认上述这些基本原则,但由于原则所依托的陪审制及对抗制与大陆法系纠问式的一些基本原则相背离而大部分最终被抛弃或难以有效践行……各种原则与陪审制结构之间的张力已在大陆法系国家引起了一些重大问题"②。

在中国新的人民陪审员制度下,我们可以构想一套全新的"审判秩序"。

### (一) 审判中心

传统以侦查为中心的治罪型程序模式将被改革,转而走向以审判为中心的正当程序模式。人民陪审员主导的合议庭将成为证据审查、事实判断以及定罪量刑的唯一权威机构。庭审奉行言辞、对席原则,任何证据均必须提交法庭方可予以认定。陪审员通过对证据的自由评价实现从客观确信至判决责任伦理的跨越。

### (二) 控辩平衡

合议庭将处于更加中立、客观的地位,辩护律师在庭审中也将具有更

---

① Stephen C. Thaman, "The Idea of A Conference on Lay Participation", in Le jury dans le procès pénal au XXIe siècle, Conférence internationale, Syracuse, Italie, 26 – 29 mai 1999, Revue Internationale de Droit Pénal (RIDP), 1ᵉ et 2ᵉ trimestres 2001, p. 19, et s.

② Stephen C. Thaman, "Europes New Jury Systems: the Cases of Spain and Russia", in *Law and Contemporary Problems*, p. 1. 类似的观点,参见 Stephen C. Thaman, "The Idea of A Conference on Lay Participation", in Le jury dans le procès pénal au XXIe siècle, Conférence internationale, Syracuse, Italie, 26 – 29 mai 1999, Revue Internationale de Droit Pénal (RIDP), 1ᵉ et 2ᵉ trimestres 2001, p. 19。

大的空间。控辩双方必须尽力向法庭提供对己方有利的各种证据材料，并证明各自的诉讼请求。合议庭的唯一职责便是判断"谁更有理"，而无须考虑双方各自的权力背景及职责差异。控辩之外的任何案外因素都不可能进入法庭并影响裁判者的心证。

### （三）民主决策

合议庭通过多数表决的民主决策形成合议并做出判决。此一判决可视为"人民的判决"，可杜绝任何国家阴谋、政治迫害、阶层差异等因素。人民自行掌控国家司法权力，仅信奉法律与良心，不为利益所惑，不为权贵所屈。

### （四）司法至上

"人民不会犯错"，这一政治理念禁止我们将人民做出的判决交由其他职权机构审查，不管该职权机构是何种机构。司法因此获得至上的地位，既不受公权力的干预，也不受民间舆论的左右。"……虽然被证实有罪的被告人会对有罪判决不满意，但他们仍然表现顺从，因为他们不得不认识到他们无法动员亲友和普通公众反对这一判决。这种成功只有在对约束性判决的承认已制度化了的社会氛围中才能实现。这就是程序的贡献：它不需要个人确信他们得到了公正的对待，而是改变了当事人的期望结构和生存环境，通过这种方式将当事人在程序中整合起来，使得他们在最后除了接受决定以外别无选择（就像我们虽然不喜欢某种天气，还是无可奈何地接受了它）"[①]。

永远不要低估这一全新的"审判秩序"对中国司法改革的辐射效力。审判中心模式所带来的制度变革绝非简单地将法院变为"法律帝国的首都"，将法官变为"帝国的王侯"（虽然这也是应有之义），而势必涉及国家权力的重新配置、社会主义法治理念的全新阐释以及国家治理方式的变革。因此，如果说"技术可以改变制度、制度可以改变观念"，那么毫无疑问，以人民陪审员制度改革为突破口的审判中心模式的建立便是撬动中国法治建设的杠杆。显然，变革时代已经到来。

---

① 〔德〕克劳斯·F. 勒尔：《程序正义：导论与纲要》，陈林林译，载郑永流主编《法哲学与法社会学论丛》第 1 辑，中国政法大学出版社，2001。

# Adjudication Centralism: Taking the Reform of the People Assessor System as the Breakthrough Point

*Shi Pengpeng*

【Abstract】The reform of the people assessor system is of great significance to promoting democratic administration of Justice, ensuring Judicial fairness, and implementing the trial-centered reform of the litigation system. Giving reasonable play to the role of people's assessors in trial is conducive to strengthening the functions of court trial and promoting the establishment of a new trial order in China.

【Key words】Adjudication Centralism; People's Assessor; Judicial Democracy; Judicial Fairness; Trial Order

# 下 篇
## 法治的新发展

# 法治中国建设与人权保障事业的新进展

柳华文*

**【摘要】** 法治中国建设与以人为本的科学发展观和人权保障事业之间具有密切的联系。2014年10月,党的十八届四中全会通过的《中共中央关于全面推进依法治国若干重大问题的决定》勾画出中国法治与人权事业的新蓝图。中国政府加快了人权白皮书的发布频率,并以中期评估的方式推动第二个"国家人权行动"计划的落实。中国政府反腐败力度空前,这对于人权保障具有多重重要意义。人权教育颇受重视,又有5所高校被授予国家人权教育与培训基地称号。中国参与国际人权机制的工作取得了阶段性进展。

**【关键词】** 法治  人权国家  人权行动计划

近年来,"法治中国"是中国国内时政的关键词。中共中央十八届四中全会专门讨论依法治国问题,这前所未有,广受法学界乃至社会各界的期待和关注。

法治本身不是目的,以人权保障为法律价值和法治目标,才可能是真正的良法善治。法治与人权存在着相辅相成、密不可分的关系。同样,法治与人权在中国又处于新的历史阶段,在此阶段中国应更加注重以人为本,注重经济、政治、文化、社会和生态文明五大建设的全面、均衡、可持续发展,注重社会和谐与公平的发展。

笔者2014年9月17日在第七届北京人权论坛——一年一度、中国最大

---

\* 中国社会科学院国际法研究所所长助理、研究员,中国社会科学院人权研究中心执行主任。

的由中国人权研究会和中国人权基金会联合举办的国际人权交流平台——上提出,法治、发展与人权是中国道路的三个基本维度。三者相辅相成、相互制约,而且三位一体,不可或缺。①

2014年,是中国将"国家尊重和保障人权"写进宪法(法学界称为"人权入宪")10周年,也是中国第二个《国家人权行动计划(2012—2015年)》实施过半的一年。2015年,是中国全面推进依法治国的开局之年,中国的法治建设在改革中起步,在期许中前行,中国的法治与人权事业从此进入了跨越式发展的新时期。

## 一 十八届四中全会:法治与人权事业的新起点

2014年10月23日,中国共产党中央委员会十八届四中全会在北京闭幕。这是中国改革开放以来,中国共产党首次以"依法治国"为主题的中央全会。会议通过《中共中央关于全面推进依法治国若干重大问题的决定》(以下简称《决定》),这是中国法治发展历程中的一个重要节点,具有承前启后的重要意义。

《决定》规定的是中国法治和人权事业的重要纲领,其中绝大部分内容都涉及人权,有两次则是直接提及人权。第一次是在"完善以宪法为核心的中国特色社会主义法律体系,加强宪法实施"部分涉及"加强重点领域立法"的内容之中,明确提出:"依法保障公民权利,加快完善体现权利公平、机会公平、规则公平的法律制度,保障公民人身权、财产权、基本政治权利等各项权利不受侵犯,保障公民经济、文化、社会等各方面权利得到落实,实现公民权利保障法治化。增强全社会尊重和保障人权意识,健全公民权利救济渠道和方式。"第二次直接涉及人权是在"保证公正司法,提高司法公信力"部分,专门规定了"加强人权司法保障"等工作要点。其中特别规定,"强化诉讼过程中当事人和其他诉讼参与人的知情权、陈述权、辩护辩论权、申请权、申诉权的制度保障。健全落实罪刑法定、疑罪从无、非法证据排除等法律原则的法律制度。完善对限制人身自由司法措施和侦查手段的司法监督,加强对刑讯逼供和非法取证的源头预防,健全冤假错案有效防范、及时纠正机制。"

在法治国家,法治思维是解决社会纠纷的重要思维,司法应充分发挥定纷止争和伸张正义的作用。《决定》也提到了涉诉信访的问题,即"落实

---

① 参见柳华文《法治、发展和人权:中国道路的三个基本维度》,《人权》2014年第6期。

终审和诉讼终结制度，实行诉访分离，保障当事人依法行使申诉权利。对不服司法机关生效裁判、决定的申诉，逐步实行由律师代理制度。对聘不起律师的申诉人，纳入法律援助范围"。这样，既保证涉诉信访的规范性，又体现了对弱者的保障。

立法是法治的基础，是执法和司法的前提和根据，是法律保障人权的第一步。《决定》体现了全面保障公民平等享有人权的宗旨，并在强调立法的基础上，强调了全社会尊重和保障人权意识的重要性以及公民权利救济的渠道及其重要意义。

《决定》体现了中国日臻成熟的以法治保障人权的人权观。2012年6月11日，经国务院批准和授权，国务院新闻办发布了第二个"国家人权行动计划"，即《国家人权行动计划（2012—2015年）》。其"导言"中指出了制订和实施国家人权行动计划的三个基本原则：首要的是依法推进原则——人权事业是以法治为基础的，体现在立法、执法、司法、守法的各个环节当中；第二个原则是全面推进原则——人权事业是以全面、平衡的科学发展观为指导的，贯穿于我国包括经济建设、政治建设、文化建设、社会建设和生态文明建设在内的整体发展过程之中；第三个原则是务实推进原则——人权事业应立足于中国现阶段的国情和发展水平，渐进而持续地发展。

值得称道的是，《决定》没有将法治和人权仅仅作为国家和政府机关的事，而是重视公民和社会的参与，强调全民守法和全社会尊重和保障人权的意识。与此相关，权利的救济渠道和方式，在加强社会治理和社会建设的新背景下，也不能仅仅理解为司法渠道和司法方式，比如，社会组织在加强行业和基层自治方面可以发挥建设性作用。《决定》规定："完善和发展基层民主制度，依法推进基层民主和行业自律，实行自我管理、自我服务、自我教育、自我监督。"《决定》提出："加强社会组织立法，规范和引导各类社会组织健康发展。"

《决定》强调加强法治教育，"深入开展法治宣传教育，引导全民自觉守法、遇事找法、解决问题靠法。把宪法法律列入党委（党组）中心组学习内容，列为党校、行政学院、干部学院、社会主义学院必修课。把法治教育纳入国民教育体系，从青少年抓起，在中小学设立法治知识课程"。这一点，可以结合《决定》中"增强全社会尊重和保障人权意识"的要求加以理解。还要注意到，《国家人权行动计划（2012—2015年）》也规定"广泛开展各种形式的人权教育和培训，在全社会传播人权理念，普及人权知识"，包括"加强中小学人权教育。将人权知识融入相关课程，纳入学校法制教育。开展适合青少年特点的人权教育活动，推动中小学依法治校和民主管理，营造尊重人权的教育环境"。

《决定》为法治中国建设绘制了新的路线，也展现了中国人权事业新的蓝图。2015 年 2 月，中共中央办公厅、国务院办公厅印发《关于贯彻落实党的十八届四中全会决定进一步深化司法体制和社会体制改革的实施方案》，对涉及司法体制、社会建设、法治队伍等的 84 项改革举措提出明确要求，这标志着涉及"体制、环境、主体"的司法体制和社会体制改革进入实质性和操作性阶段。

## 二 国家人权行动计划：让人权通过行动获得落实

"国家人权行动计划"是中国专门以人权为主题的国家政府工作规划，从其政策精神、体例和措辞以及关于国际合作和履行国际人权条约的规定等看，其也是中国实施国际人权法的重要方式。

过去，探讨国际法在国内法的实施，比如中国批准的国际人权公约在国内的适用问题时，人们关注的是如何通过立法、修法，将有约束力的国际标准吸收和转化为国内法，再通过司法和执法工作，使之获得最终的落实。而在 1993 年世界人权大会通过《维也纳人权宣言和行动纲领》后，联合国倡导各国通过制订和实施"国家人权行动计划"的方式推动人权，这使国际人权法的国内实施，除立法外，多了一个专门的政策性文件工具。"国家人权行动计划"，是国内法和国际法在人权领域的结合，是法律在国内实施的阶段性政府工作纲领和具体举措，具有很强的针对性和可操作性。

为了及时总结各地实施《国家人权行动计划（2012—2015 年）》的情况，宣传和督促计划的落实情况，国家有关部门从 2013 年下半年至 2014 年年中，多次组织政府、媒体和学者、专家组成实施国家人权行动计划采访团，赴北京、上海、甘肃、青海、新疆、福建等地进行调研和采访。[①]

2014 年 12 月 23 日，由国务院新闻办和外交部牵头，负责"国家人权行动计划"起草和实施的国家人权行动计划联席会议举行了跨部委的行动计划实施情况中期评估会。国务院新闻办主任蔡名照在会议上发言，总结了计划实施过半的相关情况，在整体乐观的基础上，督促各部门重视和进

---

① 相关省份的新闻报道参见中国人权网：http://www.humanrights.cn/cn/zt/tbbd/49/index.htm，最后访问时间：2014 年 11 月 30 日。

一步推动对计划的落实。① 值得注意的是，落实好现行计划，可以为起草和实施未来第三个"国家人权行动计划"奠定坚实的基础。

在实施"国家人权行动计划"的过程中，中国政府继续发布人权白皮书。2014年5月26日，国务院新闻办发表《2013年中国人权事业的进展》白皮书。新的人权白皮书，总结了2013年至2014年年初，中国在实施人权行动计划、促进和保障人权方面采取的举措、获得的成就。

值得注意的还有，自1991年中国首个人权白皮书发表以来，中国政府不定期地发表人权白皮书。而针对全国综合人权状况发表的白皮书，在时间间隔上过去都超过一年，而2014年新的人权白皮书，则缩短了发布的时间间隔，改为一年一发布。这一新的举措，说明中国政府对于人权工作总结、规划和宣示的重视程度超过以往。

在法治领域，人权白皮书强调，中国首次实现城乡按相同人口比例选举全国人大代表，在加强对权力的约束、严惩贪污腐败、建设廉洁政治方面迈出了重要步伐。其还总结了劳动教养制度的废止过程。

2013年12月28日，全国人大常委会决定废止劳动教养制度，对正在被依法执行劳动教养的人员，解除劳动教养，剩余期限不再执行。这样，缺少坚实的法律基础、违背在保障公民获得充分、公正的审判之前不得剥夺公民人身自由这一人权标准的劳动教养制度就被废止了。笔者认为，这是中国法制史上标志性的事件，是中国重视公民权利保障、人权保障法治化的重要体现。而改革如何接续，社区矫正制度如何建立和配套，成为接下来法学界的探讨热点和实务部门的工作重点。根据《决定》，全国有6万多名被劳教人员获释。2011年，最高人民法院、最高人民检察院等10部委出台《违法行为教育矫治委员会试点工作方案》，兰州、济南、南京、郑州被列为违法行为教育矫治试点地区。但是，正式的社区矫正法并未出台，这是未来值得期待的重要立法。对此，十八届四中全会在《决定》中专门提到"制定社区矫正法"。

正如"国家人权行动计划"和人权白皮书所体现的，中国在推进人权工作的进程中，一直将民生放在首位，让百姓享受改革和发展带来的红利。同时，在具体的工作领域，在理念和行动上，我国法律都有一些突破和创

---

① 参见蔡名照《以中国梦为引领，努力推进中国人权事业发展》，《人民日报》2014年12月24日。有关部门和成员单位的落实情况见《落实〈国家人权行动计划（2012—2015年）〉成果材料摘编》，《人民日报》2014年12月25日。

新，比如，保障妇女、儿童权益是中国法律、"国家人权行动计划"等的重要内容，而性别主流化是与人权主流化并行的在国际社会喊得响亮的口号。"妇女权利也是人权"，这句1995年北京世界妇女大会叫响的名言使这两个社会发展趋势联系了起来。2014年，在反对家庭暴力领域，立法和司法都有一些新的亮点。

2014年11月5日，安徽省马鞍山市中级人民法院公开开庭审理一起涉家庭暴力故意杀人案件，中国应用法学研究所性别与法律研究中心主任陈敏作为家庭暴力问题专家出庭，合议庭、公诉人、辩护人分别就相关问题对其进行了咨询。这是全国首例家庭暴力问题专家到庭参与诉讼的案件。[①] 2014年11月25日是"国际消除对妇女暴力日"。这一天，备受社会各界关注的《中华人民共和国反家庭暴力法（征求意见稿）》（以下简称《征求意见稿》）终于揭开面纱，由国务院法制办公布并向社会公众公开征求意见。《征求意见稿》共6章41条，对家庭暴力的界定、家庭暴力的预防、家庭暴力的处置等做了明确规定。此前，有报道称反家暴法调整范围将包含同居、伴侣关系，甚至包括同性恋者之间的关系。从最终公布的《征求意见稿》来看，调整对象仅限于家庭成员之间。国务院法制办公室同时公布的《关于〈中华人民共和国反家庭暴力法（征求意见稿）〉的说明》指出，"有恋爱、同居、前配偶等关系人员之间发生的暴力行为，与一般社会成员之间发生的暴力行为没有实质区别，由治安管理处罚法、刑法等法律调整"[②]。

将这些人权领域的前沿问题放在中国实施"国家人权行动计划"的大背景下考察，我们可以发现，中国人权事业在宏观和微观两个层面上都在不断地向前发展。

## 三 重拳反腐：人权保障的多重意义

反腐败与人权的密切关系正在成为国际共识。2012年，摩洛哥代表134个国家在联合国人权理事会第20届会议上做了腐败与人权问题的跨区域声明，要求进一步反思人权和反腐措施的密切联系，并呼吁反腐和人权运动的相关组织互相合作。2013年3月，联合国人权理事会专门就腐败对人权的不利影响等问题进行小组讨论。联合国人权事务高级专员办公室提出了

---

[①] 赵丽萍、俞家佳：《家暴问题专家首次走进法庭》，《人民法院报》2014年11月9日。
[②] 参见国务院法制办网站：http://www.chinalaw.gov.cn/article/cazjgg/201411/20141100397718.shtml，最后访问时间：2014年11月30日。

人权与反腐工作的三个要点：（1）腐败是实现所有人权——公民、政治、经济、社会及文化权利以及发展权——的巨大障碍；（2）坚持并落实透明性、问责制、非歧视这三项原则并有意义地参与这些核心人权原则是对抗腐败的最有效方式；（3）当前迫切需要增强政府间努力的协同性以落实联合国《反腐败公约》和各国际人权公约。①

十八大以来，中国反腐工作力度前所未有，成效显著。反腐败对于人权保障的积极意义也获得了中国学者的高度评价。② 笔者认为，腐败行为破坏民主和法制，严重影响国家和社会的健康与可持续发展，直接威胁着公民几乎所有人权的实现。

从人权的视角看反腐，反腐首先是能消除对于人权的侵害，并从反面推动"风清气正"的社会风气的形成，有助于促进和保障人权的社会环境的建立。其次，反腐应该在法治的轨道上进行，依法反腐，依法办案。党纪严于国法，国法必须严格实施。对于腐败分子和相关的违法犯罪嫌疑人乃至罪犯，必须尊重其依法享有的各项人权，保证他们获得公正的审判并在司法的各个环节依法享有应有的待遇。

中共中央十八届四中全会《决定》提出，"加强反腐败国际合作，加大海外追赃追逃、遣返引渡力度"。早在2014年1月召开的中纪委第三次全会上，习近平总书记发表重要讲话，吹响了境外追逃腐败分子的号角。他指出："不能让国外成为一些腐败分子的'避罪天堂'，腐败分子即使逃到天涯海角，也要把他们追回来绳之以法，5年、10年、20年都要追，要切断腐败分子的后路。"③ 中国已经是《联合国反腐败公约》的缔约国，而且截至2014年9月，我国已与63个国家缔结了司法协助、引渡和移管被判刑人等条约。国际合作的重要意义超过以往，但是国际协议的数量和国际合作的水平还有极大潜力。

境外追逃要根据国际法开展工作，更要特别重视国际人权法的影响。目前中国排除了走私等诸多罪名适用死刑的可能性，在实践中也可能由权威部门承诺不判处死刑，这为引渡和遣返工作扫除了"死刑犯不引渡"这一国际规则引起的法律障碍。同时，整体性人权保障水平的提高，也有利于引渡、遣返、劝返等相关工作的开展。中国已是大多数联合国人权核心

---

① 参见联合国人权高专办网站：http://www.ohchr.org/ch/Issues/Development/GoodGovernance/Pages/AntiCorruption.aspx，最后访问时间：2014年11月30日。
② 参见王比学《反腐败就是维护人权》，《人民日报》2014年8月8日。
③ 李楠、陈云飞：《境外不是贪官"避罪天堂"》，《南方》2014年第16期。

公约的缔约国，但尚未批准《公民权利和政治权利国际公约》。这是联合国最重要的人权公约之一，多年来中国国内一直在认真研究、积极准备批约事宜。在当前背景下，积极考虑尽早批准这一公约，对于反腐工作中的国际法律合作，亦具有重要意义。

## 四 新增人权教育基地：人权教育获得推动

根据《国家人权行动计划（2009—2010年）》"选取若干开展人权教育较早的高等院校作为人权教育与培训基地"的要求，2011年，教育部首次批准在南开大学、中国政法大学和广州大学三所高校分别设立国家人权教育与培训基地。2013年8月，由南开大学牵头，三校还共同创建了"人权建设协同创新中心"。

第二个"国家人权行动计划"在"人权教育"一章中，进一步规定，"发挥国家人权教育与培训基地的作用。到2015年，至少新增5个国家人权教育与培训基地"。

第二批"国家人权教育与培训基地"遴选评审会2014年3月17日在北京召开。相关主管部门负责人、中国人权研究会领导、遴选评审专家小组成员以及北京大学、复旦大学、华东政法大学、吉林大学、四川大学、山东大学、武汉大学、西北政法大学、西南政法大学、中国人民大学10家参评单位的代表共40余人参加了会议。各参选高校围绕现有人权教育、研究和培训机构的设置、专业方向特色、管理运行机制、经费保障来源等向遴选评审小组进行了详细汇报，并接受了评审会领导及专家的提问。最终，中国人民大学、西南政法大学、复旦大学、武汉大学和山东大学获评新一批"国家人权教育与培训基地"。[①]

不论是综合性大学还是政法院校，各参评和获评高校的人权机构均设在法学院或者以法学院的师资力量为骨干。这表明了中国人权教育与法治教育的密切关系，也是中国依法促进人权原则贯彻实施的重要体现。虽然人权涉及跨学科的知识，需要多视角和多界别的研究与推动，但是法制是人权的重要载体，法治保障是基础。

对于国家人权教育与培训基地建设，十届全国政协副主席、中国人权研究会会长罗豪才教授说："这些年来各地人权研究机构在人权调查、研究、教育、培训等方面已经形成了良性工作机制，培养出了一批人才，锻

---

① 新当选的国家人权教育与培训基地相关情况，参见《人权》2014年第4期。

炼了队伍，服务了社会，取得了非常大的成就……我们也发现一些不足和问题，如有些机构研究视角还偏单一，没有充分动员和有效整合多学科的力量；有的机构研究力量不均衡，过于倚重少数主力，没有形成团队作战的优势；有些机构在成果转化和咨政建言方面还有不足；有些机构设置级别较低，校方重视还不够，对于开展工作有一定影响等。"[1]

在环境保护、公益诉讼等许多领域，中国高等院校都发挥了重要的教育先行、理念普及、个案推动的建设性作用。人权事业的发展离不开人权研究的深入开展、人权教育的有效普及。这种人权教育不仅针对高校学生展开，其还可以承担培训政府和司法机关官员和其他工作人员的重要任务。比如，在首批基地中，广州大学人权研究与教育中心多年来就多次成功开展针对人民警察的人权培训。

## 五　联合国人权工作的机制：中国深度参与人权国际交流与合作

联合国前秘书长科菲·安南将和平、发展和人权作为联合国改革和发展的三大支柱。人权是联合国开展全球工作的重中之重，并渗透到各个领域，其中最重要的，首推联合国人权理事会的普遍性定期审议（又称国别审议）机制。它自2006年建立以来，让所有联合国会员国以大约4年为期、轮流接受人权审议，实现了各国均在多边国际舞台汇报并接受国际审议的创举。

中国继2009年首次接受审议之后，2013年10月和2014年3月接受了第二次国别审议。笔者以非政府组织代表在现场参与了人权理事会的相关会议，更参加了中国人权研究会在2013年10月22日举办的边会。这是中国非政府组织首次主动参与并在联合国人权理事会举行正式边会，会议邀请国内外人权法专家介绍了中国的人权保障情况。全国妇联、中国非政府组织国际交流促进会也根据联合国人权理事会的程序规则，在日内瓦联合国总部举办了两场边会。

当下的中国在许多方面正处在世界舞台的中央，关于中国的国别审议备受瞩目。在2013年10月22日国别审议工作组审议中国的会议上，150多个国家报名发言，导致每国代表平均下来只获得了51秒的发言时间。

---

[1] 罗豪才2014年3月17日在第二批"国家人权教育与培训基地"遴选评审会上的发言，引自中国人权网：http://www.humanrights.cn/cn/zt/tbbd/46/4/t20140408_1164284.htm，最后访问时间：2015年7月11日。

2014年3月20日,联合国人权理事会核可中国国别审议报告的第25次会议在日内瓦举行。中国正式宣布,对各国提出的252条建议,经慎重研究和努力,决定接受其中204条建议,占建议总数的81%,这些建议涉及减贫、教育、司法改革等20多个领域。

笔者发现,核可其他国家的报告,用时可能短至10到15分钟。而核可中国报告,用了大约两个小时。境内外非政府组织在此阶段有发言机会,涉及中国,其显然存在政治歧见和对抗性的张力。人权理事会要实现它在审议规则中强调的非政治性和非选择性,并非易事。非政府组织的兴起和参与为国际人权法的实践注入了活力,但是在国际舞台上,非政府组织在发达国家、发展中国家和不发达国家之间不均衡的代表性,它们不对称的参与能力以及缺乏法律边界和自我约束的行为方式,都颇耐人寻味。

基于联合国核心人权公约定期开展的缔约国履约审议,由根据各相关公约成立的专家委员会即条约机构分别进行。在诸多国家迟交甚至不交国家报告的情况下,中国按时、认真提交报告并派出高规格和多部门参与的代表团出席审议会议,这一点是值得称道的。2014年5月,联合国经济、社会和文化权利委员会审议了中国关于履行《经济、社会和文化权利国际公约》的国家报告,同年10月,《消除一切形式针对妇女的歧视国际公约》国家履约报告的审议由消除一切形式针对妇女的歧视委员会完成。条约机构在审议后通过的《结论性意见》是我们了解这些专家委员会对中国相关领域取得的成就、关切的问题和提出的建议的重要文献。

值得一提的是,2013年11月12日,第68届联合国大会改选联合国人权理事会成员,中国以176票高票当选,超过了法国所获得的174票和英国所获得的171票,任期自2014年至2016年。中国高票当选被一些国内媒体解读为国际社会对中国在人权领域取得巨大成就的高度肯定,这没有错,同时,我们还应该将之解读为国际社会对中国作为负责任的新兴大国在联合国人权领域发挥积极和建设性作用的广泛期望。

总体而言,党的十八大以来的法治新进展很多。多少热议,多少期许,其中不乏焦灼,更有令人激动和值得憧憬的崭新愿景。

对于中国这一发展中的人口大国来说,人权是一个既美好、又有几分复杂的词汇。同其他国家一样,人权的推进在中国的理论界和现实生活中,在大方向既定的前提下,是不乏矛盾、怀疑和争议的。但是,没有人会怀疑,在理论、道路和制度上更加自信的中国,在全面发展的大背景下,将毫不迟疑地走向法治,保障人权!

# New Developments in the Construction of the Rule of Law and Safeguarding of Human Rights in China

*Liu Huawen*

【Abstract】 There are close links among the construction of the rule of law, the people-oriented scientific outlook of development, and the safeguarding of human rights. The Decision of the CPC Central Committee on Major Issues Pertaining to Comprehensively Promoting the Rule of Law, adopted at the Fourth Plenary Session of the Eighteenth CPC Central Committee in October 2014, has sketched a new blueprint for the development of the rule of law and human rights cause in China. The Chinese government has decided to increase the frequency of publication of white papers on human rights and to promote the implementation of national human rights action plans by way of mid-term evaluation; the unprecedented efforts made by the Chinese government in the fight against corruption have multiple significances for the safeguarding of human rights; human rights education has been attached greater importance to, as proud by the designation of five more colleges and universities as national-level human rights education and training bases; and China has also made new progresses in participating in international human rights protection mechanisms.

【Key words】 the Rule of Law; Human Rights; National Human Rights Action Plan

# Protection under the Law—An Evolving Fundamental Right in Finland?

*Ida Koivisto*

【Abstract】 The article discusses the concept of legal protection in the recent praxis of the Supreme Administrative Court in Finland. The concept is used mostly referring to the fundamental right (section 21 in *the Constitution of Finland*, "right to protection under the law"; so-called narrow conception of legal protection). The selected case-law is systematized in three categories. The aim is to reconstruct the applied concept of legal protection. It is concluded that the right latently relies on the so-called wide conception of legal protection. However, the scope of legal protection does not seem to be constant even on the level of ideal. Instead, it is a quantifier: using the term, an appropriate amount of legal protection is allocated to each specific case. It is also proposed that the issue of legal protection may become problematic in two senses: either as access to rights, whose level as such is proper and sufficient, or alternatively, from the viewpoint of the sufficiency of legal remedies in relation to binding international legal commitments.

## 1. Introduction: The Many Dimensions of Protection under the Law

According to the theory of legal realism law is no more and no less than what judges do. Even though this idea can be challenged, it does give useful tools for analysis. What law or what rights are really valid, or, in other words, what is the law in action? What rules do courts actually apply in their adjudication?

Fundamental rights can be considered a stumbling block for the legal realistic approach. Are fundamental rights "real" rights to begin with or just some conceptual preconditions for more detailed regulation? The correct answer is probably, and perhaps vexingly: both. Fundamental rights argumentation has increased evidently in Finland over the past 20 years. Especially the fundamental rights reform in 1995 has motivated this development and brought itinto the mainstream. Along with this process, fundamental rights have come down from the giddy realm of pure ideas and been transformed into real raw material for legal argumentation.

Subsequently, the whole doctrine of fundamental rights has been a target of intense interest among legal scholars in Finland. [1] There has even been a mention of a revolution in the culture of fundamental rights. However, some scholars have suggested that the national fundamental rights system might gradually wither away while the European human rights system would simultaneously bolster its importance. In this text, however, the fundamental rights doctrine is not the primary focus of attention. Rather, the idea is to look at one particular context, in which it manifests itself: the fundamental right to protection under the law, more specifically, in the realm of administrative law.

*Protection under the law* or *legal protection* is a special kind of concept. On the one hand, it is a fundamental right among fundamental rights (the *narrow conception*). As such, it has a legal definition in the *Finnish Constitution*. The fundamental rights approach underlines this legal definition and the sub-rights of which it consists; it is composed of a set of rights. Hence, the accent is on legal positivism. On the other hand, protection under the law is one of the essential principles which label

---

[1] Ida Koivisto, Impivaarasta Strasbourgiin-ja takaisin? ("From Impivaara to Strasbourg-and back?") Lakimies 2011, pp. 397 – 401, Tuuli Heinonen-Juha Lavapuro, Suomen oikeuden eurooppalaistuminen ja valtiosääntöistyminen 1990 – 2012 ("The Europeanisation and Constitutionalisation of Finnish Law 1990 – 2012"). In Tuuli Heinonen-Juha Lavapuro (eds.), Oikeuskulttuurin eurooppalaistuminen. Ihmisoikeuksien murroksesta kansainväliseen vuorovaikutukseen ("The Europeanisation of Legal Culture: From the Revolution of Human Rights Towards International Interaction"), Helsinki 2012, pp. 7 – 28. Markku Helin: Perusoikeuksilla argumentoinnista ("On Fundamental Rights Argumentation"), Edilex-asiantuntijakirjoitukset, Asiantuntijakirjoitukset 14.11.2012, Juha Lavapuro: Perusoikeusargumentaation kontrolloitavuudesta. ("On the Controllability of Fundamental Rights Argumentation") In Tuuli Heinonen-Juha Lavapuro (eds.), Oikeuskulttuurin eurooppalaistuminen. Helsinki 2012, pp. 144 – 177.

the rationality of the whole legal system (the *broad conception*).① That is to say, the concept cannot be reduced solely to a single, impermeable fundamental right. Following the broad conception, even the entire constellation of legal remedies in (administrative) law could be categorised as falling under the banner of protection under the law.

Furthermore, the concept is notoriously opaque beyond this duality of meanings: for example, concepts such as "advance legal protection", "subsequent legal protection", "formal legal protection", "material legal protection" and "procedural legal protection" are all used. This opacity adds to the ambiguity of the concept and is also manifest in attempts at translating the term: different languages and different legal systems accentuate dissimilar facets. In English alone, there are many ways of conceptualising legal protection.

In short, the notion of protection under the law can be interpreted from at least two different meta-perspectives. The narrow conception is economical with language, calling certain compilation of rights "protection under the law". From the systemic point of view, however, it becomes even wider. That is to say, protection under the law denotes the entire functioning of the legal system. Consequently, it is to be understood as the realisation or rights, a functioning judicial system, access to justice, legal certainty, and, at the end of the day, a just society. Interpreted like that, the narrow conception represents a means (the instrumental aspect) to ends, the broad conception (the teleological aspect).②

The hypothesis in this paper, however, is that in adjudication protection under the law as a fundamental right becomes relevant reactively. It only provokes

---

① Adrian Vermeule (Our Schmittian Administrative Law, *Harvard L. Rev*, 2006, vol. 122: 1095, pp. 1096 – 1149) uses the concepts of "thin conception of the rule of law" and "thick conception of the rule of law". He refers further to David Dyzenhaus' distinction between "rule of law" and "rule by law". According to my interpretation, the "thin" conception signifies mainly legality in the sense of legal positivism, whereas the "thick" one is based on a more substantial interpretation, opening towards morality.

② Eg. JuhaLavapuro, Perustuslain 106 §: nilmeisyysvaatimuksenvaikutuksistaoikeuskäytännössä ('On the Criterion of Evident Conflict in section 106 in the Finnish Constitution and its Influence in Case Law'), Lakimies 2008, pp. 582 – 611, p. 585. See also PekkaHallberg: Oikeusturva (PL 21 §) ["Protection Under the Law (section 21)"] in PekkaHallberg et al. (eds.): Perusoikeudet ("Fundamental Rights"), 2, uudistettupainos. Helsinki, 2011, pp. 783 – 808.

disputation or argumentation, when it is contrasted with some other right, value, or interest. However, there is an underlying paradox, which also undermines the credibility of legal realism and accordingly complicates any attempt to assess the true effect of the right: the less case law there is available, the better the more expedite the passage of the rights? Would that, consequently, mean that there is less court-confirmed (according to the realistic approach: valid) law?

## 2. Law in Books: Fundamental Right to Protection Under the Law

In Finland at least, the narrow conception of protection under the law is much more recent than the broad one. Protection under the law became an explicitly stated fundamental right in the Finnish legal system in 1995. At the same time, the functionality of fundamental rights was fixed. That is to say, from the reform onwards, tribunals and other public authorities could-under certain circumstances-assess the harmony between the constitution and inferior provisions in any individual case (*Finnish Constitution* sections 106 and 107).

Prior to that, the main form of constitutional control was, and still is, parliamentary pre-emptive scrutiny in the body called the Constitutional Committee. It gives statements on the constitutionality of the proposed legislation to the parliament prior to the formal enactment of the legislation. The adjudicatory control supplements this parliamentary one and is, as such, secondary in nature.

Hence, along with the fundamental rights reform in 1995 protection under the law became once and for all important in the norm hierarchy: It became a fundamental right, which public authorities are obliged to give effect to.[①] In a way, calling the fundamental right "protection under the law" meant a novel juridification of the concept, although it already conceptually presupposes the existence of rights. The right extends both to the judicial assessment of executive power and jurisdiction in practice. The pertinent section is as follows (according to the unofficial translation of the *Finnish Constitution*, Suomenperustuslaki 731/1999):

---

[①] Finnish Constitution section 22 is as follows: "The public authorities shall guarantee the observance of basic rights and liberties and human rights."

Section 21-Protection under the law

Everyone has the right to have his or her case dealt with appropriately and without undue delay by a legally competent court of law or other authority, as well as to have a decision pertaining to his or her rights or obligations reviewed by a court of law or other independent organ for the administration of justice.

Provisions concerning the publicity of proceedings, the right to be heard, the right to receive a reasoned decision and the right of appeal, as well as the other guarantees of a fair trial and good governance shall be laid down by an Act.

The right can be broken down into separate sub-categories, including:

—The right to have case dealt with appropriately
—The right to have case dealt with without undue delay
—The right to have case dealtwith by a legally competent court of law or other authority
—The right to have a decision pertaining to his or her rights or obligations reviewed by a court of law or other independent organ for the administration of justice
—Public access to proceedings
—The right to be heard
—The right to have a reasoned decision
—The right of appeal
—Other guarantees of a fair trial and good governance

The two salient meta-categories of protection under the law are the *right to a fair trial* and the *right to good governance*. That might be inferred from the formulation "other guarantees". However, section 21 extends beyond the catalogue of the explicit sub-rights. The wording is not exhaustive, leaving room for alteration and interpretation.

Judging from case law, *the right of appeal* seems to form the crux of the fundamental right to protection under the law. To elucidate its substantial meaning, it is probably useful at this point to describe briefly the Finnish system of administrative appeals. Basically, it is constructed as a three-step system. The first step is a formal administrative decision, given by an administrative agency, in which individual rights, duties and benefits are legally defined. This decision can be appealed at a district administrative court by the parties involved within 30 days' time. Usually, any new decision made by administrative court, can be further appealed at the Supreme Administrative Court ("SAC"), which gives the decisive ruling.

However, this description of the process is a simplification for several reasons. First of all, there might be even a fourth step in the appeal. That, however, is a matter of interpretation. Namely the administrative agency in charge of the original decision can in certain cases revise its own (initial) decision. This is done following the Administrative Procedure Act and as such is not a form of court proceedings. The *raison d'être* for this action is, however, that of protection under the law. Secondly, as a first degree instance of appeal, many separate appellate bodies do exist. They function prior to or instead of the district administrative court in certain social insurance matters. Thirdly, in some areas the Supreme Administrative Court requires leave to appeal in order to reconsider the case. Fourthly, in administrative law, the *res judicata* effect is not water-tight; a new process concerning the same matter can be started in the relevant administrative agency all over. Other exceptions exist, but they fall beyond the scope of the paper.

## 3. Law in Action: Remarks on Case Law of the Supreme Administrative Court on Protection Under the Law

Professor Tuomas Ojanen has argued that the core content of the section 21 is basically equivalent to article 6 (1) of ECHR[1] and the concomitant case law of the European Court of Human Rights. According to Ojanen, the courts should first find

---

[1] *European Convention of Human Rights*, article 6 (1): "Right to a fair trial 1. In the determination of his civil rights and obligations or of any criminal charge against him, everyone is entitled to a fair and public hearing within a reasonable time by an independent and impartial tribunal established by law. Judgment shall be pronounced publicly but the press and public may be excluded from all or part of the trial in the interests of morals, public order or national security in a democratic society, where the interests of juveniles or the protection of the private life of the parties so require, or to the extent strictly necessary in the opinion of the court in special circumstances."

out what the article 6 requires in any specific case and only after that check if section 21 provides more extensive protection. ① If we look at the case law of the Supreme Administrative Court in Finland, can we detect argumentation following that formula? Is protection under the law a "real" fundamental right, and if so, in which respects? What conclusions can be derived from the praxis of the SAC? The methodological idea is to reconstruct the applied conception of protection under the law.

In what follows, I have built the argumentation on the basis of certain manifestations of protection under the law in the case law of SAC. The cases are relatively recent and are selected to illustrate the many different facets of the right. However, I will not present the cases here in detail, although some of them will be discussed briefly. Instead, I have placed the cases in three different categories- the right of appeal and the prohibition against appeal, effective remedy before national authorities, and balancing interests-to facilitate their analysisas larger totalities. ② Finally, I will present some conclusions.

## 3. 1. The Right of Appeal and the Prohibition Against Appeal

As said, the very crux of the fundamental right appears to be the right of appeal. The scope of that right is assessed in four recent cases (SAC 2008: 25, 2011: 39, 2012: 53 and 2012: 54), in which the *fundamental right to protection under the law (the right of appeal) is in tension with the prohibition against appeal* under the State's Civil Servants Act. In those matters, there has been a general prohibition against appeal. ③ The puzzling question in these cases is whether the conflict is evident between section 21 and an inferior provision containing the prohibition against appeal. In other words, the cases are reviewed from the section

---

① Tuomas Ojanen, Eurooppa-tuomioistuimet ja suomalaiset tuomioistuimet *European Courts and Finnish Courts*, Lakimies, 2005 pp. 1210 – 1228.

② It is important to note that all the cases I have looked at are united by the theme of protection under the law argumentation. However, not all cases can be neatly categorized under the systematizations described above. Other perspectives to the topic might be—partially overlapping with the previous ones " the sufficiency of the legal remedies ", " the need of protection under the law ", "fundamental rights" and also mere "protection under the law".

③ The State's Civil Servants Act has been partly revised in April 2013, rendering a wider right of appeal. However, not all prohibitions were abolished. The cases discussed here were given prior to the reform.

106 point of view.① Under which conditions is the prohibition against appeal in civil servant matters in harmony with the fundamental right of appeal-if any?②

Two examples of "non-evident" conflicts between an act (States Civil Servants Act) and the constitution can be mentioned here. First of all, prohibition against appeal has been upheld in cases, which deal with *applying for public offices*. The prohibition was motivated with two arguments. First, no-one is said to have a subjective right to be appointed to a public office. Therefore, a right of appeal would not be necessary. The second argument is more pragmatic and resembles a slippery slope fallacy. This argues that in the event of a right of appeal, the state would be overwhelmed by constant and endless appeal processes. Consequently, the prohibition was not considered unconstitutional in these cases (e. g. SAC 2011: 39), and the above-mentioned motivations for upholding the prohibition were considered legitimate. ③

---

① Section 106 deals with the primacy of the Constitution in the case of conflict. It provides that "if, in a matter being tried by a court of law, the application of an Act would be in evident conflict with the Constitution, the court of law shall give primacy to the provision in the Constitution". However, primarily the encountered conflicts should be eliminated via interpretation. That means that the public authorities should favour the interpretation, which best fulfills the fundamental rights of the party in question.

② The construction of evident conflict has been considered problematic in many ways. First of all, it makes a conflict scalar instead of a binary phenomenon. In other words, a provision can be in accord, in conflict or in evident conflict with the constitution. Consequently, it is not clear, how a court should proceed, when a "non-evident" conflict is encountered. Secondly, the evident conflict criterion places national fundamental rights in an asymmetrical position with respect to international human rights, which, in order to trump a provision, do not require a conflict to be evident. Juha Lavapuro, Uusi perustuslakikontrolli *The New Control of Constitutionality*. Helsinki, 2010, pp. 179 – 224, Martin Scheinin: Perustuslakiehdotus 2000-ehdotus ja lakien perustuslainmukaisuuden jälkikontrolli: puoli askelta epämääräiseen suuntaan *Constitution 2000-proposal and the ex post facto Control of Constitutionality—a Half a Step Towards a Vague Direction*, Lakimies, 1998, pp. 1123 – 1131. TuomasOjanen: Perustuslain 106 § : netusijasäännäs-toimivuuden ja muutostarpeidenarviointi *Section 106 in the Finnish Constitution-Assessment of the Functioning and the Need for Revision*, In Perustuslaki 2008-työryhmänmuistio *The Constitution 2008-Work Group's Memorandum*, Helsinki, 2008, pp. 131 – 151.

③ The legitimacy of the prohibition against appeal is a matter of human rights and the ECHR case law. In particular, the norm created in the case VilhoEskelinen and others vs. Finland (2007) has to be taken into account. It outlines the acceptability of the prohibition. According to it, a prohibition: i) must exist in national legislation and ii) needs to have legitimate justification. If these circumstances are at hand, the benefits of an individual must be withdrawn.

The second category of cases, in which "non-evident" conflictshaveemerged between a provision in an act and section 21, concerns the *original decision's inadmissibility to appeal*. Namely, a decision, which can be appealed (according to the *Administrative Proceedings Act*), is "a measure which has resolved the matter or rendered it inadmissible. " Conversely, if an administrative decision does not "resolve a matter or render it inadmissible", it is excluded from the scope of the right of appeal. That was the main result in the case SAC 2012: 53, in which a civil servant's office was relocated to another section of a ministry without his consent. This relocation was regarded as a measure of work supervision and not a proper administrative decision, because the office was not particularly allocated to a specific section in the ministry.

However, the court has once (in SAC 2008: 25) stated an evident conflict, rendering a right of appeal regardless of the explicit prohibition against appeal in the Civil Servants Act. This case has formed a point of reference to later cases. However, in a similar case (SAC 2012: 54), the conflict was no longer regarded as evident and instead, the controversy was eliminated via interpretation. The result, nonetheless, was the same as in SAC 2008: 25: the right of appeal was granted. That leads to ask the question as to whether the conflict can be evident only once. Both of these cases concerned altering a civil servant's position without her consent. This alteration was considered more invasive than in the case SAC 2012: 53, fulfilling the admissibility condition. Consent was required according to the law, but even when it was not given, the decision could not be appealed.

The interpretation of the prohibition against appeal forms a complex doctrine in civil servant cases. After analysing the cases, it seems that three factors need to be taken into account. 1) Is the civil servant already in post or is she applying for it? The scope of the protection under the law is dissimilar in these two cases. 2) Does the decision regard the rights and duties of the civil servant and thus constitute an official administrative decision or is it merely a matter of work supervision? 3) Is the prohibition against appeal in accord with the case law of the European Court of Human Rights?

It is evident that section 21 does not always trump prohibitions against appeal. According to current case law of the SAC, the framework for resolving the question of prohibitions against appeal seems to be in flux. The "evidence" of a conflict is itself a subject to debate.

## 3. 2. Effective remedy before national authorities

Another important sector of protection under the law is the demand for *an effective remedy before national authorities*. It remains some what ambiguous, whether the right of appeal and the right to effective remedy amount to the same thing or are conceptually distinct: one from the viewpoint of national fundamental rights system, the other from the European human rights system. Moreover, section 47 in the EU charter of fundamental rights (ECFR) requires the national legal systems to guarantee both a right to an effective remedy and to a fair trial.

Interestingly, the right to an effective remedy has stood out in the case law of the SAC even at the expense of the right of appeal, although "effective remedy" is not mentioned in section 21 of the Constitution. Let us take two examples.

Firstly, the case 10. 12. 2009/3524 handled a situation, where, according to an act, a civil servant did not have the right of appeal, but neither was appealing clearly prohibited. His office was in the President of the Republic's secretariat where he was given a formal warning. The administrative decisions, which could be appealed, were listed in the act. Giving warning was absent from that list. The SAC interpreted the act in the light of section 21 of the constitution and expanded the scope of the right of appeal to extend also to giving warning. In so doing, the SAC created an adhoc right of appeal. That is to say, it reviewed the case via the construction of an effective remedy using the section 21 as the institutional support.

Secondly, a similar decision was reached in a case which regarded a violation of EU law. Section 47 in the ECFR requires an efficient remedy before the national authorities. Therefore, in the case SAC 2012: 4, the existence of such a remedy was put under scrutiny. In the casein question the legal conundrum was to determine what the correct procedure in resolving a certain administrative disagreement would be. The disagreement concerned harm compensation. A certain form of compensation, defined in *Accident Insurance Act*, was argued to be measured in a discriminatory way under national law (the instructions drafted by the Ministry of Social Affairs and Health used different criteria for men and women), thus violating EU law.

The law-neither nationally nor in the light of the EU system-did not specify a single correct procedure or remedy to be applied to resolve the disagreement. The SAC decided that since no directly applicable provisions existed, the case could be resolved through administrative litigation, even though there was no a clear competence norm allowing it. The motivation for this choice was to reinforce the applicant's protection under the law and avoid undue delay. Hence, in this case too the right to effective remedy gave a boost to expanding the scope of the right of appeal.

It might be noted here that the concept of an effective remedy has been used to open up the possibility of appealing in situations, where it would appear to be prima facie impossible. Even though the concept of an effective remedy is not mentioned in section 21, it does play an important role.

Besides the ECFR, it seems that the national right to protection under the law gains particular impetus from the ECHR. However, an important anomaly in this respect is the case SAC 2012: 75 (plenary judgment), which deals with psychiatric treatment against a patient's will. In that case, as an exception, the SAC decided not to agree with the ECHR on the sufficiency of Finnish legal safeguards (X vs. Finland 3.7.2012). In SAC 2012: 75 the concept of an effective remedy was used in a defensive way, suggesting that the Finnish system needed no revision in that respect. That is to say, argumentation on the efficiency of legal remedies does not always or necessarily lead to favouring the applicant's judicial position, although in the majority of cases it does.

The case law indicates that the construction of an effective remedy is handy for many purposes. First of all, it may serve to bolster the judicial position of the individual. That means real interpretative support for a provision, like rendering a right of appeal when it is not allowed (or prohibited) in an Act, even dismissing the very wording of a specific provision. However, it may also be used for defending the legitimacy of the Finnish system of legal remedies before the ECHR, leaving the question of the legal status of the party in the margin, as in the case mentioned above. ①

---

① Ojanen (Lakimies 2005, p. 1218) argues that Finnish courts tend to lean on human rights provisions in a negative sense. That means looking at human rights from the viewpoint of not breaching them. In other words, human rights are not necessarily used as inspiration for bolstering the judicial position of individuals. Martin Scheinin (General Introduction, in Martin Scheinin eds., *International Human Rights Norms in the Nordic and Baltic Countries*, Dordrecht, 1996, pp. 11 - 26), for one, talks about the phenomenon of human rights minimalism.

## 3. 3. Balancing interests

Protection under the law can also have argumentative potential in cases, where a strong juxta position between the rights of an individual and some public interest exists. That may mean matters of public order, national security etc. The cases I have studied involve questions of nationality and asylum—actually, they all deal with foreigners' rights in the Finnish legal system. In these cases, a fair balance between the two contradictory values is sought by using the argumentation of protection under the law.

For example, the case SAC 2011: 77 dealt with the legal finality of an administrative decision and its legal implications. In the case in question the immigration office had granted a child Finnish nationality. However, later it made a new decision, abolishing the original one, and redefined the child as stateless. The SAC argued that the immigration office did not have the right to independently and proactively redefine the citizenship without a distinct application from the party. By doing so, the immigration office would violate the party's protection under the law and the principle of avoiding statelessness. Accordingly, the original decision was upheld by the court and the latter one was abolished. It should be noted that protection under the law implicitly includes the connotations of legal certainty and fairness; the concept was used so as to protect the position of the individual in a particularly vulnerable situation.

Another perspective on these problems is manifest in a line of cases (SAC 2007: 47, 2007: 48 and 2007: 49), which pertained to the restriction ofa party's access to documents. In these cases in question, the parties were not provided with the relevant documents due to an alleged threat to national security. In other words, the principle of equality of arms was not fulfilled. The SAC argued that this procedure was acceptable on condition that administrative court had to have a chance to see the documents—drafted and compiled by the National Security Police—and take them into account in its discretion.

Peculiar to the cases in this category is that protection under the law has a character of a certain kind of a legal principle. That is to say, the concept of protection under the law is used to balance opposite interests between an individual and that of the society in a broad sense, typically related to security.① Thus, protection under the law becomes a principle of interpretation which emphasize fairness and opening the broad conception of protection under the law. In addition, an interesting philosophical dimension emerges: protection under the law becomes an argumentative tool, by which use the inclusion and exclusion of the legal system can be regulated.②

## 4. Conclusions: Determining the Quantity and Quality of Protection Under the Law

The cases I have considered differ from each other in many ways. Regrettably, they could not be described in greater detail here and which would have made the reasoning more transparent. However, some general conclusions of the functions concerning the fundamental right to protection under the law can be drafted. In what follows I offer two conclusions or sets of conclusions.

The first conclusion is that the extent of protection under the law is not constant even as an ideal. Instead, a tendency to regulate an optimal quantity of in each pertinent case can be supposed to exist. Two factors in particular seem to affect the formation of the scope here. Firstly, the more deeply the public authority interferes in the domain of individual freedom in the form of an administrative decision, the broader the scope of protection under the law. That means not only contesting the scope of protection under the law but also actively regulating it.

In addition, protection under the law includes a hidden "counter-ideal" of economy and scarcity, which also gives raise to qualification: terms like "minimum standard of protection", "minimalism", "expansive vs. restricted interpretation" etc. are in regular use. Famously, fundamental rights are not absolute and they can be limited. However, from the perspective of protection under the law, not only are the limitations themselves interesting, but so are their

---

① Compare with Robert Alexy's (Theorie der Grundrechte, *Theory of Fundamental Rights*, Suhrkamp, 1988 famous argument, according to which fundamental rights are legal principles. Furthermore, legal principles are optimizing commands.

② Lavapuro, Valtiosääntöinenmanagerialismijaperusoikeudet, *Constitutional Managerialism and Fundamental Rights*, Oikeus, 2010, pp. 3 – 27, KaarloTuori, Foucault'noikeus, *Foucault's Law*. Vantaa, 2002, p. 108.

motivations.

The optimum circumstance for protection under the law is defined through these limitations and sometimes also expansions. In particular, the rights of an individual may conflict with the public interest, as mentioned before. In MarttiKoskenniemi's thinking, this limitation, derogation or relativisation of rights is undermining their very credibility. According to him, the scope or the conditions, under which the limitations are applied, is not clearly defined. In the ECHR system, for example, the relationship between the rights and the derogation from themis circumscribed by the clause "*in accordance with law*" and "*necessary in a democratic society*". ① Evidently, the criteria are indeterminate.

This could be construed as the political economy of protection under the law. Indeed, the right becomes a tool for quantification. By applying fundamental right argumentation, an appropriate amount of protection under the law can be regulated: the quantity may be inadequate, adequate or superfluous. The latter two are not explicitly mentioned, but these categories, it is suggested, exist implicitly.

The idea of too little protection under the law appears, perhaps rather obviously, in cases in which the available legal remedies are considered insufficient. The regulation of protection under the law is visible in cases relating to prohibition against appeal, in the problems of effective remedy as well as in situations where protection under the law has gained the status of a proportionality principle, alleviating any dichotomous reading of law.

Protection under the law is indirectly regarded as adequate of sufficient in cases, where the fundamental right is not considered to have been breached or where a provision is not in (evident) conflict with section 21. This also applies to situations, in which the case—specific extent of protection under the law is not problematized at all.

---

① MarttiKoskenniemi, *Human rights, politics and love*, Mennesker&Rettigheter, 4/2001, pp. 33 – 45. Koskenniemi argues that it is difficult to come up with a more politically loaded criterion than that. Scheinin, Perusoikeuskonfliktit, *Conflicts Between Fundamental Rights*, in Tuuli Heinonen-JuhaLavapuro (eds.): Oikeuskulttuurineurooppalaistuminen, Helsinki, 2012, pp. 125 – 141, ends up with a contrary conclusion (p. 125): "A major part of alleged fundamental rights conflicts are illusory and can be avoided by clarifying terminology."

Perhaps the most interesting category is the one of excessive protection under the law. It goes without saying that this term is not used. However, there are signs of the existence of such a category. For instance, the justifications for prohibition against appeal in civil servant matters might be mentioned here. Furthermore, matters in which administrative decisions are considered to be measures of work supervision, can be seen as a part of that category.

Both the SAC and the Committee for *Constitutional Law* are at least indirectly arguing that there are good reasons for restricting protection under the law: mostly they refer to the need for efficiency, economy, avoiding delay as well as the public interest. "Efficiency" is interestingly two-dimensional: it can be both a part of the ideal of protection under the law (the invoking idea of timeliness) and a *real-politik* counter-argument (invoking the idea of cost-effectiveness). On top of that, the question of the scope of legal argument also has very clear economicramifications: it costs money.

The second conclusion partly overlaps with the first i.e. the quantification of protection under the law. I would argue that even the narrow conception of protection under the law-the legal definition-refers indirectly to the broad conception, the system principle that is. Namely, an interesting vertical division comes into play when assessing the adequacy of protection under the law. What precisely is it that is problematic about protection under the law? Is it 1) the access to rights, which as such are good and sufficient (i.e. seen from the perspective of realization of rights; the broad conception?); or 2) the adequacy of Finnish legal remedies themselves in relation to international legal requirements (i.e. seen from the perspective of the quality of rights; the narrow conception?).

Moreover, the case law indicates that any questions about how section 21 is realised are, in a way, secondary in nature. Namely, in cases where it has proven problematic, an initial disagreement typically involves some other issue, like the rights of a civil servant or an asylum seeker's legal status. Protection under the law becomes relevant, when this disagreement has not been optimally resolved. Consequently, in such cases, the relevant question is not "what" but "how". More theoretically, the problem does not lie in *justice*per se but in *access to justice*. In many cases, that can be even further reduced to *access to court*.

The Finnish legal order must be in accord with EU law and the European

Convention on Human Rights, and in this context especially paragraphs 6 and 13. On the other hand, section 21 of the Finnish Constitution is not identical with the ECHR paragraphs, but wider in scope. Are these purely national components of the fundamental right less developed, because there is no "fourth degree" to supervise their realisation?

The same question can be formulated with the language of "evident conflict" between the constitution and lower-order legislation. It can be argued that a norm-hierarchical ideal of coherence does exist, but one whose disruptions or disturbances manifest themselves as evident and not-evident conflicts between the constitution and other provisions. Hence, might it be suggested that a demand for "effective remedy" is a meta-level criterion with respect to section 21? If so, it is possible that the Finnish standard of protection under the law would not realize protection under the law in the broad sense. All in all, it seems that by applying the section 21, an optimal scope of protection under the law in the broad sense is sought.

At the most general level, the article shows that the fundamental right to protection under the law in the Finnish legal system is very much alive and well in adjudication discourse; it is law in action. Even though some interpretations of its respective contents are in some cases incoherent, it is evident that argumentation on fundamental right has become and an important tool for pursuing justice and stability. As such, there are clearly benefits to be gained from criticism in the process of developing and refining the doctrine of protection under the law.

# 法律保护：芬兰的一项进化中的基本权利？

艾达·科伊维斯托

【摘要】本文讨论了芬兰最高行政法院近期实践中的法律保护的概念。这一概念主要指基本权利（《芬兰宪法》第21条规定了"受到法律保护的权利"这一概念，即法律保护的所谓的狭义概念）。为重建法律保护这一应用概念，本文将所选的案例法分为三个类别加以分析，并得出结论：这一权利潜在地依赖于法律保护的所谓的广义概念。但是，即使在理想层面上，法律保护的范围似乎也并不是一成不变的。它只是一个"量词"：人们使用它将恰当分量的法律保护分配到每个具体的案件之中。本文还提出，法律保护可能在两个意义上出现问题：它可以被视为享有权利的权利，在这一意义上其层次是恰当和充分的；它也可以被从法律补救的充分性的角度来理解，而这一理解与具有约束力的国际法律承诺相关。

# Employee Participation—Observations on the Legal Framework in Finland and the EU

*Ulla Liukkunen*

〖Abstract〗 This article gives an overview of the regulatory approach to employee participation in Finland and in the European Union (EU). The focus of the analysis is on employee information and consultation as well as employee representation in company administration. Striking a balance between unity and diversity has been an important objective when the EU has established a regulatory framework for employee participation. The EU legislature has increasingly placed emphasis on anticipating and managing changes through timely and meaningful employee information and participation. However, a certain tension exists between maximisation of corporate competitiveness and protection of employee participation rights. In Finland, the Act on Cooperation within Undertakings provides, for example, a cooperation procedure which has to be taken when the employer is considering measures which may lead to termination of employment contracts on financial or productive grounds. The *Finnish Act on Personnel Representation in the Administration of Undertakings* enables employee participation in company supervisory, executive or advisory bodies of undertakings. The roles and practical relevance of these two laws greatly differ.

## I. Introduction

Employee participation-information and consultation plus employee representation in company administration-has gradually established itself as one of the core areas of European Union (EU) labour law.① It has not only brought about a cross-border dimension to the employee participation systems of the EU Member States but has also set out a minimum level of rights to information and consultation, to be respected by each Member State. The current approach of the EU legislature to strengthening employee participation rights is based on the view that participation rights are fundamental social rights. The right to information and consultation is acknowledged as a fundamental labour right in the *EU Charter of Fundamental Rights*, which was made binding by the *Treaty of Lisbon*.② The EU Charter does not include the right to employee participation in company administration.

Employee participation is based on the idea that employees should be given an opportunity to express their views on decision-making that affects their work and workplace. In general, employee participation may refer to a wide range of mechanisms through which employee involvement can be arranged. In the following, employee participation is mainly discussed as the right of employees to be informed and consulted about issues that relate to their work and workplace but it also refers, depending on the context, to employee participation at board level, meaning employee representation in the company administration.

Globalization is often viewed as the cause of much turbulence, which also seems to threaten some of the key components of labour law. For companies, globalization of the economy is believed to have created a need for constant restructuring. For employees, it increasingly often means greater pressure to adapt to changes. In recent years, restructuring has taken new forms. In particular, the increase of cross-border restructuring has caused uncertainty in the European labour market and has become a growing challenge for national legislatures and the EU legislature alike.

---

① This article is largely based on Liukkunen, U., Yritystoiminnan muutokset ja yhteistoiminta. Tutkimus kansallisesta ja transnationaalista työoikeudesta, Forum Iuris, 2013. [ Corporate Restructuring and Employee Information and Consultation. A Study of National and Transnational Labour Law].

② According to Article 27 of the Charter, "workers or their representatives must, at the appropriate levels, be guaranteed information and consultation in good time in the cases and under the conditions provided for by Community law and national laws and practices". The Charter became an integral part of EU law with the *Treaty of European Union*.

The EU legislature has increasingly begun to place emphasis on anticipating and managing changes through providing a regulatory framework for timely and meaningful employee information and consultation. According to the social policy approach adopted by the EU, if changes are anticipated, then social problems that typically affect employees and their employability due to restructuring can be avoided. A number of EU legislative instruments seek to improve employee participation rights with a view to advancing their being prepared for changes in both work and workplace. The objective for better change management also encompasses appropriate social support measures to secure re-employment of dismissed employees. Thus the EU regulatory approach governs notifying the labour authorities about planned collective dismissals. Within the EU, managing changes has taken the concrete form of developing employee participation rights in corporate restructuring. [1] For its part, EU regulation on employee information and consultation aims to anticipate and manage change seven in cases where decisions that affect employees are taken in another Member State than that in which they are working.

The following overview of employee participation is divided into three parts. To begin with, the regulatory approach to employee participation in Finland is briefly addressed. The focus is on information and consultation and employee representation in company administration. The third element in the Finnish system of employee participation, which is not discussed in this article, is financial participation. This is based on a separate *Act on Personnel Funds*[2]. Secondly, the way employee participation in the broad sense is regulated at the EU level is discussed. And thirdly, some views are offered on the influence of EU labour law and the question of the relevance of employee participation in terms of corporate governance.

---

[1] See also Communication from the Commission to the European Parliament, the council, the European Economic and Social Committee and the Committee of the Regions EU Quality Framework for anticipation of change and restructuring, COM (2013) 882 final, which emphasizes, on p. 5, that " [t] imely information and consultation of workers is of particular importance in anticipating change and duly preparing for and managing restructuring. "

[2] Henkilöstörahastolaki (934/2010).

## II. Overview of the Finnish Regulatory Approach to Employee Participation

Traditionally, different methods have been used to arrange employee participation and its institutional framework in Europe. Well-established collective bargaining and employee participation systems are characteristics of the Nordic labour law model. Finland and other Nordic countries have high union density and established industrial relations institutions that have significantly contributed to the stability of the labour market.

The Nordic labour law model is characterized by well-established employee participation at the workplace level. Unlike many other European countries, Danish, Finnish, Norwegian and Swedish legislation governs employee participation in the form of information and consultation at the workplace level and employee representation incompany administration. ①

Among the different ways of arranging employee information and consultation and its institutional framework in Europe, the regulatory approach to employee information and consultation at the workplace differs from the continental European model based on establishing works councils. In the Nordic countries, employee information and consultation is mainly carried out through employee representatives. In Finland, employee representation is primarily provided by trade union representatives, or elected representatives if there are no union representatives.

The *Finnish Act on Cooperation within Undertakings* of 2007② provides rules on employee information and consultation for private companies with twenty or more employees. ③ The Act applies to a corporation, foundation andnatural person engaged in financial operations, regardless of whether the operation is intended to be profitable or non-profitable. The regulatory approach is based on the understanding that those who work should be allowed to have an impact on their work and workplace. Before an employer makes a decision which affects

---

① Although Norway is not a member of the EU, it is bound by the Agreement on the European Economic Area (EEA), which means that it also takes part in the EU internal market.
② Laki yhteistoiminnasta yrityksissä (334/2007).
③ On certain issues, the Act also applies to undertakings that employ at least thirty persons.

employees' position, employee representatives must be informed and consulted. A cooperation procedure has to be taken when the employer is considering measures which may lead to notice of termination, lay-offs or reducing a contract of employment to a part-time contract, affecting one or several employees and sought on financial or productive grounds.

The Act was reformed at the beginning of the millenium. [1] One of the objectives of the reform was to make information and consultation (or to use the terminology in the Act, cooperation between undertakings and their personnel) more efficient. The key element of the cooperation system, as emphasized by the national legislature, is the right of employees to information and consultation prior to the employer's decision-making. [2] It is noteworthy that the reform also paid particular attention to the objective of anticipating and managing change through timely employee information and consultation. The national legislature thus paid attention to the objectives that the EU legislature has used when developing a regulatory framework for employee participation.

As the last Nordic country to do so, Finland in 1990 enacted a Law enabling employee representation in company administration. The *Act on Personnel Representation in the Administration of Undertakings*[3] enables employee representatives to take part in decision-making in matters that are important to company business operations, finances, and the position of personnel in the company. Personnel representatives have the right to participate in decision-making in company supervisory, executive or advisory bodies. In contrast to other European countries, in Finland the law also enables employee participation in the managing group of a company: indeed, this alternative has quite often been used.

The *Act on Personnel Representation in the Administration of Undertakings* enables election of employee representatives to the board or the management group of

---

[1] When the reform was carried out, information and consultation in groups of undertakings was separated into a new act, the *Act on Cooperation within Finnish and Community-scale Groups of Undertakings* (Laki yhteistoiminnasta suomalaisissa ja yhteisönlaajuisissa yritysryhmissä, 335/2007).

[2] In the reform, the protection afforded to employee representatives was also improved but the most heavily discussed substantive change was lowering the threshold of application of the Act on Cooperation within Undertakings from thirty to twenty.

[3] The *Act on Personnel Representation in the Administration of Undertakings* (Laki henkilöstön edustuksesta yritysten hallinnossa, 725/1990).

companies employing at least 150 workers. The Act applies to Finnish joint-stock companies, cooperatives and other economic societies, insurance companies, commercial banks, cooperative banks and savings banks. The point of departure for arranging employee representation in company administration is an agreement between the company and its personnel. The agreement sets out on which body in the company the workers should be represented. Depending on what has been agreed, employee representation takes place on the supervisory board, the managing board or the management group or a similar body of the company.

The personnel groups supporting the agreement on employee representation must represent the majority of employees. If no agreement is reached between the employer and personnel, two personnel groups representing the majority of employees may demand employee representation. However, in this case, it is the employer which decides the body of the company where employee representation takes place. The number of personnel representatives may be one quarter of the number of the rest of the members of the body in question. Employee representatives to the selected administrative body are nominated by personnel groups. If the personnel groups do not agree on common representatives, an election takes place. The candidates in these elections are nominated by the personnel groups. Employee representatives must always be chosen from among employees in the company involved, so trade union officials and others who are not employed by the firm cannot be elected. Employee representatives basically have the same rights and duties as the other members of the administrative body involved. However, they may not participate in making decisions on the election, dismissal or contract terms of the management, conditions of personnel employment, or industrial action.

Employee representatives are released from their regular work for meetings of the company body in question as well as for necessary preparatory work. They are compensated for their expenses and receive a fee for attending meetings outside their normal working hours. Importantly, employee representatives enjoy strengthened job security so that they cannot be dismissed on the basis of their duties as employee representatives.

The roles and practical relevance of the two laws on employee participation discussed above differ greatly. As the weakening economic situation has lately led to several collective dismissals, the *Act on Cooperation within Undertakings* has often been viewed as a procedural piece of legislation containing rules on co-operation negotiations that the employer has to conduct with its employees or their representatives in order to be able to carry out dismissals based on economic or organisational grounds. Those provisions of the Act which emphasize on the need for regular information and consultation at the workplace level have gained much less attention. Nevertheless, empirical studies confirm that at those workplaces which have taken due care of their regular statutory information and consultation obligations, situations involving changes have been easier to deal with by virtue of the Act *on Co-operation within Undertakings*. ①

Whereas the experience of the *Act on Co-operation within Undertakings*, and its predecessors, has been fairly widely studied in academic research, employee representation in company administration has not received similar attention. In addition, the linkage between employee participation at board level and corporate governance has not been widely addressed in legal research in Finland. ② The question of the role of employee representation at board level has attracted rather limited attention even though the EU legislature has developed new pan—European company forms with rules that also concern employee representation in company administration.

## III. Europeanisation of Employee Participation

Striking a balance between unity and diversity has been an important objective for the EU when establishing Union-level regulation on employee participation. The EU legislature has been committed to respecting the diversity of national employee participation models in Europe. So the Union has not been aiming at total harmonisation of national laws, and Member States have been able to maintain the basic structures and institutions of their information and consultation systems. As a result, some EU Member States use a works council system whereas others do not. Nevertheless, an EU Directive of 2002 sets out the minimum rules

---

① These studies were carried out by Martti Kairinen and his research groups at the Law Faculty of Turku University. The main findings of the studies are summarized in Liukkunen, U., fn. 1.

② See, however, Liukkunen, U., Globalisaatio, EU ja henkilöstön osallistuminen, [Globalization, the EU and Employee Participation], 2006.

on employee information and consultation so that unified regulation concerns issues where employees have to be informed and consulted. [1]

The increasing relevance of employee information and consultation within the EU can be seen in its inclusion in the EU Charter of Fundamental Rights and in the growing number of EU Directives in the field. The principal model of employee participation advanced by the EU is based on employee information and consultation. The EU has no general regulation on national-level employee participation in company administration. The explanation of the chosen regulatory approach lies in the lack of a unified view among Member States on the issue, which is seen in the diversity of national approaches. Some EU Member States, such as Finland and other Nordic countries, have enacted general legislations on employee representation in company administration.

In essence, EU labour law has established the right of employees to be informed and consulted via a set of directives that regulate information and consultation at both national and cross-border levels. The need for cross-border regulation of employees' rights is connected to the internationalization of companies driven by economic integration and also to the related need to regulate cross-border company mergers and transfers at EU level.

The most substantial change brought about by the EU has been the transnational dimension of employee participation rights. Cross-border information and consultation rights are regulated in particular in the European Works Councils (EWC) Directive, which requires that the personnel of large undertakings and groups of undertakings operating in more than one European Economic Area (EEA) country should be regularly informed and consulted on certain issues. [2]

---

[1] See Directive 2002/14/EC of the European Parliament and of the Council of 11 March, 2002 establishing a general framework for informing and consulting employees in the European Community-Joint declaration of the European Parliament, the Council and the Commission on employee representation.

[2] See Directive 2009/38/EC of the European Parliament and of the Council of 6 May, 2009 on the establishment of a European Works Council or a procedure in Community-scale undertakings and Community-scale groups of undertakings for the purposes of informing and consulting employees. The initial Directive on European Works Councils was Council Directive 94/45/EC of 22 September 1994, on the establishment of a European Works Council or a procedure in Community-scale undertakings and Community-scale groups of undertakings for the purposes of informing and consulting employees.

The Directive on European Works Councils has often been called the "flagship" of EU labour law. It applies to European undertakings and groups of undertakings that have together at least 1000 employees within the EEA States and at least 150 employees in two different EEA States. The model of employee participation offered by the Directive is quite simple: each undertaking (or group of undertakings) has to set up a European Works Council which consists of employee representatives from each EEA country where the undertaking has the required number of employees. The undertaking and the employees' representatives may alternatively agree on some other forms of employee information and consultation.

European Works Councils have been characterized as innovative transnational institutions. This refers to the potential embedded as they enable various forms of undertaking-specific arrangements for information and consultation. However, it is sometimes said that in practice two typical models of European Works Councils are identifiable, one being the French model which ensures that European Works Councils jointly comprise managers and employee representatives and the other being the German model where European Works Councils comprise only employee representatives. [1] What enables different arrangements for employee information and consultation is that the regulatory approach of the Directive on European Works Councils is quite flexible and emphasizes freedom of contract. As a result, each undertaking's employee participation model can be tailor-made to what best suits its needs. However, the Directive also sets out subsidiary rules of a mandatory nature. These apply if no agreement is reached on the arrangement for information and consultation between the undertaking and its personnel.

It is noteworthy that the European regulatory architecture of cross-border employee participation rights relies largely on private international law rules which, for example, determine which Member State's law is applicable to the establishment of a European Works Council and to the conduct of related negotiations between the undertaking and personnel sides. Private international law has contributed to establishing the current regulatory framework, which is based

---

[1] See Waddington, J., *European Works Councils and Industrial Relations: A Transnational Industrial Relations Institution in the Making*, 2010, p. 67.

on applying the rules of each Member State's national legislation along with the harmonized rules in the Directive. The former are used to determine, for example, determining employee representatives.

Whereas the EU's employee information and consultation legislation also contains provisions on regular obligations of employers to inform and consult employees, and, in the case of the European Works Councils Directive, obligations of the central administration of Community-level undertakings and groups of undertakings, employee representation in company administration has been regulated by the EU in specific cases. Regulation of the right to participate in company administration has been connected to the development of EU company law, the most famous example being EU legislation on the European company.

European companies (Societas European, SE) and European cooperative societies (Societas Cooperative Europaea, SCE) are Europe-wide forms of company through which it is possible to engage in business throughout the entire EEA, in the name of a single company. ① A question essentially related to adoption of legislation on these European company forms in the EU was how the participation rights at board level should be protected. Difficulties in resolving this issue hindered completion of the legislative project on European Companies until 2001. When legislation on the European company was finally enacted, the point of departure adopted was that a precondition for establishing a European company is that board-level employee participation is ensured. In a European company, employee participation must be arranged taking into consideration the existing participation models in companies participating in the establishment of a European company. To put the matter in a nutshell, EU legislation on board-level employee participation in European companies is based on the principle of continuity: employees' existing rights cannot be reduced as a result of cross-border restructuring. Hence, EU legislation ensures not only employee information and

---

① See Council Regulation (EC) No 2157/2001 of 8 October, 2001, on the Statute for a European company and Council Directive 2001/86/EC of 8 October, 2001, supplementing the Statute for a European company with regard to the involvement of employees. See also Council Regulation (EC) No 1435/2003 of 22 July, 2003, on the Statute for a European Cooperative Society (SCE) and Council Directive 2003/72/EC of 22 July, 2003, supplementing the Statute for a European Cooperative Society with regard to the involvement of employees.

consultation but also employee representation in the company administration if employee participation already existed in acompany involved in establishing a European company. [1]

A similar regulatory approach to that used in the European company and European cooperative society legislation has been used by the EU in the case of cross-border mergers of limited liability companies. [2] Thus, the legislation on employee participation at board-level has a linkage to streamlining business operations and the most central company law reforms in the Union in terms of realizing EU economic freedom of establishment. [3] The regulatory approach adopted has been based on ensuring continuity of board-level employee participation rights in the establishment of a European company or European cooperative society and in the case of cross-border mergers. The continuity principle of protection of employee participation rights in the EU can be seen as one important element in creating a stronger European basis for employee participation rights. Importantly, it also demonstrates a sought for balance between EU fundamental economic freedoms and social rights in a complex regulatory framework where the latter has often been superseded by the former. [4]

It should be noted that recently, the European labour law debate on corporate governance has come to emphasize the role of employee participation in the broad sense of the word. Not only employee participation at board-level but also employee information and consultation are understood as elements of advancing better corporate governance. At the same time, the present EU legislative framework has been criticized for being fragile because cross-border corporate restructuring might endanger employee participation at board-level in Europe. The present diversity of national regulatory models in the EU enables companies from different Member States participating in restructuring to seek restructuring arrangements which enable

---

[1] See, for example, Barnard, V., *EU Employment Law*, Fourth Edition, Oxford University Press, 2012, pp. 676–677.
[2] See Directive 2005/56/EC on cross-border mergers of limited liability companies.
[3] See Liukkunen, U., "Collision Between the Economic and the Social—What Has Private International Law Got to Do with It?" in Pia Letto-Vanamo and Jan Smits (eds), *Coherence and Fragmentation* in *European Private Law*, Sellier, 2012, p. 144.
[4] See ibid., pp. 143–146.

them to avoid employee participation at board-level since some EU Member States have a national system of employee representation at company administration whereas others do not. Additionally, the case law of the European Court of Justice (CJEU) on freedom of establishment has come to offer some possibilities for circumventing board-level employee participation through establishing a company under the law of a Member State which does not have a system of board-level participation.[1]

## IV. Conclusion

Informing and consulting employees at the right time has become an essential part of protecting employees during times of change in the EU. Simultaneously, EU legislation on employee participation rights builds on maintaining existing Member State legislative traditions and related diversity. The EU regulatory approach thus acknowledges that each national labour law model is deeply embedded in the related industrial relations and labour market model developed through different historical stages.[2] In Finland, EU legislation on employee participation has brought about cross-border participation rights. It has also strengthened the already strong information and consultation rights at the undertaking level.

The present regulatory approach of the EU is, however, not without problems as legislation which affects employee participation rights often also has other purposes than those deriving from Union social policy. These purposes derive from economic objectives. EU legislation on company law seeks to boost economic integration through enabling new ways of cross-border corporate restructuring. At the same time, the objective is to provide employees with participation rights that also apply in cross-border restructuring situations.

The purpose of EU legislation is, on the one hand, to establish a general framework for regulation of employees' participation rights, employee information and consultation, and also to a certain extent employee representation in company administration in the Member States. On the other hand, the purpose is to promote movement of companies within the Union. As a result, a certain tension

---

[1] See Case C-212/97, Centros; Case C-208/00, überseering and Case C-167/01, Inspire Art.
[2] See Liukkunen, U., Globalisaatio, EU ja henkilöstön osallistuminen (Globalization, the EU and Employee Participation), 2006.

exists between maximisation of corporate competitiveness and protection of employee participation rights. This tension may in certain restructuring processes take effect as weakening employee participation rights.

Altogether, the EU has come to play an important role in regulating employee participation, which has meant that differences between levels of information and consultation rights among Member States have evened and a minimum level of employee participation rights has been established on a Union-wide basis. As noted at the beginning, the current approach is based on the view that information and consultation rights are fundamental social rights, as indeed is confirmed in the Charter of Fundamental Rights of the EU. However, we have yet to see how this fundamental right status of employee participation rights will concretize in the field of EU collective labour law and what its impact at the Member State level will be.

# 员工参与: 芬兰和欧盟的法律框架

尤拉·柳库恩

【摘要】 本文概述了芬兰和欧盟员工参与的规制模式，重点分析了员工的知情权和参与磋商的问题，以及员工在公司管理中的代表问题。欧盟建立员工参与规制框架的一个重要目标就是在统一性与多样性之间找到平衡。欧盟立法机构越来越重视通过及时和有意义的员工知情权及参与机制预期和处理各种变化，然而，在公司竞争力最大化和员工参与权的保护之间存在一定的紧张关系，例如，芬兰《企业内部合作法》提供了一个雇主在因经济或生产原因而考虑采取可能导致雇佣合同终止的措施时所必须履行的合作程序。芬兰《企业管理中的员工代表法》使员工能够参与企业的监督、执行或顾问机构。这两项法律在其作用和实际相关性方面有着很大的不同。

# 中国职工参与公司治理的本土路径选择

陈 洁*

**【摘要】** 任何一种职工参与公司治理机制都是一国特定文化和传统的产物。从公司治理视角出发，一国职工参与公司治理路径的选择尤其要考虑本国的法律传统、本国公司特有的股权结构以及公司治理的路径依赖。在中国的立法文本和法律实践中，职代会的虚置、职工董监事制度设计的不完善和职工持股的异化，致使中国目前职工参与公司治理的力度较弱，但现行的相关制度设计大体上适合中国国情以及中国经济发展状况。未来中国公司立法在把握好职工参与公司治理的度的同时，要努力实现职工参与公司治理目标的准确设定与参与机制的合理安排。具体而言，完善职代会、在国有独资和国有控股企业中完善职工董事、监事制度可能更符合中国历史与现实的选择。

**【关键词】** 公司治理　职代会　职工董事　职工监事

作为人力资本和物质资本相结合的机制，职工参与公司治理是当今世界公司治理的发展趋势。然而，由于任何一种公司治理都高度依赖一国的政治、经济、社会、文化、历史背景以及既有的法律规则体系，因此，不同国家职工参与公司治理的模式和机制大不相同。即便在同属"共同决策式"的大陆法系内部，德国和法国的企业委员会模式也各不相同；至于英美法系内部，虽然英美同属"利益相关者"模式，其实英国与美国职工参与公司治理的实施机制也不相同。可以说，在职工参与公司治理的路径选

---

\* 中国社会科学院法学所研究员。

择上，罔顾不同制度环境和企业文化背景的完全移植势必造成相关治理机制的"水土不服"。就中国而言，面对全球化资本市场的竞争压力以及公司治理趋同的大背景，如何立足本国的经济发展现状，尊重本国既有的法律传统，选择适合本国国情的职工参与模式与实现机制是推动本国公司治理以及深化市场经济改革的一个重要课题。

# 一 对中国现行《公司法》下职工参与公司治理的立法梳理[①]

## （一）中国现行《公司法》关于职工参与公司治理的基本规定

作为社会主义国家，中国历来重视维护企业职工的合法权益，积极推动职工参与企业民主管理的制度建设。在中国，职工参与公司管理具有广泛的宪法和法律基础。中国的《宪法》、《工会法》、《劳动法》和《公司法》等为职工参与企业民主管理构建了基本的法律框架。其中，《公司法》作为规范现代企业运行的基本法，对职工参与公司治理做了全面具体的规定。《公司法》涉及职工参与公司治理的法条主要有8条（第18、44、51、67、70、108、117、142条），具体分述如下。

第一，关于职工参与公司治理的一般规定。《公司法》第18条第2款规定："公司依照宪法和有关法律的规定，通过职工代表大会或者其他形式，实行民主管理。"第18条第3款规定，"公司研究决定改制以及经营方面的重大问题、制定重要的规章制度时，应当听取公司工会的意见，并通过职工代表大会或者其他形式听取职工的意见和建议。"上述规定明确了职工参与是公司民主管理的一种形式，确立了职工参与公司治理的法律地位，同时规定了职工参与企业民主管理的具体途径是通过职工代表大会或者其他形式。换言之，职代会是中国企业职工参与公司治理的基本组织形式。

第二，关于集体谈判。《公司法》第18条第1款规定："公司职工依照《中华人民共和国工会法》组织工会，开展工会活动，维护职工合法权益。公司应当为本公司工会提供必要的活动条件。公司工会代表职工就职工的劳动报酬、工作时间、福利、保险和劳动安全卫生等事项依法与公司签订集体合同。"该规定明确了工会的职能与运行机制，即职工加入工会，工会代表员工与企业签约。集体谈判制度的目的就在于通过加强职工的谈判力

---

① 鉴于中国理论界与实务界熟悉并习惯使用2005年《公司法》的条文序号，故本文还是援用2005年的《公司法》版本，而未采用2013年新修订的《公司法》版本。

量来解决劳资的对立。

第三，关于职工监事。《公司法》第 51 条①、第 70 条②、第 117 条③规定，除股东人数较少或者规模较小不设监事会的有限责任公司外，中国公司都要设置职工监事，且监事会中职工代表的比例不得低于三分之一。监事会中的职工代表由公司职工通过职工代表大会、职工大会或者其他形式民主选举产生。对于国有独资公司，监事会成员中的职工代表由公司职工代表大会选举产生。

第四，关于职工董事。《公司法》在职工董事的设置上根据所有制的性质予以区别对待，即国有公司强制设置职工董事，非国有公司则任意设置职工董事。具体来说，《公司法》第 67 条规定，④"国有独资公司设董事会"，"董事会成员中应当有公司职工代表"，"董事会成员中的职工代表由公司职工代表大会选举产生"。此外，《公司法》第 44 条规定⑤："两个以上的国有企业或者两个以上的其他国有投资主体投资设立的有限责任公司，

---

① 《公司法》第 51 条："有限责任公司设监事会，其成员不得少于三人。股东人数较少或规模较小的有限责任公司，可以设一至二名监事，不设监事会。监事会应当包括股东代表和适当比例的公司职工代表，其中职工代表的比例不得低于 1/3，具体比例由公司章程规定。监事会中的职工代表由公司职工通过职工代表大会、职工大会或者其他形式民主选举产生。"

② 《公司法》第 70 条："国有独资公司监事会成员不得少于五人，其中职工代表的比例不得低于三分之一，具体比例由公司章程规定。监事会成员由国有资产监督管理机构委派；但是，监事会成员中的职工代表由公司职工代表大会选举产生。监事会主席由国有资产监督管理机构从监事会成员中指定。监事会行使本法第五十四条第（一）项至第（三）项规定的职权和国务院规定的其他职权。"

③ 《公司法》第 117 条："股份有限公司设监事会，其成员不得少于三人。监事会应当包括股东代表和适当比例的公司职工代表，其中职工代表的比例不得低于三分之一，具体比例由公司章程规定。监事会中的职工代表由公司职工通过职工代表大会、职工大会或者其他形式民主选举产生。"

④ 《公司法》第 67 条："国有独资公司设董事会，依照本法第四十七条、第六十七条的规定行使职权。董事每届任期不得超过三年。董事会成员中应当有公司职工代表。董事会成员由国有资产监督管理机构委派；但是，董事会成员中的职工代表由公司职工代表大会选举产生。董事会设董事长一人，可以设副董事长。董事长、副董事长由国有资产监督管理机构从董事会成员中指定。"

⑤ 《公司法》第 44 条："有限责任公司设董事会，其成员为三人至十三人；但是，本法第五十一条另有规定的除外。两个以上的国有企业或者两个以上的其他国有投资主体投资设立的有限责任公司，其董事会成员中应当有公司职工代表；其他有限责任公司董事会成员中可以有公司职工代表。董事会中的职工代表由公司职工通过职工代表大会、职工大会或者其他形式民主选举产生。董事会设董事长一人，可以设副董事长。董事长、副董事长的产生办法由公司章程规定。"

其董事会成员中应当有公司职工代表；其他有限责任公司董事会成员中可以有公司职工代表。董事会中的职工代表由公司职工通过职工代表大会、职工大会或者其他形式民主选举产生。"《公司法》第108条也规定①："股份有限公司设董事会……董事会成员中可以有公司职工代表。董事会中的职工代表由公司职工通过职工代表大会、职工大会或者其他形式民主选举产生。"

第五，关于员工持股计划。《公司法》第142条规定：②"公司不得收购本公司股份。但是，有下列情形之一的除外：（一）减少公司注册资本；（二）与持有本公司股份的其他公司合并；（三）将股份奖励给本公司职工；（四）股东因对股东大会作出的公司合并、分立决议持异议，要求公司收购其股份的。公司因前款第（一）项至第（三）项的原因收购本公司股份的，应当经股东大会决议……公司依照第一款第（三）项规定收购的本公司股份，不得超过本公司已发行股份总额的百分之五；用于收购的资金应当从公司的税后利润中支出；所收购的股份应当在一年内转让给职工。"员工持股计划实质上是将员工转换成了股东，或者说是使员工兼具股东身份。这和严格意义上的基于利益群体角色划分的职工参与公司治理制度其实并不完全相同。

## （二）对中国现行《公司法》关于职工参与公司治理立法的评述

**1. 《公司法》对职工参与公司治理的制度形式全面涉及，但立法整体目的不明，功能不清**

任何法律制度及其规则的设定都反映和体现着立法者所要寻求的价值

---

① 《公司法》第108条："股份有限公司设董事会，其成员为五人至十九人。董事会成员中可以有公司职工代表。董事会中的职工代表由公司职工通过职工代表大会、职工大会或者其他形式民主选举产生。本法第四十六条关于有限责任公司董事任期的规定，适用于股份有限公司董事。本法第四十七条关于有限责任公司董事会职权的规定，适用于股份有限公司董事会。"

② 《公司法》第142条："公司不得收购本公司股份。但是，有下列情形之一的除外：（一）减少公司注册资本；（二）与持有本公司股份的其他公司合并；（三）将股份奖励给本公司职工；（四）股东因对股东大会作出的公司合并、分立决议持异议，要求公司收购其股份的。公司因前款第（一）项至第（三）项的原因收购本公司股份的，应当经股东大会决议。公司依照前款规定收购本公司股份后，属于第（一）项情形的，应当自收购之日起十日内注销；属于第（二）项、第（四）项情形的，应当在六个月内转让或者注销。公司依照第一款第（三）项规定收购的本公司股份，不得超过本公司已发行股份总额的百分之五；用于收购的资金应当从公司的税后利润中支出；所收购的股份应当在一年内转让给职工。公司不得接受本公司的股票作为质押权的标的。"

目标。从形式上看，中国《公司法》努力吸收域外经验，尤其是美、德立法经验，借鉴模仿域外国家的制度安排，对职工参与公司治理的具体形式，从集体谈判到职工代表大会（企业委员会）、再到共同决策（职工董事和职工监事）进而到员工持股计划都做了面面俱到的涉及。这种全方位多角度的制度设计，一方面固然体现了中国立法对职工参与公司治理的肯定和重视，另一方面也恰恰折射出立法者对职工参与公司治理制度的认识不清以及由此导致的立法思路的混乱。例如，《公司法》强行要求所有公司都要设职工监事，但细察中国《公司法》中的监事会职能，竟然没有一项是与员工福利等有关的职责。那么职工监事制度的立法目的何在？与此相似，董事会职权中也没有涉及员工福利，那么，这种职工董事设立的目的又是什么？有学者指出，为了让员工对关乎自己的福利政策表达不同意见而设立职工董事的目的是值得怀疑的。"就保护雇员利益而言，劳动合同法、社会保障法、劳动安全法和反歧视法恐怕能比职工参与公司监控更有效；就保护消费者利益而言，有效的法律措施恐怕是管制产品安全、强化产品责任的损害赔偿和强制披露产品成分和性能，而不是让消费者代表进入公司董事会。"①

此外，虽然中国《公司法》规定了职工监事的存在，但立法规则中又未明确监事会要向股东会负责。同时，《公司法》对监事适用与董事一样的诚信义务，这会导致职工监事并不能代表职工，而只能为公司的利益考虑。上述种种职工参与公司治理的制度安排，体现出中国相关立法不伦不类"拼凑"的特点，② 根本无法实现职工参与公司治理从法律规范的目的到功能以及权利义务、责任配置的内在协调统一。

2.《公司法》对职工参与公司治理的立法设置分野不明，且不同层次的立法内容参差不齐

由于中国正处于经济转型、体制转轨时期，现代企业制度以及社会保障制度等也都处在转型、转轨之中。反映在《公司法》中，职工参与公司治理的制度往往与劳动政策、社会保障制度等紧密联系，相关制度规范呈现相互交叠、分野不明的状态。事实上，很多本属于劳动合同、社会保险、劳动保护、安全生产等的制度安排都在《公司法》中得到了体现，而这些

---

① 刘连煜：《公司治理与公司社会责任》，中国政法大学出版社，2001，序言部分。
② 参见邓峰《普通公司法》，中国人民大学出版社，2009，第612页。

义务其实无须由《公司法》加以确认。例如，《公司法》第 17 条规定："公司必须保护职工的合法权益，依法与职工签订劳动合同，参加社会保险，加强劳动保护，实现安全生产。公司应当采用多种形式，加强公司职工的职业教育和岗位培训，提高职工素质。"再如，《公司法》第 18 条规定："公司职工依照《中华人民共和国工会法》组织工会，开展工会活动，维护职工合法权益。公司应当为本公司工会提供必要的活动条件。公司工会代表职工就职工的劳动报酬、工作时间、福利、保险和劳动安全卫生等事项依法与公司签订集体合同。"这两个法条的内容应属于《劳动法》、《劳动合同法》和《工会法》的范畴，是否有必要由公司法规定值得商榷。

此外，近年来，为配合《公司法》的实施，国务院国有资产监督管理委员会在 2006 年 3 月 3 日发布《国有独资公司董事会试点企业职工董事管理办法（试行）》，2006 年 5 月 31 日全国总工会发布《关于进一步推行职工董事职工监事制度的意见》，2006 年 9 月 29 日内蒙古自治区也通过《内蒙古自治区公司职工董事职工监事条例》，此后，还有很多地方相继出台关于职工董事、监事制度的规范性文件。这些部门规章、地方性法规的规定内容参差不齐，互有冲突，极大地影响了职工参与公司治理制度实施的协调性和有效性。

3. 《公司法》对职工参与公司治理的立法多为宣示性条款，缺乏相应的制度支持

《公司法》对职工参与公司治理的制度设计，缺乏相应的权利义务分配和责任机制，这导致很多的制度安排变成摆设，难以发挥其应有的作用。例如，《公司法》第 18 条规定，"公司依照宪法和有关法律的规定，通过职工代表大会或者其他形式，实行民主管理。公司研究决定改制以及经营方面的重大问题、制定重要的规章制度时，应当听取公司工会的意见，并通过职工代表大会或者其他形式听取职工的意见和建议"。这里，职代会的性质与职能是什么？职代会与工会的关系又是什么？《公司法》的规定显然都不明确。如果说，根据法条的规定可以模糊地推出职代会享有提出意见和建议的权利，但是，该法条对"听取职工的意见和建议"的措辞也相当含糊，对听而不取或不听也不取的情形如何处理没有规定相应的应对措施。事实上，由于《公司法》没有明确职代会的法律地位，对侵犯职代会职能的法律后果也未做规定，实践中公司职代会制度往往形同虚设。此外，《公司法》第 18 条对"实行民主管理"没有任何界定。如果将职代会定性为公司民主管理的机构，在职代会的职权范围没有明确的情况下，也就无法通

过职代会职权的相关规定去理解民主管理的含义。可以说,《公司法》对职工参与公司治理的规定缺乏责任配置、具体责任条款以及配套制度,立法规定整体上不够协调,其宣示性的意义远甚于实践中的操作价值。

综上分析,中国目前正处于经济转型时期,由于法律规则在短时期内的爆发式的增长,渊源众多、形式多样、制度结构日趋复杂的规则之间的抵牾矛盾在所难免,因此,必须从整体制度目标设定的角度来解释、协调现行法,才能使错综复杂的法律规则所建构的法律秩序尽量成为一个无矛盾的统一体。

## 二 中国职工参与公司治理路径选择的本土因素考量

任何一种职工参与制,都是一国特定文化和传统的产物。从公司治理的视角出发,一国职工参与公司治理路径的选择尤其要考虑本国的法律传统、本国公司特有的股权结构以及公司治理的路径依赖。

### (一) 中国法下职工参与公司治理的法理分析:与英美"职工持股模式"的不相容

1. 对职工与公司法律关系的审视

人力资本和利益相关者理论是以美国为代表的发达国家推行职工持股计划的最重要的理论基础。"人力资本理论"认为,人是推动经济增长和发展的真正动力,而企业就是"一个人力资本与非人力资本的特别合约",因此,人力资本应该是与物质资本平等的社会资本形态。至于"利益相关者理论"则认为职工是公司最为重要的利益相关者,他们基于人力资本所有者的身份使其具备了分享公司治理权的资格。

在中国,尽管《公司法》第 5 条明确规定公司要承担社会责任,而且 2002 年 1 月中国证监会发布的《上市公司治理准则》规定在上市公司中引入"利益相关者治理模式"[①],但是,在中国从传统社会向现代社会的转型

---

[①] 2002 年 1 月证监会发布的《上市公司治理准则》第 81 条规定:"上市公司应尊重银行及其它债权人、职工、消费者、供应商、社区等利益相关者的合法权利。"第 82 条规定:"上市公司应与利益相关者积极合作,共同推动公司持续、健康地发展。"第 83 条规定:"上市公司应为维护利益相关者的权益提供必要的条件,当其合法权益受到侵害时,利益相关者应有机会和途径获得赔偿。"第 85 条规定:"上市公司应鼓励职工通过与董事会、监事会和经理人员的直接沟通和交流,反映职工对公司经营、财务状况以及涉及职工利益的重大决策的意见。"

过程中，对私权的确认和保障一直是中国法律制度发展的主旋律。中国公司法的发展轨迹就是一个典型的张扬私权、加强对股东权益的保护、激励个体投资热情的过程。在中国目前的法律框架下，根据传统的民商法原理，职工与公司是彼此独立、地位平等的合同当事人，职工与公司之间是雇佣合同关系，二者通过合同实现的是劳动力使用权的转让和受让。职工与公司双方可以就劳动时间、劳动报酬、休息、休假等工作条件协商决定，但职工仅对公司享有合同债权而并无参与公司治理的权利。因此，尽管《公司法》对社会责任做了宣示性的规定，但在"人力资本所有权"尚未得到法律的认可之前，《公司法》进行公司权利配置的逻辑基础只能是财产所有权。事实上，英美职工持股计划通过让职工持有公司股份，使职工在同时具备雇员和股东双重身份的前提下参与公司治理，隐藏在这种制度设计背后的也依然是对财产所有权的尊崇。①

此外，如果我们在中国现行的法律框架下检讨上市公司治理中的利益相关者模式，则会发现该模式其实存在两个突出问题。其一，利益相关者模式的构造基础在于公司董事对公司所承担的受信义务。受信义务是英美法特有的观念，在大陆法系的中国不具有实践基础和理论上衔接的可能性。其二，利益相关者模式的实现是以公司独立董事的配备为前提的。中国虽然在上市公司中规定有独立董事制度，但在其他公司中并没有相应的设置，因此该模式在中国现阶段不具有普遍推广的意义。②

2. 中国国企改革对职工与企业关系的重新定位

以公有制为主体、多种经济成分共同发展是中国的基本经济制度。这种制度决定了长期以来中国在经济生活中是依所有制性质对企业进行分类并建构相应的企业运行体制的。在居于主流的国有企业和集体企业中，社会主义国家劳动者当家做主、企业职工是企业主人翁的理论，导致职工对企业深重的依附关系。随着中国改革开放的深入，中国的企业改革经历了放权让利、承包制、股份合作制、股份制的过程。在国企向现代企业演进的进程中，"产权明晰"成为现代企业的基本特征和要求。所谓"产权清晰"，主要有四层含义：有明确的产权主体对相关资产行使占有、使用、处置和收益等权利，有清晰的产权边界，厘清产权关系，权责相等。企业的"产权明晰"，意味着职工与公司之间的关系逐渐由公有制下的行政性劳动

---

① 参见石旭雯《职工参与公司治理的法律分析》，《辽宁师范大学学报》2008 年第 3 期。
② 参见郭占红《职工参与公司治理法律制度研究》，中国社会科学出版社，2009，第 164 页。

关系转变为市场性劳动关系。在市场性劳动关系下，职工成为独立的市场主体，具有不同于企业的独立的利益。中国职工终于由抽象的领导阶级变为具体的受雇者。

客观而言，中国国企改革推动的职工角色的回归在本质上是中国经济社会发展促成的每个人作为相对独立的个人意识的觉醒，这种觉醒对中国的社会发展来说无疑是值得肯定和发扬的。从法理角度分析，在公司治理范畴中，虽然职工是受雇者，但受雇者也是与投资者一样平等的法律主体，他们是以不同方式参与公司治理的合作者，这种认识对于建构中国合理的公司治理机制、形成和谐的公司运行状态，是非常重要的前提性的主体制度定位。

3. 中国职工持股制度的异化

中国的职工持股制度是在20世纪80年代中期伴随国有企业的股份制改造而诞生的。当时先从国有小型企业开始试点，而后向全国推行。中国企业职工持股制度主要有四种表现形式：定向募集公司中的内部职工股、非上市公司中的内部职工股、上市公司中的内部职工股和股份合作制中的内部职工持股。这些形式归结起来，其目的主要有三：一是为实现企业股权结构多元化以及解决所有者缺位的问题；二是在企业困难时期通过职工持股解决企业的资金危机；三是解决职工福利问题。此种背景下的职工持股计划，导致中国实践中的职工持股集资与获利的功能较强，但作为激励机制推动职工参与公司治理的功能较弱。此外，实践中，由于这一制度还涉及商法、民法、税法、劳动法、证券交易法等诸多领域，职工持股在具体运行中逐渐暴露出许多问题，诸如内部职工股上市之后严重冲击股票市场，短期的谋利驱动使职工根本不关心企业的长远发展，严重背离了职工持股计划的初衷，加之许多发行职工股的企业动机不纯，职工股的购买缺乏自主性，职工股沦为企业圈钱的工具，等等。[①] 鉴于上述种种，1998年底，中国证监会发布通知，停止上市公司内部职工股的发行。目前实践中，采用职工持股制度的非上市公司，通常以章程或契约来限制职工股份的转让或者在职工退职时强制其向公司出售其股份，以确保职工参与意识的维持和股东结构的稳定。由此可见，坚持以财产所有权为依托是当代中国职工参与公司治理模式的基本前提。

---

① 参见张靖《论我国职工持股制度的〈公司法〉构建》，中国民商法律网，http://www.civillaw.com.cn/article/default.asp? id = 18948，最后访问日期：2015年2月15日。

## （二）中国上市公司股权结构与资本市场的特性：与德国"共同决策模式"的间离

公司治理结构实质上受制于公司的股权结构。各种公司治理模式总是对应于特定的公司股权结构。公司股权结构的含义至少包括两个方面的内容：一是各股东所持股份占公司总股份的比例有多大，即股权集散度；二是公司股份由哪些股东持有，即股权特性。前者是股权结构量的体现，后者则是股权结构质的体现。①

尽管德国"共决制"的职工参与模式无疑深受德国集体主义意识形态的影响，但实际上，德国的"共决制"与德国公司特有的股权结构和融资渠道具有直接关系。② 从股权集散度上讲，中国与德国上市公司都有股权相对集中的特点，但股权特性的差异与融资机制的差异导致中国上市公司中职工参与公司治理的模式不能完全沿用德国的"共同决策模式"。

1. 股权特性差异

中国公司脱胎于计划经济时代的国有企业和集体企业，中国资本市场最初的安排就是为国企脱困服务的，因此，中国大多数上市公司是由国有企业改制而来的。

中国A股上市公司的股权高度集中于第一大股东，且第一大股东同时为国有股股东。这是中国上市公司股权结构的基本特征。鉴于国家本身是一个抽象的概念，不具有行使其股权的能力，因此必须由代理人来代表国家行使其股权。由于作为国家股权的代理人只有监控权，没有剩余索取权，因而代理人往往缺乏足够的经济利益驱动去监控经营者，也就不能真正代表国家切实行使股东权力和承担相应责任。所以，在中国上市公司治理结构中，国家股东实际上是缺位的。而在德国，尽管其上市公司股权结构的典型特征也在于法人股占主导地位，但其法人股既可能来自外部的单一股东持股（如大银行对公司的持股），也经常产生于公司同其他法人之间的交叉持股。实践中，德国银行除了经营存贷业务、信托业务外，还可以直接进行股权投资，这使德国银行可能拥有大量的股票投票权，使其在公司监事会中占有很多席位，足以影响公司的经营决策。可以说，德国银行对公司的持股和干预，使德国公司内部的各相关利益主体监控公司经营成为可能。尤其在股东利益和职工利益发生冲突时，监事会中大股东的代表可以

---

① 参见张兆国等《试析我国上市公司股权结构的治理效应》，《中国软科学》2003 年第 12 期。
② 参见张舫《职工参与公司控制质疑》，《现代法学》2004 年第 2 期。

与职工代表分庭抗礼，防止职工代表与经营者结成同盟，损害股东利益。但在中国，国有大股东显然难以发挥上述作用。

此外，与欧美公司的机构投资者和德、日公司的法人股东相比，中国上市公司相当数量的法人股份还由非银行金融机构（投资公司）持有，诸如共同基金、养老基金等机构投资者的持股量微乎其微。而无论关联法人或是投资公司还是其他法人股东几乎都是国有身份，但其最终受益者却不明确。这样的股权特性决定了目前法人股东在中国公司治理结构中的作用是非常有限的。[1]

2. 资本市场的监督效能差异

在股东内部监督不力的情况下，外部资本市场监督将起到重要的替代作用。从资本市场的比较来看，以银行为中心的资本市场与以证券市场为中心的资本市场之间显然存在重大的体制差异。[2] 在中国，随着大力发展资本市场，证券市场成为公司的一个重要融资渠道。完善的经理人市场、公司并购市场和证券市场体系形成外部制约体系，努力对管理者形成有效约束已经成为中国资本市场发展的目标。[3] 而在德国，由于德国的银行规模很大，银行对公司经理层的监督对公司治理起着非常重要的作用。德国银行与公司的亲密关系使德国的公司更倾向于向银行贷款融资，而不是利用证券市场融资。这导致德国的证券市场不发达，大股东高比例持股的现象长期存在。而且，德国的"共决制"为公司收购造成障碍，削弱了外部资本市场的监督机制。因此，从长远发展看，在中国上市公司中实行"共决制"不符合中国资本市场的发展方向，全面接受德国的"共决制"无疑会造成一系列的问题。

### （三）公司治理的路径依赖：中国现有模式的惯性作用

由于公司法的规则和财产法、合同法、证券法等其他法律体系的嵌入关系，并且其和司法系统、法官的思维习惯等制度实施体系融合在一起，故而在转轨的时候产生了成本，从而导致先前的选择制约此后的选择。比博绍克和罗伊提出，在公司法上存在着两种路径依赖，分别是结构驱动的路径依赖和规则驱动的路径依赖。结构驱动是由于规则制定的参与者的理

---

[1] 参见张兆国等《试析我国上市公司股权结构的治理效应》，《中国软科学》2003年第12期。
[2] 参见〔美〕杰弗里·N. 戈登、马克·J. 罗主编《公司治理：趋同与存续》，赵玲、刘凯译，北京大学出版社，2006，第153页。
[3] 参见蒋建湘《我国国有公司股权结构及其法律改革》，《法律科学》2012年第6期。

性选择和集体行动导致的,既得利益者因并不能从转轨之中获得较大的收益而排斥改革。规则驱动来自于法律规则系统中的两个特点,主导性的法律规范的力量和"细节中的魔鬼"带来的"橘逾淮为枳"。①

1. 中国《公司法》下公司治理架构的特殊性

中国存在和任何一种世界主流法律体系均不相同的公司治理。在公司的机关设置和职权划分上,中国《公司法》采用了类似金字塔式样的结构安排:在这一结构中,基础机关是由公司全体股东共同组成的股东大会,有权决定公司的所有重大事项;中间机关是董事会和监事会,分别承担公司的实务决策权以及监督权;顶层机关是法定代表人,公司章程可以约定由董事长或者经理担任公司的法定代表人;② 在上市公司之中,还要求采用独立董事制度,这明显受到了美国法的影响。从上述形式上的三角形治理结构的安排分析,中国的公司治理模式既不同于美国的"一元制"模式,也不同于德国的垂直式"二元制"模式。

2. 中国不同所有制企业职工参与的差异性

中国有关职工参与的立法从计划经济时代的职工主人翁模式开始,到社会主义市场经济的职工参与公司的董事会和监事会止,经历了不同的职工参与模式。因企业所有制不同而导致的职工参与方式的差异一直存在。在我国所有的企业类型中,职工参与的程度随企业的性质所含公有制因素程度的高低而出现差序格局。具体而言,在全民所有制企业里,职工参与企业的经营机制以职代会为中心,并辅以工会、工厂管理委员会等其他参与机制;在集体所有制企业中,职工参与的机制则以职代会为主,并辅以工会的参与机制。私营、三资企业中职工参与程度最低,只有工会参与机制。这是由于中国各个企业统一适用工会法,因此在工会这一方式上的职工参与程度理论上是相当的。企业管理委员会是专门为全民所有制企业设立的。职代会条例的适用也是针对全民所有制企业,其他企业在理论上只是参照适用。实践中,在非公司制和非公有制企业中,除了工会之外,几乎没有职工参与的形式。③

综上所述,由于不同的历史渊源和立法背景,中国的职工参与在立法上形成了不同的模式,客观而言,我们应当承认这些模式具有一定的合理

---

① 邓峰:《中国公司治理的路径依赖》,《中外法学》2008年第1期。
② 参见叶林《公司法研究》,中国人民大学出版社,2008,第190页。
③ 参见郭占红《职工参与公司治理法律制度研究》,中国社会科学出版社,2009,第153页。

性。一方面，该制度为企业与职工之间的信息交流提供了渠道，有利于企业与职工建立相互信任关系；另一方面，它对公司股东的控制权并没有产生太大的影响，不会增加决策成本，也不会削弱外部市场的监督功能。也正因此，中国现行《公司法》规定的职工参与制度，大体上是一种适合中国国情的立法。[①] 不过，需要改进的是，在以法律制度的形式把握好职工参与公司治理的度的同时，要努力实现职工参与公司治理目标的准确设定与参与机制的合理安排。

## 三 完善中国职工参与公司治理的机制设计

中国法律和实践中职代会的虚置、职工董、监事制度设计的不完善和职工持股的异化，致使中国目前职工参与公司治理的力度较弱。事实上，由于中国目前缺乏职工直接参与治理的社会环境和企业认同，没有所有权作为依托的职工参与制度很难得到私人投资公司的认同，因此，职工董事、监事制度的全面普及还不切实际。也正因此，完善职代会、在国有独资和国有控股企业中完善职工董事、监事制度可能更符合我国历史与现实的选择。

### （一）明确职代会的性质与职能

作为中国职工参与公司治理的基本组织形式，职代会制度的完善对维护职工利益以及实现公司和谐运行和可持续发展具有重要意义。当前中国《公司法》下职代会制度的完善至少要包括以下几个方面。

第一，职代会的性质与设立的前提。公司法应当直接将职代会定性为职工参与公司治理的机构，而不是所谓的"民主管理机构"。此外，考虑到中国中小企业居多，因此，可以适当地放宽职代会设立的标准。立法上可以职工人数作为职代会设立的标准，具体的标准可以参考目前地方立法中的规定，例如，以50人为基准，超过50人的企业应设立职代会，低于50人的企业设立职工大会等。

第二，关于职代会的职能。立足中国国情，借鉴域外经验，公司法规定的职代会的职权至少应当包括以下三点。（1）知情权和提出意见、建议权。不管是公司日常的经营事项，还是公司的重大决策，公司职工都应该享有知情权和提出意见、建议权。（2）对涉及职工重大利益事项的否决权。

---

[①] 参见张舫《职工参与公司控制质疑》，《现代法学》2004年第2期。

(3) 选举和罢免职工董事和职工监事。(4) 对管理人员的民主评议监督。①

第三,职代会与股东会、董事会、监事会的协调机制,例如:职代会应与监事会配合监督公司的经营管理,通过职工监事定期沟通公司信息,给监事会做出决策提供科学参考,董事会制定涉职工利益的文件时,应先向职代会告知有关情况,听取职代会的意见和建议;对职代会提出的异议,董事会应将相关决策连同职代会的建议和意见交由股东会确认;等等。总之,对涉及职工重大利益的事项,立法应该促进董事会和股东会在职工支持的基础上进行决策。

### (二) 加强国有公司中职工董事制度的可操作性

在职工董事的设立方面,《公司法》规定,职工董事的设立已经不再有所有制的局限,不仅公有制企业、混合所有制企业,而且非公有制企业都可以通过选举职工董事进入董事会,实行民主管理。但从现实角度分析,职工董事在非公有制企业中很难实施。

如前所述,职工董事参与公司治理应限定在国有企业中,尤其在国有上市公司中推行职工董事制度较为可行。目前的法律对职工董事的任期、权益保护、罢免条件等都没有规定,尤其是对职工董事的比例没有规定,这导致公司完全可以只设立一名职工董事来规避法律,从而使职工董事参与公司治理沦为摆设。

借鉴域外经验,职工董事与其他董事的地位应当是平等的,但基于其职务性质,那些涉及雇员的人事性和社会性的利益问题则主要应由职工董事负责。此外,职工董事在公司董事会中的规模应根据公司的职工人数按照一定比例来确定。结合我国目前的公司发展现状,同时考虑到职工进入董事会难免会增加集体决策的成本,在依据公司职工人数确定职工董事数量的同时,也应规定职工董事一定的比例上限,例如可设定职工董事最高比例为1/4。除职工董事人数规定外,公司法对职工董事的任职条件、罢免程序、法律责任等也需进一步细化。

### (三) 加强国有公司中职工监事制度的可操作性

中国职工监事制度的设置是对德国双层制公司治理结构的借鉴。但是,由于中国缺乏像德国那样强大的工会组织和职工管理委员会作为职工监事制度的依托,职工监事制度效能不彰。目前《公司法》对职工监事的适用

---

① 参见李勇、郭占红、白宇《职工代表大会参与公司治理的立法完善》,《国家行政学院学报》2013年第6期。

范围、产生程序、权利义务、法律责任等都缺乏细致的规定。未来立法至少要注意以下一些内容。

1. 职工监事的人数

与职工董事的制度完善相一致，以人数来确定监事会的规模可以为监事会提供可靠的法律保障。《公司法》规定公司监事会中职工监事的比例不少于1/3，"不少于"的措辞不严谨，给公司限制监事会作用的发挥提供了可能。立法可以在这一基础上根据公司的职工人数逐渐提高比例，但也应限定最高比例。

2. 职工监事的产生条件

职工监事应符合一定的任职条件，例如，必须在企业工作一定期限，同时其产生应经职代会全体代表过半数通过。

3. 职工监事的职权

职工监事应具有与非职工监事相同的职权，还应承担其对职代会的责任，例如，应定期向职代会汇报工作、听取职代会的意见并反馈到监事会，表达职工的利益。此外，要确保职工监事在履行职务时的合法权益，例如，其担任职工董事、监事的期间计入工作时间，公司对其解聘要经过职代会的同意等。

4. 职工监事的罢免

公司对职工监事的解聘要经过职代会的同意。如果认为职工董事、监事没有认真履行职责，一定比例的职工代表或一定比例的公司职工可以向职代会提出罢免。

# Choice of Native Approaches to Employees' Participation in Corporate Governance in China

*Chen Jie*

【Abstract】 Any mechanism for employees' participation in corporate governance is a product of the culture and tradition of a specific country. In choosing an approach to employees' participation in corporate governance in a country, consideration must be given to the legal tradition, the corporate shareholding structure, and the path dependence of corporate governance of that country. In China, because of the mere nominal existence of employees' congress, the defects in the design of the system of employees' directors and supervisors, and the alienation of employees' stock ownership, currently the employees' participation in corporate governance is relatively weak, although the design of the relevant institutions is, on a whole, suitable for the national conditions and the level of economic development in the country. In the future legislation on employees' participation in corporate governance, China should provide for appropriate degree, precise objective, and reasonable institutional design of participation. More specifically, improving the employees' congress system and the system of employee's directors and supervisors in solely state - owned enterprises and state holding enterprises is perhaps an approach more suitable to the history and reality in China.

【Key words】Corporate Governance; Employees' Congress; Employees' Directors; Employees' Supervisors

# An introduction to the non-discrimination law of the European Union in the Finnish labour law context

*Marjo Ylhäinen*

[**Abstract**] This article provides an introduction to the non-discrimination law of the European Union in the Finnish labour law context. The article deals with the non-discrimination directives in the special context of Finnish labour law. The non-discrimination law of the European Union has multiple dimensions and there are several ways to systematize the complexity of legal rules in this field. The article focuses on giving an overview of these questions. The questions are divided into three categories the principle of equal treatment of men and women, the prohibition of discrimination on other grounds and the application of the non-discrimination principle and equal treatment within labour law. This systematisation shows that although the many international commitments on non-discrimination and equality long before joining the European Union, the impact of European Union law on Finnish legislation has been significant. Implementing the non-discrimination directives has had effects on legislation which has also served as a booster for legal change on the level of legal culture.

## 1. Introduction

The principle of equality has been—in some form at least—one of the fundamental principles of Western democratic societies since the declaration of independence of the United States in 1776 followed by the declaration of human *rights in* 1789 during the French Revolution. ①Especially in the 20th century the principle of equality was strengthened and supplemented by the principle of non-discrimination, a principle that was expressed and complemented in several international charters, declarations, conventions and decisions that have been accepted by for example the United Nations and the International Labour Organization. ② Both equality and non-discrimination as legal principles serve the objective of achieving full parity between all people.

In Europe two central institutions have contributed to the legal principles of equality and non-discrimination. Firstly, the Council of Europe (COE) and the European Court of Human Rights, with the Convention for the protection of human rights and fundamental freedoms as the main instrument, have contributed significantly to equality and non-discrimination on the European level. Secondly, the European Union and development of its fundamental freedoms and non-discrimination legislation in the form of directives as well as development of the European Social Charter into a legally binding document strengthens the principles of equality and non-discrimination in the member states. ③ The legal efficacy of both the human rights convention and the non-discrimination directives owe a great deal to the Human Rights Court as well as to the Court of Justice of the European Union: these have both had a remarkable effect on the development and interpretation of human rights and non-discrimination principles in their case-law.

Non-discrimination law at the European level can be defined as including non-discrimination principles according to the European Court of Human rights as well as the non-discrimination law of the European Union. ④ Although these two legal regimes have a slightly different scope of application, nevertheless it is evident that

---

① Equality is closely connected to the concept of justice. Aristotle famously stated the formal equality principle "treat like cases as like" as part of his ethic and conception of justice. *Aristotle's Nicomachean Ethics*, part V, section 3.

② The ideas of both equality and non-discrimination as legal principles are well sedimented in the legal cultures of Europe. The sedimentation of legal principles on the level of legal culture, which is constructed on the idea of positive law, requires legislation, judicial praxis and passing of time. See Tuori, Kaarlo, *Critical Legal Positivism*, Ashgate, 2002.

③ The Lisbon Treaty, (*Treaty on European Union*, *TEU*) Article 6 (1).

④ See, Douglas-Scott, Sionaidh, "The European Union and Human Rights after the Treaty of Lisbon", *Human Rights Law Review* (2011) 11 (4): 645–682 pp. 646–647.

since the Lisbon treaty these two regimes are legally connected within the jurisdiction of the European Union and should be considered as complementing each other in the member states.① This is the wide definition of EU non-discrimination law.

However this introductory article will focus on the non-discrimination law of the European Union in the narrow sense. The article deals with the non-discrimination directives in the special context of labour law and especially Finnish labour law.② The non-discrimination law of the European Union has multiple dimensions and even the above mentioned framing leaves a wide range of rules and principles to be considered. Several possible ways can be used to systematize the complexity of legal rules in this field. In an introductory article like this it is in any case necessary to make simplifying assumptions and definitions in order to give an overview of these questions.

With a view to systemizing the multidimensional question of non-discrimination law in the labour law context, the questions here are divided into three different categories. Firstly comes the principle of equal treatment of men and women, which is expressed in the principle of equal pay and in the prohibition of discrimination on the grounds of pregnancy, parenthood or family responsibilities.

Secondly comes the prohibition of discrimination. This is based on fundamental human rights, which forbid discrimination on the grounds of race, ethnicity, religion, origin, disability or other personal qualities as well as on the basis of personal conduct related to, for example, union membership and religious practice and which safeguards the fundamental freedoms of speech and opinion.

---

① *Handbook on European non-discrimination law*. European Union Agency for Fundamental Rights 2011 s. 11.

② Finland became a member of the European Union in 1995 but implementation and harmonization of the legal system had already begun before that as Finland become a full member of the EFTA (European Free Trade Association) in 1994. However, the history of non-discrimination in Finnish labour law is older than EU membership and has its origin especially in conventions of the International Labour Organization (ILO). Relevant conventions here are Convention number 100 (1951) that governs equal pay of men and women (ratified in Finland 1963), the non-discrimination convention number 111 (1958), convention number 156 (1981) concerning equal treatment of men and women regardless of their family responsibilities 6/1981) and article 5 in convention number 158 (1982) that regulates termination of employment.

The separation of parental rights and non-discrimination on the grounds of pregnancy, motherhood and family relations into one category and the other non-discrimination grounds into the other category does not imply that these categories differ by their nature as human rights. However, at least in the Finnish—and perhaps even in the European—context a qualitative difference stands between these two categories regarding how strongly these discrimination grounds are embedded in the legal system.

The third category, on the other hand, differs from the first two. The third category of application of the non-discrimination principle within labour law relates more directly to the nature of employment. It encompasses prohibition of discrimination in the form of less favourable treatment on the basis of type of employment (e. g. fixed-term, part-time, hired work). ①

The structure of the text follows the categorization mentioned above. Due to the close relation between the first two categories, I will deal with the basics of these two categories separately and after that briefly sketch the basic concepts common to the non-discrimination principle in both categories. After that I will briefly describe the issue of equal treatment between employees.

## 2. Equality and non-discrimination

### 2. 1. Equality

In order to separate the different kinds of aims and measures that are necessary in seeking to achieve full parity between women and men it is necessary to contextualize the concept of equality. Quite commonly, equality is contextualized by referring to three different stages of equality. The stages or levels of equality are formal equality, equality of opportunity and substantive equality. ②

---

① See also Hepple, Bob & Barnard, Catherine, "Substantive Equality", *The Cambridge Law Journal*, 2000, 59, pp. 562 – 585.

② The concept of equality can be analysed in many ways. The threefold division in this text serves to clarify the different aims of legal regulation. For example, Anttila analyses equality using only two different categories: formal equality and substantive equality. Substantive equality consists of different categories. Among these are the categories of equality of opportunity and equality of results. Anttila Outi, Kohti tosiasiallista tasa-arvoa, *Towards substantive equality*, Suomalaisen lakimiesyhdistyksen julkaisuja A- sarja, Vammala, 2013 s. 46 – 50.

The fundamental right of everyone to be treated equally before the law represents the level of formal equality. Its ideological background lies in classical constitutionalism and the Aristotelian idea of equality. It contains the idea of equal treatment as "similar cases must be treated similarly" or likes must be treated alike. This formal concept of equality can be found in the background of the concept "less favourable treatment" and in legal regulation regarding direct discrimination. ①

Equality as a guarantee of the same opportunities for every member of society refers to actions—whether on a legislative or practical level—that aim to even up such differences between women and men that prevent full use of a person's faculties and full use of their potential. The rules of non-discrimination aim to fulfil this task. The ideological background to this kind of equality is still rooted in liberalism and is quite strongly based on the idea of everyone taking responsibility for their own actions as long as the starting points are guaranteed to be as equal as possible.

The third level, substantive equality, aims at achieving true parity between people. ②Here, the different kinds of possibility to use positive action are the most important tool, while the ideological foundation is more communitarian than liberal. ③

## 2. 2. Equality between men and women

The first specific principle concerning equality and non-discrimination within the law of the European Union can be traced back to the founding treaty of the European Economic Community in 1957. The Treaty contained a provision④ stating the principle of equal pay between men and women for equal work. The equal pay principle has been on the agenda of the European Union ever since as

---

① Hepple & Barnard, 2000, p. 562.
② However, a blurred line exists between the equal opportunities approach and substantive equality. The former has developed towards a more substantive approach due to case-law and especially development of the doctrine of comparison. See Hepple & Barnard, 2000, p. 564.
③ For a critique of the communitarian concept of equality, see Lund, William R. "Communitarian Politics and the Problem of Equality", *Political Research Quarterly*, 1993, 46, No. 3, pp. 577 – 600, p. 584 and p. 585.
④ Article 119 EEC Treaty, now Article 157 TFEU.

well as being one of the top issues of gender equality in Finland. ① It is also a starting point for gender equality in the industrial market and labour law.

In Finland the *Act of Equality* between men and women was enacted in 1986 after quite along debate and came into force in 1987. Within the scope of labour law the *Gender Equality Act* aimed to promote women's position in the industrial market and to increase equality between men and women. The Act had its background first and foremost in the CEDAW agreement. ② Before specific legislation on equality between men and women, equality and non-discrimination issues were regulated only by the *Employment Act* (1970). Provision 17.3 § of the *Employment Act* prohibited discrimination on the grounds of, for instance, sex. It also obliged the employer to treat all employees equally. The original law of gender equality has been changed and amended several times since 1987. EU legislation as well as the case law of the European Union Court has modified both the rules as well as the interpretation of the act. ③

*The Gender Equality Act* has wide applicability in employment and therefore as part of labour law. The Act applies whether the question of discrimination arises during recruitment, in the course of employment or on termination of employment. It is one of the issues to be considered when assessing a lawful ground of dismissal. It is also applicable in both the private as well as the public sector and is applied both to employees and civil servants.

Three kinds of provision concern gender equality. Each of these aims at realization of gender equality on different levels-formal, levelling opportunities and substantive equality. Equality between men and women is expressed as one of the fundamental rights in the constitution. ④

On the level of equality of opportunity, the *Gender Equality Act aims* to ensure

---

① The equal pay programme is once again part of the government platform, 2012 – 2015 for equality. Hallituksen tasa-arvo-ohjelma 2012 – 2015. Loppuraportti. Helsinki 2015. Sosiaali- ja terveysministeriön raportteja ja muistioita 2015: 1, Government programme for equality 2012 – 2015. [Final report, Ministry of Social Affairs and health reports 2015: 1].

② *The United Nations Convention on the Elimination of All Forms of Discrimination against Women* (1979).

③ The latest changes in the *Gender Equality Act* were made in 2014 when the *Equal Treatment Act* was renewed.

④ *Constitution of the Republic of Finland* Article 6.4 §.

and enhance equality by banning discrimination on the grounds of sex.[①] These provisions have a close connection to the whole process of employment. Job opportunities must be addressed to both sexes and the required qualifications may not be discriminatory. For example military service, which is in practice mostly done by men, cannot be required nor is the employer allowed to ask questions about plans concerning family bonds or pregnancy. During employment the employer must guarantee similar conditions of work to both genders including the same wages and other compensation for the same job. This also applies to educational opportunities provided by the employer as well as to promotion. Additionally, ending an employment contract may not be based on grounds of sex, while special protection for pregnant women appears in the *Employment Act*.[②]

Thirdly, the Act contains provisions that oblige the employer to take different kinds of action in order to actually enhance the position of women.[③] An employer with over 30 employees must make an equality plan which defines the principles of enhancing equality in that particular workplace. Under new article 6 b) the employer is also obliged to prepare a salary report in order to make any differences between wages paid to women and men transparent. This provision aims at better control of unjustified wage differences. From the point of view of the employer, the different stages of equality mentioned above oblige the employer in somewhat different ways to perform actions that can be regarded as non-discriminatory and equality-enhancing. Neglecting obligations is also differently sanctioned. If a court finds a violation of non-discrimination provisions, penalties may follow. However, neglecting to prepare an equality plan or salary report is not sanctioned.

Despite the fact that the principle of gender equality is quite thoroughly carried out in Finnish regulation, many issues are still left unresolved due to structural segregation between men's and women's jobs and structural discrimination: these are very hard to overcome. Two major issues regularly appear on the political

---

① It should be noted that according to the gender equality act, discrimination on the ground of sexual identity or expression of sexual identity are also forbidden. Moreover, sexual harassment is defined as gender discrimination under the *Gender Equality Act*. The *Gender Equality Act* 1 § and 7.6 §.
② Protection against unlawful dismissal on grounds of pregnancy and parental leave is regulated by the *Employment Act* 13: 9.
③ *The Gender Equality Act* 6 §.

agenda. First, the principle of equal pay for equal work regardless of employee gender is still awaiting realization. ① The other problem is the situation of young women who have a hard time finding permanent jobs and therefore constantly face the threat of unemployment. ②

## 2. 3. The principle of equal treatment

As pointed out earlier, the non-discrimination principle has been part of Finnish labour law since enactment of the Employment Act in 1970. This act was replaced by a new *Employment Act in 2001* and the provision on non-discrimination (article 2: 2. 1 in the new *Employment Act*) was still there obliging the employer to treat all employees equally. This obligation was supplemented by a non-discrimination clause stating the grounds of discrimination. These were age, health, nationality or ethnic origin, sexual orientation, language, religion, opinion, family relations, union action and political action. It also contained the rather open ended statement that discrimination on "other similar types of ground" was also forbidden.

However, due to the EU directives on non-discrimination③ with their much wider scope of application than merely working life, a special act on equal treatment was passed in 2004. Preparation of that act was rather complicated as opinions were many and varied on how the directive should properly be implemented in Finnish legislation. The legislative process was so full of disagreement that the Parliament simultaneously with the legislative process declared that Finland should as soon as possible renew all non-discrimination legislation. However it took almost ten years before a new act on equal treatment was passed.

---

① markkina-asemaan ja samapalkkaisuuteen [ The impact of changes in the labour market on the position of women and men in the labour market and on equal pay ], Reports and memoranda of the Ministry of Social Affairs and Health 2015: 10.

② [ A fixed-term employee is most probably a highly educated young woman ]. YLE news 29. 5. 2013. http://yle. fi/uutiset/todennakoisin_ patkatyolainen_ on_ korkeasti_ koulutettu_ nuori_ nainen/6663638. [ referred: 17. 3. 2015. ] Official Statistics of Finland (OSF): Labour force survey [ e-publication ], ISSN = 1798-7857, December 2014, Appendix table 52, Employees aged 15-74 by type of employment relationship and sex in 2012 – 2014, Helsinki: Statistics Finland [ referred: 17. 3. 2015 ].

③ Council Directive, 2000/78/EC, establishing a general framework for equal treatment in employment and occupation and Council Directive, 2000/43/EC, implementing the principle of equal treatment between persons irrespective of racial or ethnic origin.

The new *Equal Treatment Act*, which entered into force at the beginning of 2015, also replaced the non-discrimination clause in the Employment Act. The old provision containing a non-discrimination clause was replaced by a reference to the *Equal Treatment Act*. This was made to clarify the scope of those two acts and also followed the same logic that had been used in the *Gender Equality Act*.

One of the major renewals in the *Equal Treatment Act* was the widening of the coverage of compensation for all violations of prohibited grounds of discrimination. Violation of any non-discrimination ground: age, health, disability, nationality, origin, sexual orientation, language, religion, opinion, family relations, union action, political action and "other similar type of ground" is now sanctioned. The personal purview was also widened to cover discriminatory acts which result from close personal relationships. ①

According to the new act the employer is also obliged to make a plan for equal treatment, similar to the one legislated in the gender equality act, in order to enhance equal treatment and diminish discrimination. The employer also has an obligation to make reasonable changes in the working environment in order to enable an employee with some disability to work.

Systematization of equality and division of the provisions into three categories is also used while enacting the *Equal Treatment Act*. The Act also contains three kinds of provision. These represent different levels of conception of equality and equal treatment.

## 3. Some key concepts

### 3.1. Direct and indirect discrimination

One of the most important and concrete impacts that EU directives have had on non-discrimination law in Finland and in the Finnish labour law context lies in the concepts of direct and indirect discrimination. Direct discrimination is taken to occur where one person is treated less favourably than someone else has been or would be treated in a comparable situation and on grounds that are considered to be discriminatory. Direct discrimination occurs when people in similar situations

---

① See also Case C-303/06 S. Coleman v Attridge Law and Steve Law.

are treated differently. ①

Indirect discrimination, on the other hand, means discrimination as a result of treating similarly people who are in different situations. Indirect discrimination is indirect because the result of such treatment leads to discrimination. However the effects of different treatment should be quite significantly negative. The definition of indirect discrimination also refers to "an apparently neutral provision, criterion or practice" that might cause persons some particular disadvantage compared with other persons because of their age, ethnic origin, sex or other grounds of discrimination. ②

In considering indirect discrimination, two things are of the essence. Firstly, indirect discrimination as a legal definition is needed in order to enhance the principle of equality as fully as possible by broadening the concept of discrimination in so far as possible in situations where substantive equality is not achieved. Secondly, the definition of indirect discrimination is closely attached to structural discrimination, which often appears in neutral forms but causes discrimination as its actual effect.

The definition of direct discrimination is fairly clear. A fairly typical example in the context of labour law would be not hiring a pregnant women or aged job seeker despite their best suitability for the job in question, paying lower wages for the same job to workers of a certain race than to others, or choosing persons to be dismissed solely because they are of a different nationality. ③

The line between direct and indirect discrimination is not always clear, while difficult questions might still arise about the meaning of the concepts themselves. The concept of indirect discrimination is much more complex than that of direct discrimination but the difficulty is also dependent on the ground of discrimination. For example family relations or parental responsibilities are easily

---

① Interpretation of the concept of direct discrimination is also found in the practice of the European Court of Human Rights. Case No. 42184/05 Carson and Others v. UK, case No. 57325/00 D. H. and Others v. the Czech Republic and case No. 13378/05 Burden v. UK.
② Case law of European Human Rights Court, see case No. 33401/02 Opuz v. Turkey and case No. 17209/02 Zarb Adami v. Malta.
③ Discrimination on the grounds of pregnancy is always direct discrimination. See ECJ case C-177/88 Dekker paras 12 and 18.

recognizable causes of indirect discrimination. ①

Outlining typical situations where indirect discrimination can occur in the labour law context would be for example requirements for job seekers that are not attached to the job in question but that are used in order to avoid, for example, job seekers with disabilities. An example of an apparently neutral provision could be a collective agreement provision that-whilst neutral in itself-would in a certain situation treat employees differently because their situation differs due to some ground of discrimination. ②

Both direct and indirect discrimination require comparison. In principle, when discrimination is suspected, for example in a situation involving employment, there should be two persons, or two groups, representing different personal qualities that would be relevant from the point of view of the grounds of discrimination, for example difference in age, sex, religion, union membership, and so on. The question of comparators has been brought up quite often in the Court of Justice of the European Union, which has clarified the requirements for comparison. ③

The question of comparators is one of the most disputed and well established in cases when discrimination is suspected on the ground of sex. The Court of Justice of the European Union has ruled in several cases that despite lack of male comparators in the case of pregnancy, there has been discrimination on the grounds of pregnancy. ④

In the context of equal pay for equal work, on the other hand, one of the key questions is to find out what equal work means. In an important case, the ECJ

---

① The gender-neutral character of parenthood and family relations has contributed to the definition that these are grounds of indirect discrimination.
② Labour Court in Finland cases 2014 – 115, 2014 – 116, 2014 – 117.
③ ECJ Case C – 13/94 P. v. S. and Cornwall County Council and ECJ Case C – 256/01 Allonby v. Accrington and Rossendale College.
④ See ECJ Cases C – 177 Dekker v Stichting Vormingscentrumvoor Jong Volwassenen ( VJV-Centrum) Plus, C – 294/04 Carmen Sarkatzis Herrero v. Instituto Madrile? o de la Salud ( Imsalud), Case C – 191/03 North Western Health Board v Margaret McKenna, and C – 284/02 Land Brandenburg v. Ursula Sass. For example in Finland the Supreme Court ruled in 1992 that pregnancy cannot be considered as discrimination on the grounds of sex because no male comparator is available since only women can get pregnant. Finnish Supreme Court case 1992: 7.

commented that there were notable similarities between work carried out by women who were psychologists and men who were psychiatrists. However the Court ruled that, despite the similarities of the tasks, the education that the male psychiatrists had received compared to the educational background of the women allowed them to make decisions which the women could not and therefore there was an objective reason to pay higher salaries to the men.

## 3. 2. Objective reasons for less favourable treatment

In the context of labour law the question of objective treatment when it is less favourable can be conceptualized in the tension between the prerogative of the employer and the principle of non-discrimination. The latter modifies the context of the former also in areas that traditionally fall outside the scope of labour law. The principle of non-discrimination is actually quite simple; no-one should be treated less favourably on grounds of discrimination. The principle of the prerogative of the employer would in this context be put simply as the employer's right to make managerial decisions including the right to make decisions concerning workers.

Defences of less favourable treatment in the context of labour law actually refer to objective reasons which make performance by the employee, otherwise considered as discriminatory, acceptable. These reasons are first and foremost intertwined with the requirements of the work to be done. Whether the question concerns educational skills, working history, or personal qualities, these might all be justifiable causes as long as the requirements relate to the work and are not overly valued. The question of defences of less favourable treatment might also arise when decisions about working conditions are made or when a decision on dismissal is involved. In such circumstances, if the question of discrimination is raised, the employer must be able to justify its decisions with objective reasons. For example, the criteria under which an employer chooses employees for extra education must relate to the requirements of the employees' tasks and their personal skills. In the case of redundancies the selection process for employees to be dismissed must be related to the employer's business needs (preferring for example workers with special skills that the employer needs) and not to discriminatory personal qualities of employees.

## 3.3. Positive action

Positive action means favouring in two different ways. It can mean either favouring characteristics that easily lead to discrimination, or using these characteristics as criteria when making decisions. It also means improving the disadvantaged position of a particular group in society in general. The first type of positive action measures can be used in the context of employment.

Positive action allows differential treatment to achieve equality. Positive action means taking measures that enhance the situation of the members of a minority group, for example at the workplace. Positive action is one of the major tools that aim to improve substantive parity. In non-discrimination law this tool has many applications at the legislative level. This tool has also become increasingly important in enterprises. Additionally, a clear tendency exists to maximize the use of this tool whenever necessary.

However, according to the case law of the ECJ such measures should be reasonable and should be used according to the proportionality principle.① Evaluating this is—in the labour law context—usually connected to consistency of the employer's conduct. Positive action cannot be used in an ad hoc manner, but has to be used coherently.

## 4. Treating employees equally

The Employment Act prohibits discrimination on the grounds of the type of employment contract e.g. fixed-term or part-time. This provision is based on Directives 1999/70/EC and 97/81/EC.② This category of non-discrimination differs from those dealt with above as there are no requirements of personal qualities as grounds of discrimination nor is there a straight connection to human rights. Nevertheless in the labour law context this category certainly has relevance as a principle of non-discrimination. However, it is only applicable during employment.

Furthermore, it should be noted that in some cases important connections can exist

---

① Case C-407/98 Abrahamsson and Anderson v Elisabet Fogelqvist.
② Council Directive 1999/70/EC concerning the framework agreement on fixed-term work and Council Directive 97/81/EC concerning the Framework Agreement on part-time work.

between indirect discrimination and fixed-term or part time employment. Usually this question comes up when at group level it is evident that a certain kind of employment contract is connected to sex, age or other grounds of discrimination.

The provision in the Employment Act obliges employers not to treat less favourably employees with fixed-term or part time contracts unless there is an objective reason for such treatment. The conditions of work as well as wages or wage related benefits should be in accordance with the employment conditions that a permanent, full time employee enjoys. However, unfavourable treatment is also tied up with hours and duration of work. The principle of pro rata temporis means that this non-discrimination principle is relative. Benefits and conditions should be offered in relation to the fixed time of the contract. To offer a simple example: an employee must be paid equal pay for equal work but the basis for wages can vary according to hours. Or the employee cannot be left outside benefits that are bound with the passage of time simply because of the type of contract, but termination of the contract can be taken into account.

Implementation of directive 2008/10/EC on temporary agency work[1] in the Employment Act should have brought the principle of non-discrimination to this context as well. The principle of equal treatment in article 5 requires that "The basic working and employment conditions of temporary agency workers shall be, for the duration of their assignment at a user undertaking, at least those that would apply if they had been recruited directly by that undertaking to occupy the same job."

The question of sufficient implementation of Article 5 can be raised. There are no direct provisions that would ensure equal treatment of hired workers. However most of the time the true requirement here will be fulfilled through the obligation to follow the conditions of a collective agreement.[2]

## 5. Concluding remarks

Although the fact that Finland was bound by many international conventions on non-discrimination and equality long before joining the European Union, the impact of European Union law on Finnish legislation has been significant. Implementing the

---

[1] Council directive 2008/104/EC on temporary agency work.
[2] *The Employment Act* 2: 9.

non-discrimination directives has had effects on legislation which has also served as a booster for legal change on the level of legal culture.

Some changes in legal practice and legal thinking around this specific field of labour law can also be recorded especially in the field of gender equality. Firstly, the operations of officials that supervise enforcement of the two acts, especially the work of the equality ombudsman, nowadays enjoys quite well established status as a preliminary discloser of violations of the Gender Equality Act and is also known for promoting gender equality in working life. [1] In the practice of the labour court, gender equality has also had some interpretative impact on disputes over regulations in collective agreements. [2]

# 芬兰劳动法语境中的欧盟反歧视法

玛丽奥·伊尔哈伊南

【摘要】本文介绍了在芬兰劳动法的特殊语境下的欧盟非歧视指令。欧盟非歧视法律具有多重维度。本文重点介绍了使这一领域中复杂的法律规制系统化的各种方法。这些方法可分为三个类别：男女平等对待的原则，禁止基于其他理由的歧视和非歧视原则的适用，以及劳工法下的平等对待。系统化分析显示，尽管芬兰在加入欧盟之前已经在非歧视和平等方面做出了许多国际承诺，但是欧盟法律仍然对芬兰立法产生了很大的影响。实施欧盟非歧视指令对芬兰立法所产生的影响促进了其法律文化层面上的变革。

---

[1] Supervision of compliance with the Equal Treatment Act is divided in two. Regarding working life, the Act is supervised by occupational health and safety officials. In other areas it is supervised by the equal treatment ombudsman (minority ombudsman until 31.12.2014). Differences in organizing supervision were criticized by parliamentary committees during the legislative process of the new Equal Treatment Act. See the report of the Committee for Constitutional Law 31/2014 and the report of the Committee for Working Life and Equality 11/2014. Although occupational health and safety officials are experts in the field of working life, the effect of the Equal Treatment Act in working life would benefit from expertise in the field of non-discrimination.

[2] For instance disputes over paid maternity leave. Labour Court cases 2014 – 115, 2014 – 116 and 2014 – 117.

# 社会性别主流化与我国反家暴立法中的相关问题研究

徐 卉*

**【摘要】** 本文针对家庭暴力民事案件在司法实践中存在的举证难、证明难、认定难和诉讼难的问题展开分析，指出在反家暴立法中应针对家暴案件的特殊性，在诉讼证据制度与诉讼机制上，制定特有的专项规范。在证据制度上，应以有利于保护受害人为基本原则，适用表见证明原则，增设新的证据种类，实行证据能力裁量主义。同时在诉讼机制上，建立反家暴公益诉讼机制，赋予妇联、公益法律组织、检察机关以适格的提起反家暴公益诉讼的原告主体资格，并且围绕这些反家暴公益诉讼主体设置相关配套的诉讼规范。

**【关键词】** 反家庭暴力法　表见证明　公益诉讼

2014年11月25日，国务院法制办在其官网发布了《中华人民共和国反家庭暴力法（征求意见稿）》（以下简称《意见稿》），开始向全社会公开征求意见，这是我国首次专门立法防治家庭暴力。这个巨大的进展，被认为是十多年来地方促进中央立法、妇女推动国家发展的结果。① 此后，在《意见稿》的基础上，2015年8月，国务院将《中华人民共和国反家庭暴力法（草案）》（以下称《草案》）提交全国人大常委会第十六次会议审议。2015年9月，经审议后的《草案》正式在中国人大网公布，并于2015年9月8日~10月7日向社会公开征求意见。至此，我国的反家暴立法已进入

---

\* 徐卉，中国社会科学院法学研究所研究员。
① 在中国，关于反家暴的立法论证已经历了十数年，从2000年至今，全国已有28个省（自治区、直辖市）出台了反家庭暴力的地方性法规，但是全国层面的法规一直缺失。

实质性的推进阶段。

目前,针对家庭暴力进行法律规制的必要性和重要性已在全社会层面上达成了共识。需要强调的是,反家暴立法,不应只是将散见于不同的法律法规中涉及家暴的规定进行整合,而是要有效回应反家暴的社会需求,真正达到通过法律预防和惩治家庭暴力的目的。目前全球已有125个国家将家庭暴力定为刑事罪行,在1995年召开的第四次世界妇女大会上,中国是承诺把社会性别意识纳入社会发展和决策的主要考虑因素的49个国家之一。社会性别主流化是联合国推动性别平等、性别公正的主要战略,强调国家立法和政府决策应遵循社会性别平等理念。社会性别主流化旨在实现社会性别平等,使男女两性平等地参与发展并从发展中受益,这是一切可持续发展的核心内容与终极目标之一。[①] 我国的反家暴立法也应当坚持社会性别主流化的理念,立足于社会性别平等的立场,针对家庭暴力案件的特点,制定特有的专项规范。为此,在诉讼证据制度与诉讼机制上,必须考虑以下几方面的问题。

## 一 家庭暴力案件的特殊性与证据适用问题

家庭暴力案件不同于一般的伤害行为,家庭暴力是一方为达到控制另一方的目的而采取的暴力手段。目前,国内外多学科的研究发现,家庭暴力的加害人实施暴力的动机与目的,是为了控制受害人。无论是伤害受害人,还是当着受害人的面自虐或自杀,无论是不同意分手,还是为了达到分手目的,加害人实施家庭暴力的目的,都是为了确保自己在家庭中的"霸主"地位,[②] 让受害人接受在家庭中由加害人制定规则的权力关系。

由于家庭暴力多发生在家庭成员之间,如夫妻之间、父母和子女之间、成年子女和老年父母之间、兄弟姐妹之间,以及具有或曾经有过亲密关系的恋人之间,如离异夫妻或已经分手的恋人之间,这使得家庭暴力案件具有普遍性、隐蔽性、长期性和反复性的特点。而这些特点在家暴案件中产生了一系列的证据适用难题,主要体现为:一是证据本身的数量少。家庭

---

[①] 关于社会性别主流化的概念,第四次世界妇女大会通过的《行动纲领》中的表述是:"在处理提高妇女地位的机制问题时,各国政府和其他行动者应提倡一项积极鲜明的政策,将性别观点纳入所有政策和方案的主流,以便在做出决定以前分析对妇女和男子各有什么影响。"

[②] Lundy Baneron, *Why Does He Do That*? Berkley Publishing Group, 2002. 转引自陈敏《关于家庭暴力认定难的思考》,《法律适用》2009年第2期。

暴力行为一般都发生在家庭内部，具有隐蔽性。由于家庭关系的特殊性及家庭暴力的私密性，家庭暴力发生时并不容易被外人所知晓，因此家庭暴力发生时往往缺乏直接的目击证人，在这方面，受害人除了可以提供伤情鉴定外，难以找到其他有力证据或者不愿意再提供其他关于家庭隐私的证据。家庭暴力的长期性，也往往使证据遭到毁损或遗失。由于通常情况下家庭暴力给受害人造成的伤情并不严重，很多为软组织挫伤甚至没有留下明显伤痕，这种肉体的轻伤害性往往造成受害人疏于求医、求救，致使证据缺失。二是取证困难，由于家庭暴力的隐蔽性、长期性等特点，当事人很难就家暴行为取得直接证据，因此在当事人的举证中，多为间接证据。[1]由于家庭暴力发生的隐蔽性和长期性，传统证据收集难度大，而且精神暴力和性暴力行为无法用外界实物做载体，所以在家庭暴力案件中，家暴受害人往往难以提供有力的直接证据证明家暴行为的存在，法官也就很难认真对待受害人提出的家暴诉求，这致使在目前的司法实践中，家庭暴力案件普遍存在取证难、证明难和认定难的证据适用问题。

## 二 制定家庭暴力案件的特有证据规则

### （一）基本原则：制定有利于保护受害人的证据规则

保障受害人的基本人权是制定家庭暴力防治法的首要目的。反对家庭暴力的立法目的不仅仅是为了惩处加害人的暴力行为，更重要的是保护受害人权利。因此，受害人的意愿、利益、安全等都应该是这部法律的重要出发点和目的，从这个意义上来说，受害人本位作为反家庭暴力法立法的基础，也体现了我们国家保护人权、保护妇女权利的结合。[2]

从保护受害者的立法原则出发，对现行民事证据制度进行检审，我们就会很清楚地看到，依现行法律，根据"谁主张、谁举证"的原则，家庭暴力的受害者要想得到法律的保护、维护自己的权益，那么其本人不仅要向法院提交自己曾受到家庭暴力侵害的证据，如病例或伤情鉴定书等，还要向法院提交该伤害结果是由其家庭成员所致的证据，并且还要证明对自己的这种暴力伤害在平时的日常生活中不是偶尔发生的，这样才能形成一个完整的证据链，才能完成就自己所遭受的家暴提供证据的责任。这样的

---

[1] 参见雷明光、李莹《论家庭暴力案件中的证据认定》，《西北民族大学学报》2005年第5期。

[2] 参见陈明侠《制定家庭暴力防治法的基本原则》，《妇女研究论丛》2012年第3期。

证据规则显然忽视了家庭暴力案件的特殊性，在举证责任、证据的采信与认定方面并没有考虑家庭暴力案件隐秘性的特点，要求受害人负全部举证责任将置其于不利地位，使其正当权利难以得到有效维护。实践中，很多家庭暴力案件因缺乏证据无法立案或得到公正审理。

有鉴于此，在反家暴立法证据规则的制定中，必须明确以有利于保护受害人为原则，制定适用于家庭暴力案件的专项诉讼证据规则，其核心问题则是家庭暴力法律事实所涉及的证据规则的认定问题，包括在证据的搜集、认定、证明标准等方面降低受害人的举证困难，合理分担证明责任，以切实保护受害人的合法权益。

### （二）适用表见证明原则

民事诉讼中，通常的证明标准是证据的优势分量，即为了胜诉，负有举证证明责任的当事人，通常是原告，其所出示的证据必须比对方当事人出示的证据更可信和更有说服力，或者表明要证明的事实更加具有存在的可能性。如果各方证据的证明力不相上下，则被告胜诉。但是，基于前述家庭暴力案件的特殊性与证据适用中存在的问题，适用优势证据规则的证明标准，要求受害人负全部举证责任，不仅使其处于不利地位，也给法院依法审判带来困难，结果可能是受害人的合法权益得不到应有保障，而施暴人却轻易地躲避了法律的制裁。为此，在家庭暴力民事案件中，应适用较优势证据规则标准更低的表见证明原则。

所谓表见证明，是指因一定的事实经过，依高度盖然性的经验法则，必然产生一定的结果，因而推定行为人的行为有过失、或行为与该结果的发生具有因果关系的要件事实存在，从而减轻该事实主张的一方当事人的举证责任。具体而言，是指若某一事实的发生，在生活经验法则上体现为一定的原因，而且通常皆朝一定的方向演变发展，即被认为是"定型事象的经过"（typischer Geschehemrablauf）时，可直接推定过失或因果关系的要件事实存在，相对人如果想推翻此表见证明，必须就该事件通常经过的相反事由，即就事件的经过有其他的可能性提供证据，使法官对原来的定型事象的经过发生疑念。

表见证明是事实推定的一种特殊情况，是因一定的事实经过，依高度盖然性的经验法则，必然产生一定的结果，因而推定行为人的行为有过失或行为与该结果的发生具有因果关系的要件事实存在，从而减轻主张该事实的一方当事人的举证责任的证据评价活动。表见证明作为事实推定的一种特殊情形，相对人在举证成功时，原来负举证责任的一方当事人，必须再度就该事件的内容加以说明,直到法官获得确实的心证为止。因此,从作用上来说,表见证明又属于证明责任的一种减轻情形。

在家庭暴力民事案件中适用表见证明原则,其目的在于减轻作为原告的受害人一方的举证责任。依此原则,只要受害者能提供一些基础性的证据,证明当事人之间存在家庭暴力行为,包括伤情照片、身体伤痕、证人证言、被告书写的不再施暴的保证书、报警记录、社会团体的相关记录纪录或证明、病历、录音录像、短消息、网络聊天记录、家属提供的证据等,而另一方当事人没有否认或无证据推翻受害者的主张,则法院即可直接推定家庭暴力事实存在,施暴人具有过失或故意,构成家庭暴力的民事责任。如果作为被告的施暴人想推翻该表见证明,则必须就其不具有过失或故意,伤害是因其他意外事件而引起的等事项承担举证责任,直至动摇法官的心证,待法官对该事件产生怀疑,进而要求原告方再就该事件的内容加以说明,使法官获得确实的心证后,做出判决。

在发生于河北石家庄的一起因家庭暴力而起诉离婚的案件中,我们可以看到表见证明制度的运用。该案的案情大致是:妻子甲起诉丈夫乙对其实施家庭暴力,并要求法院判决离婚。妻子甲身高170cm,自脖子处以下的身体都受到了不同程度的烫伤,面部也有轻微烫伤。甲称被告乙对其实施家庭暴力,将开水瓶中的开水泼到了自己的身上。而丈夫辩称烫伤原因是自己不小心将开水瓶打翻,开水溅到了妻子身上。法官在审理过程中,询问丈夫乙:"请问你家的桌子有170cm那么高么?"乙回答:"没有"。法官在判决中,支持了原告甲的诉讼请求,判决认定被告对甲实施了家庭暴力,其依据是:如果被告辩称的理由成立的话,那么只有在桌子有170cm左右的高度时,不小心把水瓶碰倒了才可能烫伤到原告的面部和脖子,但是事实上桌子并没有那么高,所以被告的理由不成立。

在该案的事实认定上,法官根据原告身高,依据一般的经验规则认为,开水瓶倒了造成原告烫伤这一事实,只有在放置水瓶的桌子达到170cm的高度时才有可能发生,而原被告家的桌子没有那么高,从而推定被告的暴力行为才是原告烫伤的原因,这一事实推定其实适用了表见证明原则。[①]

在某些案件无直接证据可供利用,而事实真伪的可能性又很大以至于

---

① 该案为《中华人民共和国家庭暴力防治法》项目专家建议稿起草小组在河北省石家庄市调研所得,引自夏吟兰主编《家庭暴力防治法制度性构建研究》,中国社会科学出版社,2011,第356页。

足以认定的情况下适用表见证明原则,更有利于争点的发现和事实的正确认定。在不改变法定的举证责任分配规则的前提下,运用表见证明这一事实推定方法认定家庭暴力事实,不仅可以减轻当事人的举证负担,还更有利于争点的发现和事实的正确认定,符合家庭暴力民事案件的特点。① 而对于对方当事人来说,其并没有因此受到任何不公正的对待。当事人的证明责任并未发生转移,对方当事人只需提出可以动摇法官心证的反证即可推翻表见证明。② 由此可见,作为减轻证明责任、降低证明标准的原则与方法,表见证明原则充分适应了家庭暴力案件的特点。

由于法官可以通过具有高度盖然性的生活经验推导得出结论,因此,表见证明省却了当事人对推定事实提出证据的责任,也免去了法官对推定事实的具体审查义务。法官所依据的生活经验法则因具有高度的盖然性,为日常生活实践所反复验证,所以具有被公众所认可的正当性。法官通过表见证明认定待证事实,在坚持司法公正的前提下,保证了诉讼效率,避免了因当事人在难以证明的事实上纠缠不清而造成诉讼拖沓,从而防止对司法资源造成无谓的浪费。而且,在家庭暴力民事案件中适用表见证明原则,加大了法官的司法能动性,强化了对家庭暴力的司法干预,更利于实现司法的公正与效率。③

### (三) 增设新的证据种类,实行证据能力裁量主义

家庭暴力是一门涉及社会学、心理学、医学、女性学的跨学科知识,而目前司法界以及整个社会普遍对家庭暴力领域中的专门知识了解不够。事实上,不仅社会上对家庭暴力仍存在许多误解,包括法官在内也可能无法理解受虐妇女杀人行为的合理性,因为一个"理性"的人是不会让自己长期挨打的,而且,一个"理性"的人如果无故挨打,应当会立刻逃离打人者。在家暴案件的审理中,如果没有专家提供的知识与意见,法官很可能无法理解施暴者与受暴者之间的暴力关系,也很难对案件事实做出正确的判断。

为了更好地保护受害人的合法权益,有必要在反家暴立法中增设新的

---

① 参见夏吟兰主编《家庭暴力防治法制度性建构研究》,中国社会科学出版社,2011,第352页。
② 参见肖建国、李婷婷《论表见证明制度》,载《证据学论坛》第14卷,法律出版社,2008,第105页。
③ 参见夏吟兰主编《家庭暴力防治法制度性建构研究》,中国社会科学出版社,2011,第353页。

证据种类，包括关于暴力及其后果的专家证词，以及能说明当事人惯习，诸如吸毒、赌博等的品格证据。增设这两类证词，不仅能够帮助法官分析受暴人行为的合理性——为什么不离开施暴者，为什么不采取其他措施，为什么相信会有即刻的死亡威胁或严重的身体伤害，给法官公正裁判提供重要的参考，而且可以显著解决精神暴力、性暴力在证据收集上的困难。①

同时，人民法院在审理家庭暴力案件中，在证据采纳的原则上，应当坚持证据能力裁量主义，即要求司法人员根据案件的具体情节确定证据能力，对于主张家庭暴力事实存在的当事人所做的陈述或提供的其他证据，人民法院均应根据案件的具体情况进行审查判断，审查这些陈述中是否包含自相抵触之处，或有前后不一致的事项。经审查判断后，如认为这些陈述或证据与案件具有关联性，就应采纳该证据；如认为某些陈述或证据与案件不具有关联性，则应裁定拒绝采纳，并在裁定中说明拒绝采纳的具体理由。

实行证据能力裁量主义是与家庭暴力案件的特点相一致的。与证据能力裁量主义方式相对立的是证据能力的法定主义方式。法定主义方式是以客观的、明示的法律规则宣示证据的适格性，排除司法人员的主观随意性，因而明确且易于操作、执行，但是缺乏灵活性；裁量主义方式则相反，其要求司法人员根据案件的具体情节确定证据能力，是一种更灵活更有弹性的方式。在家庭暴力案件中，受害人向公安机关或公诉人做了第一次陈述，但是到了临近审判时，受害人可能又会收回她的先前陈述，或者在审判中，受害人做出与先前陈述相抵触的陈述，或者与先前陈述不一致的陈述，这种情形在家庭暴力案件的审判中经常发生。因为受害人长期受到施暴人的虐待，她们在精神和心理上都有着与普通人不一样的反应，比如，根据受虐妇女综合征理论，受虐妇女往往经历了三个明显的暴力阶段：气氛日趋紧张阶段，严重暴力事件阶段和相爱－忏悔阶段。在第一第二个阶段，施暴人实施了语言或身体攻击，到了第三个阶段，施暴人可能会道歉，表现得很温柔、很后悔并且送礼物，做出承诺。由于施暴人在此阶段的行为增强了受虐妇女认为他会改变的希望，并鼓励受虐妇女维持他们之间的关系，所以受虐妇女会认为施暴人已经回心转意，因此会试图收回她先前做出的陈述，或者做出与之前不一致的陈述。而且，社会环境对于受害人的反应也会对其产生影响，在受虐妇女的求助过程中，如果接触的警察、公诉人

---

① 参见陈敏《关于家庭暴力认定难的思考》，《法律适用》2009 年第 2 期。

对家庭暴力持漠然态度,这种态度会加剧受虐妇女的无助感,迫使她们又退回到暴力关系中,相应地,她们会变得消极、逆来顺受,产生多一事不如少一事的心理,因而撤回先前的指控。① 关于受虐妇女的这些理论都解释了,为什么在家庭暴力案件中,受害人会做出前后相矛盾的、不一致的陈述,所以,对于受害人的这些陈述及其他相关证据,法院必须以证据能力裁量主义的方式,根据案件的具体情况进行审查判断,不能仅因其前后不一致、自相抵触而拒绝采纳。

对家庭暴力案件中的证据以证据能力裁量主义的方式要处理,是根据家庭暴力案件的特点而做出的专项规定。在家庭暴力案件中,法律应强调法院更灵活、更弹性地运用自由裁量权确定证据能力,适用更少限制性的宽泛的证据采纳标准,这样才更有助于对家庭暴力案件的公正审理,有助于对受害人的司法保护。

## 三 建立反家暴公益诉讼机制

### (一) 家庭暴力是社会公害

我国传统的家庭一体化观念认为,在家庭内发生的事都是内部问题,应在家庭内部解决。因此,不少人对家庭暴力还抱着这是"个人私事"的观念。"清官难断家务事"、"法不入家门",甚至不少执法人员也以此为由,对家庭暴力案件不予过问和干预。但是,家庭暴力绝非个人私事,而是社会公害。家庭暴力是对妇女人权的侵犯,其影响远远超出了家庭范围,其严重性和危害性,给社会的发展带来了巨大的阻碍。

全国妇联的一项调查表明:在中国 2.7 亿个家庭中,30% 存在家庭暴力,施暴者 9 成是男性;发生在夫妻间的家庭暴力受害者 85% 以上是妇女;每年有 10 万个家庭因为家庭暴力而解体。全国妇联和国家统计局 2011 年 11 月发布的第三期中国妇女社会地位调查数据和其他研究表明,有 1/4 到 2/3 的妇女在一生当中会经受一种形式的配偶暴力,包括身体暴力、精神暴力、经济控制以及性暴力。家庭暴力不仅是侵害家庭成员人身权利的违法行为,并且是影响家庭和睦、社会稳定的消极因素,其社会危害性非常严重。家庭暴力不仅严重危害妇女的身心健康,而且对儿童产生极为深刻的

---

① 参见〔美〕波拉 F. 曼格姆《受虐妇女综合症证据的重新概念化:检控机关对有关暴力的专家证词的利用》,黄列译,《环球法律评论》2003 年第 2 期。

负面影响。在暴力环境中长大或被暴力侵害的孩子，很容易以暴抗暴，其暴力行为往往加剧。而家庭暴力又是滋生社会暴力的温床，家庭暴力危害的实际上就是整个社会，因此，家庭暴力是国际社会公认的"社会毒瘤"，是名副其实的社会公害。

作为社会公害，家庭暴力是一个复杂的社会现象，对家庭暴力的干预也应作为一个系统工程来对待，需要众多机构和组织针对家庭暴力的复杂性，在各自的权限范围内予以干预。而转变公众、舆论、各机构对家庭暴力的传统认识，给予家庭暴力受害人有效而充分的社会救助，对加害人采取必要的矫治和处罚等，这些目标的达成除了要以政府为主导，公、检、法、司等国家机关各司其职之外，社会组织的广泛参与也十分重要，家庭暴力的防治应当是一个全社会参与的、综合性、体系化的工程。

（二）以公益诉讼防治家庭暴力

针对家庭暴力这一社会公害，在国际上，通过提起公益诉讼惩治家庭暴力，已是一种普遍的做法。不仅在美欧这些法治发达国家，而且这一做法在南亚、拉美、非洲等发展中国家都获得了普遍支持。反家暴诉讼作为公益诉讼的一种类型，不仅推动了许多国家的立法，使家庭暴力入罪，确立了保护令这种新型的司法救济措施，而且对于原告主体资格、诉讼中证据的使用、司法认知等司法程序的问题，均带来了重大的改革和影响。

以美国为例，自20世纪70年代起，在全美各地，都不断涌现妇女组织提起反家暴诉讼的案例，并由此改变了美国刑事司法制度的面貌。在美国，以保护令的形式来保护家庭暴力的受害人始于20世纪80年代。此前，家庭暴力中的受虐妇女只能依赖于传统的民事救济方式，如通过强制令、限制令和治安保证书等方式获得临时性的救济。但是，对于家庭暴力的受害人来说，这样的保护显然是远远不够的。因为，这些措施作为解决民事纠纷的救济途径，在其适用中，执法部门不应当予以介入，所以，如果施暴人与受害人并没有分居，也不是正在办理离婚手续，那么法院就不会签发禁止一方与另一方接触的命令。而且，即便是因情况严重，法院签发了强制令或限制令，然而违反这些命令的行为，就其严格意义而言，仍属于民事违法行为。因此，这种命令所能够给予的保护是非常有限的。如果施暴人违反了命令的规定，继续对受害人实施暴力行为，那么受害人所能够获得的救济就只有向民事法庭提出动议，表明施暴人违反了法院的命令，要求法院认定其为民事违法行为，并给予制裁。显然，这样的做法既费时，又费钱，受害人往往必须为此聘请律师。且至为关键的是，在法庭为动议举行听证以前，受害人通常无处寻求保护，而这段时间有时又可能长达几个星期。况且，即使法官认定当事人违反了法庭命令，作为民事违法行为，也并不需要判处监禁，通常只是对违反法庭命令的施暴人处以罚款制裁，更多的则是对他进行告诫并告诉他不能再犯。由此可见，传统的民事保护方式无法为家庭暴力受害人提供及时有效的救济。自20世纪70年代起，众多妇女组织提起的反家暴公益诉讼层出不穷，唤起了全社会对于家庭暴力作为社会公害的认知意识，使得刑事司法体制对家庭暴力做出了回应。随着家庭暴力的刑事化以及执法部门对家庭暴力的介入，到了80年代中期，美国的各州都颁布了法律，规定应当为家庭暴力受害人签发保护令。而且，大多数州都通过了立法，规定违反这些保护令是一种刑事犯罪。此后，以保护令方式为家庭暴力的受害人提供救济便成为大多数国家通行的一种做法。

在美国的反家暴公益诉讼中，通常是由妇女组织作为原告，代表家暴的受害人提起诉讼，这些妇女组织经常使用多机构联合提起的诉讼策略，并且在法庭审理中大量使用社会科学证据。这些社会科学证据说明受虐妇女的经验既因为她个人的经历和关系而呈现出个体化的特性，在普遍低估妇女经验的社会和法律制度的语境下也与其他妇女的经验具有共性。受虐妇女的经验一般是在作为普通人的法官和陪审员的通常理解之外的，在案件的审理中，法官和陪审员应当力求理解那些提交给他们的证据，以便克服那些关于女性的神话和典型形象所起到的偏颇影响。最为重要的是，所有这些证据都应当以这样的方式提交——即证据提交旨在将注意力聚焦于理解妇女行为的合理性上，而不是基于那些旧式的或者新式的关于受虐妇女的刻板印象来解释其行为。① 如在1999年喀考拉诉喀考拉案（*Cachola v. Cachola*）中，美国现代法律辩护与教育基金会联合其他11个当地和美国国内的反家暴组织，代表本案中被殴致聋的妇女向法院提出诉讼请求，其中包括请求法庭颁发保护令，要求法院将对她经常滥用暴力的丈夫和儿子从家里驱逐出去。但是一审法院拒绝签发保护令，结果这位妇女为了逃避丈夫的暴力，从家中逃出，住在女儿的家中。为此，作为原告的这些反家暴组织，向上诉法院提交了一份长达几百页的辩论要点书。结果，纽约州上诉法院推翻了下级法院的判决，认为让施暴者留在家里而受害者却要离开家庭，无异是对施暴者的最佳奖赏。反家暴组织在辩论要点书中列举了

---

① *R. v. Malott* (1998), S. C. J. No. 12 (S. C. C.).

大量证据，说明家庭暴力是如何导致受害人流离失所无家可归的。该报告还引用了社会科学以及学术上的研究成果，说明将施暴者驱逐出家庭的法令能有效防止被害妇女落到流离失所的境地。①

### （三）妇女权益与公共利益之辩：反家暴公益诉讼的正当性

随着 2012 年《民事诉讼》的修改，公益诉讼已经正式入法。《民事诉讼法》第 55 条规定："对污染环境、侵害众多消费者合法权益等损害社会公共利益的行为，法律规定的机关和有关组织可以向人民法院提起诉讼"。该条款被许多专家学者和媒体评价为中国公益诉讼制度迈出的跨越性一步。继而，在 2013 年 10 月修改的《消费者权益保护法》中，第 47 条规定："对侵害众多消费者合法权益的行为，中国消费者协会以及在省、自治区、直辖市设立的消费者协会，可以向人民法院提起诉讼。" 2014 年新修订后的《环境保护法》第 58 条规定："对污染环境、破坏生态，损害社会公共利益的行为，符合下列条件的社会组织可以向人民法院提起诉讼：（一）依法在设区的市级以上人民政府民政部门登记；（二）专门从事环境保护公益活动连续五年以上且无违法记录。符合前款规定的社会组织向人民法院提起诉讼，人民法院应当依法受理。提起诉讼的社会组织不得通过诉讼牟取经济利益。"这三项法律规定，被认为是目前我国现行法律中关于公益诉讼制度的明确规定。

显然，目前我国法律对于公益诉讼的适用范围，仍仅限于环境保护和众多消费者权益保护这两种诉讼类型，而对于《民事诉讼法》第 55 条中的"对污染环境、侵害众多消费者合法权益等损害社会公共利益的行为"的表述，哪些事项应列入"等损害社会公共利益的行为"中，目前我国的法学理论界和实务界仍然是存在争议的。

在我国，对于公益诉讼所致力于保护的"公共利益"存在着一种误解，即认为所谓"公共利益"，应当是指不特定多数人的利益，而像反家暴诉讼这种主要是以维护妇女、老人、儿童这些特定群体利益为目的的诉讼活动，不应属于公益诉讼的范畴。然而实际上，现代社会公益诉讼中的"公共利益"恰恰是限定于弱势群体的利益，而非指向全体社会成员的利益。

尽管公益诉讼或许可以追溯到更久以前，但在国际上，专家、学者和观察家们都一致认为，现代意义上的公益诉讼发端于美国 20 世纪 50 ~ 60 年代的民权运动，当时的目的是挑战针对黑人的种族隔离和种族歧视政策。

---

① 257 A. D. 2d 27, N. Y. App. Div. (1999).

到了 20 世纪 70 年代之后,公益诉讼逐渐成为一种全球景象,它也从最初的为取消种族隔离而提起的诉讼扩展到为保护所有社会弱势群体、边缘化群体——环境、消费者、女性、有色人种、未成年人及类似的诸多利益——而施行的一类特殊的诉讼机制。在世界范围内,无论公益诉讼在不同国家中呈现出怎样不同的样貌和形态,其根本的立足点都没有变化,就是限定于保护社会弱势群体的利益。

或许有读者会提出疑问,何以公益诉讼中的"公益"竟仅限于弱势群体而非全体社会成员的利益?又或者,这样特定的弱势群体、边缘化群体的利益是否可以被认为代表了社会的公共利益?

事实上,公益诉讼中的"公共利益"所指的并非一种整体上的、泛化的公益观。其根据在于,现代社会中,由于社会分层、利益分化和各种利益集团的形成,社会并非是一个整全性的社会,而公共利益也不是整全性的公共利益。社会弱势群体的出现,必然降低全社会的公共利益水平。同时,强势利益集团则更可能影响公共政策的指向,并且使政策偏离公共利益这一根本方向。因此,根据经济学的"木桶原理",整个社会的公共利益水平实际上取决于弱势群体这一短板在社会中的利益状况。相应地,也就产生了为提高社会公共利益程度,而代表弱势群体、以公共利益的名义提起的公益诉讼。这也就是为什么在世界各地,旨在维护妇女、老人、儿童这些弱势群体权益的反家暴诉讼,在公益诉讼中占有很重要的地位,并具有特定的诉讼模式和程序规范的原因。[1]

有鉴于此,我国在反家暴立法中,应当明确规定反家暴公益诉讼机制,扩大家暴案件的原告范围,赋予妇联、公益法律组织、检察机关以适格的原告主体资格,并且围绕这些反家暴公益诉讼主体设置相关配套的诉讼规范,如证据规则、调解规则、诉讼费用规则等。只有这样,才能强化对弱者利益的保护,消除基于社会性别的歧视和暴力行径,在全社会层面上达到防治家庭暴力,实现对家庭暴力零容忍的反家暴立法原则和国际准则。

---

[1] 参见徐卉《通向社会正义之路——公益诉讼理论研究》,法律出版社,2009,第 333 ~ 335 页。

# Gender Mainstreaming and Anti-domestic Violence Law in China

*Xu Hui*

【Abstract】 In practice, it is very difficult in China to bring an anti-domestic violence case to the court because the victim does not have sufficient means to gather evidences or to effectively demonstrate her case. The author analyzes the specific features of anti-domestic violence cases and argues that it is necessary to introduce prima facie case as the proof standard, providing for new kinds of evidence, including expert and social science evidence, and open the door for public interest litigation.

【Key words】 Anti-domestic Violence law; Prima Facie Case; Public Interest Litigation

# 我国见义勇为认定标准和程序的完善

谢增毅[*]

**【摘要】** 见义勇为是中华民族的传统美德，也是社会主义核心价值体系的重要组成部分，对发展社会主义先进文化、构建和谐社会具有积极的促进作用。见义勇为不仅是道德问题，也是重要的法律问题。见义勇为的认定是见义勇为制度的基础性工作。完善见义勇为认定体系有利于正确识别见义勇为行为、保护见义勇为人员的权益、明确相关当事人责任、鼓励见义勇为行为。应考虑多重因素，完善见义勇为行为的认定标准，并从认定机构、认定程序、认定时效、认定证据等方面完善见义勇为行为的认定程序。

**【关键词】** 见义勇为　认定标准　认定程序

见义勇为是中华民族的传统美德，也是社会主义核心价值体系的重要组成部分，对发展社会主义先进文化、构建和谐社会具有积极的促进作用。见义勇为不仅是道德问题，也是重要的制度和法律问题。近年来，各地区、各部门在认定见义勇为行为、鼓励和表彰见义勇为行为、保护见义勇为人员权益方面做了大量工作，陆续出台了法规政策。但在实践中，见义勇为工作仍存在政策措施不统一、认定体系不完善、权益保护不到位等亟待解决的突出问题。

见义勇为的认定是见义勇为制度的基础性工作。完善见义勇为认定体系有利于正确识别见义勇为行为、保护见义勇为人员的权益、明确相关当

---

[*] 中国社会科学院法学研究所研究员。

事人责任、鼓励见义勇为行为。因此，完善见义勇为认定体系是完善我国见义勇为制度的重要内容。

## 一 当前我国见义勇为认定体系存在的主要问题

### （一）认定标准不统一

目前我国大部分省份都制定了有关见义勇为的条例、规定或办法，并对见义勇为进行了界定，但不同省份关于见义勇为的定义却存在很大差别，认定标准非常不统一。各地方的差异主要表现在以下几个方面。

第一，见义勇为的行为类型不统一。有些地方规定见义勇为行为的范围较为宽泛，规定见义勇为是"保护国家利益、公共利益、集体利益或者他人人身、财产安全的行为"，例如山东省；有些地方规定见义勇为行为包括两大类型，即"制止正在发生的违法犯罪行为或者救人、抢险、救灾等行为"，例如安徽省；有些地方规定见义勇为包括"与正在发生的违法犯罪作斗争或者抢险救灾的行为"，没有明确包括"救人"，例如北京市；有的地方规定见义勇为包括"制止正在发生的违法犯罪行为或者抢险救灾、救死扶伤的行为"，例如河北省；有些地方的见义勇为仅包括"同违法犯罪行为作斗争的行为"，不包括抢险救灾、救人，例如内蒙古。从大部分省份的规定看，见义勇为主要包括两个类型，即同违法犯罪行为做斗争以及抢险救灾、救人。

第二，见义勇为的主体称谓不统一：有些地方对见义勇为的主体使用"人员"的概念，例如安徽省、山东省、广东省、北京市等；有些地方则使用"公民"的概念，例如辽宁省、内蒙古、重庆市等。相比而言，"人员"的概念更为中性，"公民"则往往和一国国籍相联系。因此，在使用"公民"的省份，"见义勇为"的荣誉是否可以授予外国人或无国籍人则存在疑问。

第三，见义勇为的身份限定不统一：多数地方要求见义勇为人员必须是"不负有法定职责、特定义务"的人，例如安徽省、山东省、重庆市；有些地方则规定行为人必须是"不负有法定职责、特定义务或者约定义务"的人，例如宁夏；有些地方则要求行为人必须是"不负有法定职责、法定义务"的人，例如辽宁省；有些地方仅要求行为人"在履行特定职责之外"，例如内蒙古；有些地方则没做具体要求，例如北京市。对见义勇为主体所负职责和义务的限定将直接影响见义勇为行为的主体资格。

第四，见义勇为的主观要求不统一：关于见义勇为人员的主观状态，有些地方要求见义勇为人员必须"不顾个人安危",例如内蒙古、北京市;有些地方则要求见义勇为人员必须"挺身而出",例如山东省、福建省、贵州省;有些地方则不做类似的要求,例如,安徽省、辽宁省、重庆市等。对行为人主观状态的要求也会直接影响对见义勇为行为的认定。

第五,对见义勇为行为要求的程度不统一:一些地方要求见义勇为行为必须是"表现突出"或"事迹突出"的行为,例如辽宁省、重庆市、山西省;较多的省份则没有类似的要求,例如,安徽省、内蒙古、山东省等。

第六,见义勇为的行为属性不统一。一些地方在法条中明确规定见义勇为必须是"合法行为",例如福建省、贵州省;大部分省份则未做此规定。

从上可见,目前我国不同地方见义勇为的内涵和外延存在较大差别,见义勇为的构成要素和认定标准也存在较大差异。

### (二) 认定机构不统一

大部分省份规定,各级人民政府负责对见义勇为人员的奖励和保护工作,社会管理综合治理工作机构负责奖励和保护见义勇为人员的日常工作,其他有关部门按照各自职责,做好见义勇为人员奖励和保护的相关工作。安徽省、辽宁省、内蒙古、山东省、重庆市等省(市)采用此种模式。个别地方规定公安机关负责见义勇为的日常工作,例如福建省;个别地方规定民政部门负责见义勇为的日常工作,其他有关部门密切配合,例如北京市;有的地方并没有明确指定具体的负责部门,例如宁夏回族自治区规定,见义勇为人员的奖励和保护由县级以上人民政府负责,具体工作由本级人民政府确定的相关机构实施。

大部分省份由社会管理综合治理工作机构或公安机关负责见义勇为行为的日常工作的主要原因是,目前大部分省份立法认可的见义勇为行为类型多与社会管理综合治理工作机构或公安机关的主管业务有关。例如,宁夏的条例规定见义勇为的行为类型包括:"(一)同正在危害国家安全、公共安全或者扰乱社会秩序的违法行为作斗争的;(二)同正在侵害国家、集体财产或者他人人身、财产安全的违法行为作斗争的;(三)抓获或者协助有关机关抓获逃犯或者犯罪嫌疑人的;(四)为保护国家、集体财产或者他人人身、财产安全,抢险、救灾、救人的;(五)依法确认的其他见义勇为行为。"[1] 上述行为中,前三类行为都属于社会管理综合治理或公安机关的

---

[1] 《宁夏回族自治区见义勇为人员奖励和保护条例》(2010) 第5条。

业务范围，第四类行为和综治机构或公安机关的工作也密切相关。因此，由综治机构或者公安机关认定见义勇为行为，因这些机关机构更熟悉业务，执法手段更强，证据或证人容易获取，见义勇为的认定更易开展。但由综治机构或公安机关认定见义勇为行为也存在"既当运动员又当裁判员"的弊端，因为在上述行为中，综治机构或公安机关往往也是事件的主体之一，其客观性和公正性可能受到影响。北京市由民政部门负责见义勇为行为的日常工作的做法颇具特色，其优点是因民政部门是社会福利和社会救助的主管部门，由其负责有利于为见义勇为行为人提供后续救助和福利等权益保障措施，且民政部门一般不直接参与见义勇为事件，立场较为中立；其缺点是民政部门远离行为现场，执法手段和技术水平不及公安机关，调查等行为不易开展，使其在行为认定上处于劣势。

### （三）认定程序不统一

见义勇为的认定程序一般包括申请、评审、认定、再次认定（复议）、公示等程序，但不同省份的规定差异较大。

大部分省份对认定的基本程序做了规定，例如，有地方规定，行为人或者其亲属可以申报见义勇为行为，任何单位和个人可以举荐见义勇为行为。申报人、举荐人对确认结果有异议的，可以向上级人民政府申请再次确认。见义勇为行为没有申报人、举荐人的，县（市、区）人民政府确定的相关机构可以依照职权直接办理。① 可见，除了行为人或其亲属可以申报见义勇为行为外，其他机构或人员也可以举荐，政府相关机构也可以主动办理。

有些地方对见义勇为行为的认定过程更为严格，设立了评审程序，例如，安徽省的条例规定，申报的受理单位即县级综治机构在接到申报、举荐后，应当及时调查核实，组织评审委员会进行评审，提出是否确认的意见。评审委员会由人大代表、政协委员，人民法院等机构的专业人员以及其他方面的人员组成。② 而有些地方仅将评审程序适用于行为复杂的情形，例如：山东省的条例规定，县级以上综治部门会同见义勇为基金会或者见义勇为协会，作为见义勇为行为的确认机构；对情况复杂、争议较大的确认申请、举荐，见义勇为确认机构应当组织由有关机关、专家学者、人大代表、政协委员参加的评审委员会进行评审，对符合见义勇为条件的，做

---

① 《宁夏回族自治区见义勇为人员奖励和保护条例》（2010）第6、7条。
② 《安徽省见义勇为人员奖励和保护条例》（2011）第11条。

出拟确认的评审意见。①

关于申请人、举荐人异议程序，各省份的规定差异也较大：安徽的条例规定了见义勇为认定的复核程序，并明确规定了申报人、举荐人可以依法申请行政复议或者提起行政诉讼；② 有的地方明确规定，对确认结果有异议的，可以申请行政复议或提起行政诉讼，例如福建省的条例的规定③；有的地方则规定行政机关的确认为最终确认，例如，宁夏的条例规定，申报人、举荐人接到书面确认通知后，对确认结果有异议的，可以向上级人民政府申请再次确认，再次确认为最终确认，④ 山东的条例也做了类似的规定；⑤ 有的地方则没有规定当事人是否可以申请行政复议或提起行政诉讼，例如辽宁省的条例规定，由县级综治机构负责见义勇为行为的调查、核实和确认工作，申报人对不予确认有异议的，可以向市级社会综治机构申诉，由市级综治机构完成调查、核实工作，并没有明确规定申请人有异议的可以提起行政复议或行政诉讼；⑥ 有的地方仅仅规定由县级政府见义勇为评定委员会确认见义勇为，并没有关于复核、再次确认或者行政复议、行政诉讼的规定，例如广东省的规定。⑦

由于见义勇为的认定程序事关行为人以及其他相关人的权利义务，因此，认定程序不统一和不完善的现象亟待改进和完善。

### （四）认定时效不统一

申请人或举荐人在什么期间内可以申请或举荐见义勇为行为，事关行为人的基本权利，目前各地方的做法各不相同。

宁夏回族自治区、山东省的条例规定，申报、举荐见义勇为行为应当自行为发生之日起1年内提出，特殊情况不超过2年。⑧ 安徽省的条例规定，申报、举荐见义勇为应当自行为发生之日起6个月提出，特殊情况下不超过2年。⑨ 辽宁省的条例规定，申报见义勇为的时限为6个月，特殊情况

---

① 《山东省见义勇为人员奖励和保护条例》（2012）第9、11条。
② 《安徽省见义勇为人员奖励和保护条例》（2011）第15条。
③ 《福建省奖励和保护见义勇为人员条例》（2011）第6、8条。
④ 《宁夏回族自治区见义勇为人员奖励和保护条例》（2010）第7条。
⑤ 《山东省见义勇为人员奖励和保护条例》（2012）第9、11、14条。
⑥ 《辽宁省奖励和保护见义勇为条例》（2013）第9条。
⑦ 《广东省见义勇为人员奖励和保障条例》（2012）第12条、15条。
⑧ 《宁夏回族自治区见义勇为人员奖励和保护条例》（2010），第6条，《山东省见义勇为人员奖励和保护条例》（2012）第10条。
⑨ 《安徽省见义勇为人员奖励和保护条例》（2011）第11条。

不超过 1 年。① 福建省的条例规定举荐、申请确认见义勇为行为的，应当自行为发生之日起 2 年内提出。② 广东省的条例则规定，申请、举荐确认见义勇为行为，应当自行为发生之日起 6 个月内提出。③ 贵州省的条例的规定则富有弹性，其规定：申请、举荐确认见义勇为行为的，应当提供真实材料，并自行为发生之日起提出，一般情况不超过 2 年。④ 一些地方的条例则对申请或举荐的时间没有做出规定，例如，北京市、江苏省、四川省。此外，各地对见义勇为行为受理申请或举荐之后的处理时限以及再次确认、复核等工作时限的规定也不一致。申报、举荐见义勇为行为的时效涉及当事人的实体权益，各省份的规定相去甚远，亟待统一和完善。

## 二 见义勇为行为认定标准的完善

见义勇为行为的认定标准是见义勇为制度的核心和基础。见义勇为行为往往具有跨省域的特征，例如，行为人可能不是本地人，受益人或者侵害人也可能不是本地人，不同省份立法的差异将给法律的适用，尤其是行为的认定和权益保护带来直接的困难，特别是有关待遇的转移接续需要全国统一的立法。而且，我国是统一的单一制国家，见义勇为行为作为精神文明和社会主义核心价值体系的重要内容应该有全国统一的导向和标准，因此，我国急需根据"见义勇为"的应有含义、法学原理以及我国的经济社会条件，对见义勇为做一个统一的定义，确立统一的认定标准。

由于见义勇为行为事关道德评价和制度安排，因此，见义勇为行为的定义和认定标准需要考虑大众的道德评价和一般观念，同时也要考虑制度的科学性和可操作性。见义勇为行为的认定包含以下几个要素。

### （一）见义勇为行为的主体是"自然人"

虽然对见义勇为行为的认定涉及主观的道德评价标准，不同国家有不同标准，但有些行为是不同国家所共同推崇或鼓励的，而且从平等原则出发，除非具有特殊理由，对不同国籍的人也应当给予平等待遇。因此，见义勇为的主体应为"自然人"，包括中国人、外国人和无国籍人，而不应仅仅限于中国公民。

---

① 《辽宁省奖励和保护见义勇为人员条例》（2013）第 8 条。
② 《福建省奖励和保护见义勇为人员条例》（2011）第 7 条。
③ 《广东省见义勇为人员奖励和保障条例》（2012）第 12 条。
④ 《贵州省见义勇为人员奖励和保护条例》（2014）第 10 条。

见义勇为行为的主体资格还涉及行为人的年龄问题。未成年人的见义勇为行为是否应当给予认定？从理论上讲，对见义勇为行为的主体不应设置年龄限制，只要行为符合见义勇为的要求都可以认定，但见义勇为行为人的自身安全也应当考虑。未成年人救助能力低，自我保护能力弱，自身容易受伤害，因此在立法中不宜提倡未成年人见义勇为的行为；但只要其实施了见义勇为行为，仍可以予以认定。① 2010年宁夏条例②的规定值得肯定，其第4条第2款规定，鼓励成年人采取有效方式见义勇为，并保护自身安全。这一规定，体现了救助他人与自身保护的关系，同时也暗含了不鼓励未成年人实施见义勇为行为这一政策导向，值得借鉴和推广。

**（二）见义勇为的行为人须不负有"法定"或"特定"义务**

见义勇为的主体必须是不负有法定、约定或其他危难救助义务的自然人，这是见义勇为行为的前提，负有义务的人实施救助的行为难谓"见义勇为"。具体而言，一是负有法定救助义务的救助行为不能构成见义勇为，如《人民警察法》规定警察负有危难救助义务，《海商法》规定了船长的救助义务，这些特定主体的救助行为都不构成见义勇为行为。二是依据合同产生的约定义务的救助行为也不构成见义勇为。三是当事人之间存在特殊关系时的救助行为一般也不构成见义勇为。例如，二人相约外出钓鱼，若其中一人溺水，另一人对其负有当然的救助义务。在这些情况下，当事人之间存在特殊关系，其应承担相应的救助义务的主要原因在于：特殊关系当事人之间存在彼此的信赖，一方在与对方的社会互动关系中开启了特殊的危险，理当承担相应义务，而且，特殊关系的当事人一方往往对产生的危险具有控制能力或具有最为便利的救助条件，因此，在以上特殊关系中，当事人应承担相应的救助义务。③ 综上，可以将见义勇为的主体限定为"不负有法定义务或特定义务的自然人"，用"特定义务"涵盖约定义务或者特殊关系下当事人的义务，这种提法也为目前许多地方的规定所采用。

除了以上负有法定或特定义务的自然人之外，一般社会成员之间并不存在法定的危难救助义务。一般社会成员是否负有救助他人的义务是一个充满争议的重大问题。概括而言，如果对一般社会成员规定救助的义务，则对一般人提出了较高的道德要求，难以被社会所普遍接受。虽然国外也

---

① 参见王雷《见义勇为行为中的民法学问题研究》，《法学家》2012年第5期。
② 《宁夏回族自治区见义勇为人员奖励和保护条例》（2010）
③ 参见王雷《见义勇为行为中的民法学问题研究》，《法学家》2012年第5期。

有一些立法例规定了陌生人的救助义务,且不履行义务者可能承担刑事责任,例如德国刑法的规定以及美国一些州的法律规定,但事实上,法院很难适用这些规定,当事人受到追责的案例寥寥无几。例如,德国司法实务中对"拒不救助罪"的适用条件做了严格限制,从法院判例上看,数量极少且也多将适用范围限缩在医生等特殊身份主体之上。美国佛蒙特等州相关规定的实效同样欠佳,佛蒙特州的规定从1972年施行到2007年,尚无任何相关民事或刑事诉讼发生。美国自1996年至2006年的十年里,平均每年仅有1.6件因不救助行为引发的案件。① 因此,对一般社会成员强加危难救助义务,因其将道德过分上升为法律而存在诸多争议,也存在实施的诸多难题。

### (三) 见义勇为的行为目的必须是为了"非己利益"②

见义勇为本质上是一种利他行为,而非利己行为,为了自己利益的行为不属于见义勇为。非己利益可以包括国家利益、公共利益或他人的人身或财产利益。实践中提出的问题是,同时为了他人和本人的利益实施的行为是否属于见义勇为?例如,在辽宁,中科院沈阳科学仪器研制中心的工程师荆涛与4名歹徒英勇搏斗,身受4处刀伤,有关部门认为他从歹徒手里夺回的两个包中有一个是他妻子的,因而认定此举不构成见义勇为。③ 从法理上讲,只要不是纯粹为了个人利益,都应理解为了国家利益、公共利益或他人的利益,而且,将为他人和本人利益实施的行为纳入见义勇为也有利于鼓励见义勇为行为。

### (四) 见义勇为必须是对正在发生的危难实施的救助行为

见义勇为行为通常针对正在发生的不法侵害、自然灾害或意外事故等危难,换言之,救助的情景处于紧急状态或者受救助人处于紧急状态,受助人处于一定的危险状态,这是见义勇为的重要特征。如果受救助的对象没有处于紧急状态或者没有危险性,则救助行为属于一般的助人为乐,并非见义勇为行为。当然,要区分受助对象的紧急状态或危险性与救助行为人的危险性之间的区别。见义勇为从其本意上讲,主要突出的是救助情景的紧急状态或受助对象的危险性,并不要求救助者本身也处于一种"危险"的状态,况且,见义勇为行为人是否处于危险状态,事先往往不易判

---

① 参见王雷《见义勇为行为中的民法学问题研究》,《法学家》2012年第5期。
② 郑丽清:《法律论域下"见义勇为"概念的厘立》,《广西社会科学》2011年第4期。
③ 参见张素凤、赵琰琳《见义勇为的认定与保障机制》,《法学杂志》2010年第3期。

断,而且随时可能发生变化,因此,见义勇为并不要求行为人本人也处于危险之中。目前,一些地方对见义勇为行为的定义强调了"不顾个人安危"、"挺身而出",体现了见义勇为之"勇"。但许多地方的规定主要突出了为他人利益的目的以及受助情景的紧急性以及受助人的危险性,并不要求救助行为人也处于危险之中。实践中,见义勇为的情形较为复杂,在一些情形中双方均处于危险之中,在一些情形中,只有一方处于危险之中,而且,是否具有危险性往往不易判断或者不以主观意志为转移,例如:救助人下河救人,河水的深浅往往事先难以判断;见义勇为人员与歹徒做斗争,歹徒是否携枪或持刀,见义勇为行为人可能事先无法知晓;行为人本身是否处于危险状态,可能瞬间发生变化,且不易判断。因此,不应以救助人本身是否处于危险之中作为认定见义勇为行为的要件。当然,行为人是否"不顾个人安危"、"挺身而出"应作为认定见义勇为行为的重要参考因素。

### (五)见义勇为行为的类型

根据大多数省份的规定,见义勇为行为主要包含两种类型:一类是制止不法行为,另一类是抢险、救灾、救人的行为。两种类型的主要区别是前者往往存在违法犯罪行为,见义勇为行为人的主要目的是制止不法行为,或者使受害人免受加害人的不法侵害;后者则一般不存在违法犯罪行为或加害人,行为人主要是为了救助处于危急状态的国家或集体的财产或他人的人身和财产安全,危险往往不是来自加害人。因此,理论上见义勇为行为可以概括为制止正在发生的违法犯罪行为以及抢险、救灾、救人的行为两大类型。各地方的规定往往将其细化为五种类型,例如,上文提及的宁夏条例的规定。[①] 该规定值得其他地区借鉴。

### (六)见义勇为行为认定的"弹性"

见义勇为从其字面看,"义"和"勇"都富有弹性,且见义勇为制度的创设也具有树立楷模和道德倡导的功能,加上见义勇为行为认定后将产生法律上的权利义务关系,因此,对见义勇为行为的认定除了考虑行为的性质以外,行为的程度也是重要的考量因素。诸如,受助人所处的危急或危险程度,救助目的中国家、公共或他人利益的大小,行为人自身是否面临危险以及危险的程度,行为实施的最终效果等都是认定见义勇为行为成立

---

[①] 《宁夏回族自治区见义勇为人员奖励和保护条例》(2010)第 5 条。

与否的重要因素。换言之，见义勇为之"义"和"勇"应达到社会一般所能接受的程度，行为人之精神和表现应为一般大众所难以做到，具有"楷模"的特征，见义勇为行为才能被认定。从目前的地方规定看，一些地方要求行为人的行为须"表现突出"，这也体现了对行为程度的要求。一般的救助行为可以通过民法规则解决，不必作为见义勇为行为来认定，不需要对行为人进行表彰和宣传，并提供特殊保护。因此，不管在条文中是否要求行为人"表现突出"，在实际的认定中，仍然要考虑具体行为各方面的因素。2012年《国务院办公厅转发民政部等部门关于加强见义勇为人员权益保护意见的通知》中规定，"国家对公民在法定职责、法定义务之外，为保护国家利益、社会公共利益和他人的人身、财产安全挺身而出的见义勇为行为，依法予以保护"。该通知并没有对见义勇为下严格的定义，对见义勇为的界定较为宽松，也没有指出见义勇为的类型，但其使用了"挺身而出"的限定。因此，"挺身而出"之类的表述可以作为认定见义勇为的考虑因素。

综上，可以将见义勇为行为定义为：不负有法定职责和特定义务的自然人，为保护国家利益、社会公共利益或他人人身、财产安全，制止正在发生的违法犯罪或者抢险、救灾、救人，表现突出的行为。

## 三　见义勇为认定程序的完善

### （一）认定机构

如上所述，由综治机构（公安机关）或者民政部门作为日常负责机构和认定机构各有利弊，在全国性的立法中可以允许各省份根据自身情况决定由综治机构（公安机关）还是民政部门负责见义勇为行为的认定。

### （二）认定程序

见义勇为行为的认定程序一般应包括申请、评审、认定、认定异议、公示等。

关于见义勇为的申请，行为人或者其亲属可以提出申请，其他机构或者个人可以举荐，认定机构也可以依职权主动办理。但由于见义勇为行为的认定将对行为人或其亲属产生直接的精神或物质影响，因此应该尊重行为人或其亲属的意见，如由他人举荐或由有关机构直接办理，一般应经本人或其亲属同意。

认定机构受理申请之后便进入评审程序。由于见义勇为行为的认定既要根据客观事实,同时也具有一定的道德评判因素和法律弹性,为保证认定的客观性和专业性,对于疑难或有争议的行为,应由具有一定代表性的评审委员会进行实质性的评审,提出意见,以提高认定的权威性和公信力。评审委员会应包括综治机构(公安机关)、民政、人力资源和社会保障、宣传、教育、司法、法院等部门的代表,也可以吸收专家学者、社区工作者、公民代表等参与评审。

关于申请人、举荐人的异议程序,应当依照行政法的一般原理,允许其进行复议或提起诉讼。由于见义勇为行为的认定主要是对事实的认定,为提高专业性,对认定不服的,应当先由认定机构的上级部门进行复议,对复议不服的,再提起行政诉讼。

### (三) 认定时效

申请时效事关行为人的基本权利。由于见义勇为行为的认定涉及对证据的认定,且对见义勇为行为的宣传具有一定的时效性,因此,见义勇为行为的认定时效不宜过长;同时,时效过短可能影响申请人权利的实现。因此,可以借鉴一些地方的规定,规定申报、举荐见义勇为行为应当自行为发生之日起6个月内提出,特殊情况不超过2年。

### (四) 认定证据

认定见义勇为行为往往涉及对事实的认定,因此,相关证据的采集和使用非常重要。有关证据规则,一是要明确有关单位和个人的配合义务,即见义勇为认定机构对见义勇为行为进行调查核实时,有关单位和个人应当予以配合。二是要特别明确受益人的责任,即见义勇为行为的受益人应当如实提供见义勇为行为的证据或者其他有关情况。之所以特别强调受益人有义务提供证据的原因是,现实中受益人为避免承担相关责任,往往否认或不如实提供证据,造成见义勇为认定以及行为人权益保障方面的困难。

# Improvement of the Standard and Procedure of Identification of Courageous Acts for a Just Cause in China

*Xie Zengyi*

【Abstract】 Taking courageous acts for a just cause is a traditional virtue of the Chinese nation as well as an important component of the system of socialist core values. It plays a positive role in developing advanced socialist culture and constructing a harmonious society. It is not only a moral issue, but also an important legal issue. The identification of courageous acts for a just cause is a basic part of the work of rewarding and protecting persons taking courageous acts for a just cause. Improving the system of identification of courageous acts for a just cause is conducive to correctly understanding courageous acts for a just cause, protecting the rights and interests of the person who took the courageous acts, clarifying the responsibilities of the relevant parties, and encouraging courageous acts for a just cause. China should further improve the identification criteria of courageous acts for a just cause by taking into consideration multiple factors and improve the procedure of identification in terms of the organ, procedure and time limitation of identification and the evidence for the identification.

【Key words】 Courageous Acts for a Just Cause; Identification Criteria; Procedure of Identification

# 中国所得税制改革的走向及其制度完善

席月民*

**【摘要】** 中国所得税制发展的历史并不长,如何在国家、企业和个人之间实现社会财富的公平分配,是当前全面深化所得税制改革需要认真研究的重要问题。本文回顾了所得税制在中国的发展历史,归纳了企业所得税制与个人所得税制的现有特点,分析了中国未来所得税制改革需要重点考量的问题,包括所得税的征税范围、所得的科学分类、税收公平与量能负担原则的适用、两税合一的正当性以及国际税收协定在减少重复征税方面的补强等,最后分别从《个人所得税法》和《企业所得税法》两个方面,提出了完善中国所得税制的具体建议。

**【关键词】** 所得税制改革  企业所得税法  个人所得税法

近些年来,分配问题,特别是分配不公问题,已经引起了社会各界的高度关注。参与社会财富分配的各类主体,无论是国家、企业、个人,还是其他主体,在其参与分配的能力、权利或权力、信息等许多方面都存在突出的差异。我们必须正视分配上客观存在的这些差异,并通过财税法律制度安排,将分配差异控制在合理的限度内。2013年《中共中央关于全面深化改革若干重大问题的决定》明确指出,要深化税收制度改革,完善地方税体系,逐步提高直接税比重,这为中国未来所得税制的发展注入了新的动力。① 如何在国家、企业和个人之间实现社会财富的公平分配,是中国

---

\* 中国社会科学院法学研究所副研究员。
① 参见《中国共产党第十八届中央委员会第三次全体会议文件汇编》,人民出版社,2013,第37页。

所得税制改革需要认真研究的重要问题。

## 一 所得税在中国的发展历史及其现有特点

### (一) 所得税及其立法简史

1. 中国所得税制发展的历史并不长

中国所得税制度的创建受欧美国家和日本建立所得税制度的影响,始议于20世纪之初。"中华民国"成立以后,开征所得税的问题日益受到重视,但是立法和开征的过程十分曲折。[①] 从1910年清末的《所得税章程》到1914年"中华民国"的《所得税条例》,虽然所得税在当时引起了政府部门的重视,但因时局动乱,企业生产经营不稳定,加上税收征管条件差等原因,其时并未开征真正的所得税。1936年国民政府公布《所得税暂行条例》并自同年10月1日起施行,这才是中国历史上第一次开征所得税。1943年国民政府公布了《所得税法》,进一步提高了所得税的法律地位,并使所得税最终成为政府组织财政收入的重要方式之一。新中国成立后,1950年的《全国税政实施要则》规定了所得税,并通过工商业税(所得税部分)、存款利息所得税以及薪给报酬所得税进行征收,由于当时国营企业实行利润上缴制度,因此工商业税(所得税部分)的征收对象只限于私营企业、集体企业和个体工商户的应税所得。改革开放后,1980年中国针对外国人制定了《个人所得税法》,在国际经济交往中合理实施了中国的税收管辖权,个人所得税在组织财政收入和调节收入分配差距等方面发挥出了越来越重要的作用。当时中国又针对内外资企业分别建立了不同的企业所得税制度。入世后中国于2007年最终统一了《企业所得税法》,从而建立了公平、规范、透明的新企业所得税制。

2. 中国当前的所得税制由企业所得税制和个人所得税制两部分构成,两税都经历了由分到合的发展过程

改革开放后至2007年企业所得税制统一以前,中国对企业所得税按内资、外资企业分别立法,采取了区别对待的税收政策。外资企业在1991年7月1日前分别适用《中外合资经营企业所得税法》(1980年制定实施)与《外国企业所得税法》(1981年制定实施),其中前者税率为30%,另按应纳所得税额附征10%的地方所得税,后者则实行20%~40%的5级超额累

---

① 参见刘佐《中国所得税制的起源》,《中国财政》2010年第16期。

进税率，另按应纳税所得额附征 10% 的地方所得税。1991 年，中国完成了外资企业所得税的统一，同年 7 月 1 日起所有外资企业统一适用《外商投资企业和外国企业所得税法》，实行 30% 的比例税率，另按应纳税所得额征收 3% 的地方所得税，综合税率为 33%。内资企业在 1994 年 1 月 1 日前分别适用《国营企业所得税条例（草案）》、《国营企业调节税征收办法》、《集体企业所得税暂行条例》、《私营企业所得税暂行条例》。就国营企业而言，在 1983 年试点利改税后，1984 年起大中型企业的所得税实行 55% 的比例税率，小型企业等的所得税实行 10%～55% 的 8 级超额累进税率，国营企业调节税的纳税人为大中型国营企业，税率由财税部门企业主管部门核定。集体企业自 1985 年起实行 10%～55% 的 8 级超额累进税率，原来对集体企业征收的工商税（所得税部分）同时停止执行。私营企业所得税制改革稍晚一些，1988 年起开始征收专门针对私营企业的企业所得税，并实行 35% 的比例税率。1994 年，中国实行分税制财政体制后同时完成了对内资企业所得税的统一，同年 1 月 1 日起所有内资企业开始统一适用《企业所得税暂行条例》，纳税人包括国有企业、集体企业、私营企业、联营企业、股份制企业和其他组织，法定基准税率为 33%，年度应纳税所得额在 3 万元以下的企业以及 3 万元至 10 万元以下的企业分别适用 18% 和 27% 的照顾性税率。上述内外有别的企业所得税政策，目的在于吸引外资、发展经济，实践证明其确曾对中国的改革开放、吸引外资、促进经济发展发挥出了重要作用。2007 年 3 月，中国统一了内外资企业所得税，制定了新的《企业所得税法》，并自 2008 年 1 月 1 起施行。

在中国，个人所得税的开征依据是 1980 年 9 月 10 日五届全国人大三次会议通过的《个人所得税法》，该法历经 1993 年、1999 年、2005 年、2007 年、2011 年 6 次修改（其中 2007 年两次修改），受到了社会公众的高度关注。1986 年 1 月，中国针对个体工商户与普通居民收入差距拉大的问题颁布了《个体工商户所得税暂行条例》，该条例适用于从事工业、商业、服务业、建筑安装业、交通运输业以及其他行业的经批准开业的城乡个体工商业户。1986 年 9 月，中国发布了《个人收入调节税暂行条例》；自 1987 年 1 月 1 日起，对个人收入达到应税标准的中国公民征收个人收入调节税，并且，缴纳此税后，不再缴纳个人所得税。该条例实施后，原《个人所得税法》仅适用于在中国的外籍人员。自此，中国形成了对个人所得按主体分类课税的三税并存状态。随着经济形势的发展，这些税收法律法规逐渐暴露出一些矛盾和问题，1993 年 10 月 31 日中国修改了《个人所得税法》,同时废止了《个体工商户所得税暂行条例》和《个人收入调节税暂行条例》,实现了三税合一,自此以后该税收入以年均34%的增幅稳步增长,是1994年税制改革以来税收收入增长最为强劲的税种之一,目前已成为国内税收中的第四大税种,在部分地区已跃居地方税收收入的第二位,成为地方财政收入的主要来源。

3. 近年来,中国所得税收入在全国财政收入的比重逐年增加

据统计,中国2013年度的全国财政收入为129142.9亿元,比2012年增长10.1%,其中企业所得税收入为14443.1亿元,个人所得税收入为3918.84亿元,所得税收入共计18361.94亿元,总体上占全国财政收入的比重为14.22%。[①] 2012年度全国财政收入为117209.75亿元,比2011年增长12.8%,其中企业所得税收入为12082.18亿元,个人所得税收入为3492.61亿元,所得税收入共计15574.79亿元,[②] 总体上占全国财政收入的比重为13.29%;2011年度的全国财政收入为103740.01亿元,比2010年增长24.8%,其中企业所得税收入为10021.81亿元,个人所得税收入为3633.06亿元,所得税收入共计13654.87亿元,[③] 总体上占全国财政收入的比重为13.16%。不难看出,中国所得税总体收入逐年增长的势头十分明显,2013年企业所得税和个人所得税的增长比例分别达到19.5%和12.2%。2012年企业所得税增长了20.56%,虽然同期个人所得税因税率调整出现了负增长(-0.04%),与2010年的4837亿元相比减税效益明显,但所得税总体规模占全国财政收入的比重仍比2011年有所提高。

### (二) 现行企业所得税制的主要特点

企业所得税是就企业的应纳税所得额予以课征的一种直接税,其在中国现行税制中仅次于增值税而居第二位,在促进企业多元化发展和产业结构优化调整方面发挥着重要作用。2007年新《企业所得税法》是中国加入

---

① 参见财政部《关于2013年中央和地方预算执行情况与2014年中央和地方预算草案的报告》,中国人大网:http://www.npc.gov.cn/npc/xinwen/2014-03/16/content_1855947.htm,最后访问时间:2014年5月31日。

② 参见财政部《关于2012年中央和地方预算执行情况与2013年中央和地方预算草案的报告(摘要)》,中国人大网:http://www.npc.gov.cn/npc/dbdhhy/12_1/2013-03/06/content_1765445.htm,最后访问时间:2014年5月31日。

③ 参见财政部《关于2011年中央和地方预算执行情况与2012年中央和地方预算草案的报告》,中国人大网:http://www.npc.gov.cn/npc/xinwen/2012-03/19/content_1715299.htm,最后访问时间:2014年5月31日。

世界贸易组织后,为各类企业创造公平、规范、透明的所得税制环境的重要立法成果。① 该法共8章60条,② 其主要内容和特点如下。③

1. 从纳税主体看,对企业身份的认定引入了"居民企业"与"非居民企业"新标准

新《企业所得税法》第2条明确了该新标准的具体判断标准,即企业登记地标准和企业实际管理机构所在地标准。其中,居民企业是指依法在中国境内成立,或者依照外国(地区)法律成立但实际管理机构在中国境内的企业;非居民企业是指依照外国(地区)法律成立且实际管理机构不在中国境内,但在中国境内设立机构、场所的,或者在中国境内未设立机构、场所,但有来源于中国境内的收入所得的企业。居民企业承担全面纳税义务,就其来源于境内外的全部所得纳税;非居民企业则区分为在境内设立机构、场所和未设立机构、场所两种类型,二者虽都承担有限纳税义务,但前者除就来源于境内的所得纳税外,还需要对发生于境外但与其所设机构、场所有实际联系的所得纳税,而后者只就来源于境内的所得纳税。

2. 从税率看,基本税率显著降低,优惠税率政策导向性更切合实际

税率是计算企业所得税应纳税额的法定尺度。就税率形式而言,新《企业所得税法》规定的是比例税率,从而较好地体现了税收公平原则,对促进各类企业公平竞争具有典型意义。按照新《企业所得税法》第4条和第28条的规定,企业所得税的税率具体包括基本税率和优惠税率两种类型,其中基本税率为25%,优惠税率则分为15%和20%两档。从其各自的目的看,基本税率着眼于企业所得税的收入分配功能,而优惠税率则着眼于企业所得税的资源配置功能。新的优惠税率由过去的"内外有别"实现了"内外统一"。能够适用15%优惠税率的企业只限于国家需要重点扶持的高新技术企业。而能够适用20%优惠税率的企业具体有两种:一是符合条件的小型微利企业;二是在中国境内未设立机构、场所的非居民企业,或者

---

① 该法其实名不副实,在中国,个人独资企业和合伙企业实际上缴纳个人所得税,并不是企业所得税的纳税人。
② 需要说明的是,《中华人民共和国企业所得税法实施条例》于2007年12月6日发布,自2008年1月1日起施行,共8章133条,是中国企业所得税法的重要法律渊源之一。
③ 参见席月民《新〈企业所得税法〉解读》,《中国社会科学院院报》2007年5月8日,第3版。

虽设立机构、场所但取得的所得与其所设机构、场所没有实际联系的非居民企业。

3. 从税前扣除标准看，允许扣除项目更加合理、明晰和统一

根据新法的规定，除不征税收入、免税收入和允许弥补的以前年度亏损外，允许税前扣除的项目具体包括：（1）企业发生的公益性捐赠支出，在年度利润总额12%以内的部分；（2）企业按照规定计算的固定资产折旧；（3）企业按照规定计算的无形资产摊销费用；（4）企业按照规定摊销的作为长期待摊费用支出，即已足额提取折旧的固定资产的改建支出，租入固定资产的改建支出，固定资产的大修理支出，以及其他应当作为长期待摊费用的支出；（5）企业使用或者销售存货，按照规定计算的存货成本；（6）企业转让资产的该项资产净值；（7）企业可以在计算应纳税所得额时加以扣除的支出包括开发新技术、新产品、新工艺发生的研究开发费用，安置残疾人员及国家鼓励安置的其他就业人员所支付的工资。而禁止进行税前扣除的项目主要包括支出类、固定资产折旧类、无形资产摊销费用类、对外投资成本类以及资本弱化利息类等。

4. 从税收优惠看，多种方式确保统一实行"产业优惠为主、区域优惠为辅"的新兴政策

《企业所得税法》第25条规定："国家对重点扶持和鼓励发展的产业和项目，给予企业所得税优惠。"这是税收优惠的一般性条款，也是判断税收优惠合法与否的基本准则。新法综合运用优惠税率、免税、减税、加计扣除、加速折旧、减计收入、抵扣抵免等方法，统一建立了"产业优惠为主、区域优惠为辅"的新税收优惠政策体系。除前述统一的优惠税率和加计扣除支出项目外，新税收优惠政策的统一主要表现在：（1）统一法定的免税收入项目；（2）统一酌定的免税、减税项目；（3）统一加速折旧标准；（4）统一减计收入标准；（5）统一抵扣抵免标准；（6）统一税收优惠管理主体。

另外，新法坚持税收法定原则，专章增加了特别纳税调整的规定，使税务机关采取反避税措施实现了有法可依。为实现新、旧企业所得税制度的衔接，该法第57条还特别针对享受低税率优惠、定期减免税优惠等待遇的企业做出了过渡期安排，从而建立了本土化的企业信赖利益保护制度。[①]

---

① 参见刘剑文《新企业所得税法：八大制度创新》，《涉外税务》2007年第8期。

## (三) 当前个人所得税制的主要特点

个人所得税是对个人①取得的各项应税所得征收的一种直接税。2011年中国对《个人所得税法》做了修改,重点采取了提高工资薪金所得减除标准与调整工资薪金所得税率结构的联动调整方式,把工资薪金所得每月的减除标准调整到了3500元,工资薪金所得的超额累进税率由原来的9级调整为7级,其中的最低税率由原来的5%降低为3%,其目的除简化与完善税制外,更重要的是减轻大多数普通工薪阶层纳税人的税收负担,尤其是中低收入者的负担,同时适当增加高收入者的税负,从而在一定程度上达到调节收入分配、缓解初次收入分配压力、刺激消费需求、实现经济社会可持续发展的目标。中国目前的《个人所得税法》共15个条文,②其个人所得税制的主要特点是:③

1. 纳税人分为"居民"和"非居民"两类

区分这两类纳税人的标准有两个,一个是住所标准,另一个是居住期限标准。居民纳税义务人负有无限纳税义务,非居民纳税人承担有限纳税义务。根据《个人所得税法》第1条的规定,居民纳税人是指在中国境内有住所,或者无住所而在中国境内居住满1年的个人;非居民纳税人则指在中国境内无住所又不居住,或无住所且居住不满1年的个人。需要注意的是,现行税法中关于"中国境内"的概念,只指中国大陆,目前还不包括香港、澳门和台湾地区。

2. 在税制模式上采取了分类所得税制

中国的《个人所得税法》对所得的定义采用了纯资产增加说理论,但凡人们增加的经济收益都构成税法上的所得。根据该法第2条的规定,在中国,应纳税所得共分为11种类型:(1)工资、薪金所得;(2)个体工商户的生产、经营所得;(3)对企事业单位的承包经营、承租经营所得;(4)劳务报酬所得;(5)稿酬所得;(6)特许权使用费所得;(7)利息、股息、红利所得;(8)财产租赁所得;(9)财产转让所得;(10)偶然所

---

① 在中国,个人所得税的纳税人并非仅局限于自然人,还包括个人独资企业和合伙企业。
② 需要说明的是,《中华人民共和国个人所得税法实施条例》于1994年1月28日发布,先后于2005年、2008年和2011年进行了3次修改,现行条例于2011年7月19日发布,同年9月1日起施行,是中国个人所得税法的重要法律渊源之一。
③ 参见徐孟洲主编《税法学》,中国人民大学出版社,2005,第278~279页。

得；(11) 经国务院财政部门确定征税的其他所得。① 分类所得税制严格区分了不同类型的所得形式，并分别适用不同的税率和费用扣除标准。个人所得，难以界定应纳税所得项目的，由主管税务机关确定。

3. 比例税率与累进税率相结合

中国的《个人所得税法》在税率形式上既有超额累进税率，也有比例税率。其中，工资、薪金所得，适用7级超额累进税率，税率为3%～45%。个体工商户的生产经营所得和对企事业单位的承包经营、承租经营所得，适用5%～35%的5级超额累进税率。个人独资企业和合伙企业的生产经营所得，也适用5%～35%的5级超额累进税率。除此之外，稿酬所得、劳务报酬所得、特许权使用费所得、利息、股息、红利所得、财产租赁所得、财产转让所得、偶然所得和其他所得，均采用比例税率，税率为20%。另外，《个人所得税法》对稿酬所得，按应纳税额减征30%；对劳务报酬所得一次收入畸高的，规定可以实行加成征收，具体办法由国务院规定。

4. 费用扣除实行从宽从简原则，扣除标准统一、固定

从宽、从简的原则是中国实际情况所需，但扣除标准上采取定额扣除和定率扣除两种办法，这种统一、固定的费用扣除标准与纳税人取得的收入所必须支付的费用没有关系，与维持家庭生活的生计支出、子女教育支

---

① 其中，工资、薪金所得系指个人因任职或者受雇而取得的工资、薪金、奖金、年终加薪、劳动分红、津贴、补贴以及与任职或者受雇有关的其他所得；个体工商户的生产、经营所得包括个体工商户从事工业、手工业、建筑业、交通运输业、商业、饮食业、服务业、修理业以及其他行业生产、经营取得的所得，个人经政府有关部门批准，取得执照，从事办学、医疗、咨询以及其他有偿服务活动取得的所得，以及其他个人从事个体工商业生产、经营取得的所得，当然也包括上述个体工商户和个人取得的与生产、经营有关的各项应纳税所得；对企事业单位的承包经营、承租经营所得是指个人承包经营、承租经营以及转包、转租取得的所得，包括个人按月或者按次取得的工资、薪金性质的所得；劳务报酬所得是指个人从事设计、装潢、安装、制图、化验、测试、医疗、法律、会计、咨询、讲学、新闻、广播、翻译、审稿、书画、雕刻、影视、录音、录像、演出、表演、广告、展览、技术服务、介绍服务、经纪服务、代办服务以及其他劳务取得的所得；稿酬所得则指个人因其作品以图书、报刊形式出版、发表而取得的所得；特许权使用费所得是指个人提供专利权、商标权、著作权、非专利技术以及其他特许权的使用权取得的所得，提供著作权的使用权取得的所得也属于特许权使用费所得，但不包括稿酬所得；利息、股息、红利所得具体指个人拥有债权、股权而取得的利息、股息、红利所得；财产租赁所得通常指个人出租建筑物、土地使用权、机器设备、车船以及其他财产取得的所得；财产转让所得是个人转让有价证券、股权、建筑物、土地使用权、机器设备、车船以及其他财产取得的所得；偶然所得是个人得奖、中奖、中彩以及其他偶然性质的所得。经国务院财政部门确定征税的其他所得属于一般性兜底条款。

出以及赡养老人的支出等没有关系。这种扣除方式虽然简单、便于计算，但并未体现出应有的公平。

5. 广泛采用源泉扣缴的课征方式

纳税人各项所得的应纳款项，由支付所得的单位或个人实行代扣代缴，这种源泉控制的征税方式，具有实时课征的效果，目的在于有效地防止税收流失。

6. 实行双向申报制度

现行《个人所得税法》第 8 条规定，个人所得税，以所得人为纳税义务人，以支付所得的单位或者个人为扣缴义务人。个人所得超过国务院规定数额的，在两处以上取得工资、薪金所得或者没有扣缴义务人的，以及具有国务院规定的其他情形的，纳税义务人应当按照国家规定办理纳税申报。扣缴义务人应当按照国家规定办理全员全额扣缴申报。具体说来，按照《个人所得税法实施条例》第 36 条的规定，纳税义务人有下列情形之一的，应当按照规定到主管税务机关办理纳税申报：（1）年所得 12 万元以上的；（2）从中国境内两处或者两处以上取得工资、薪金所得的；（3）从中国境外取得所得的；（4）取得应纳税所得，没有扣缴义务人的；（5）国务院规定的其他情形。其中，年所得 12 万元以上的纳税义务人，在年度终了后 3 个月内到主管税务机关办理纳税申报。

## 二 中国未来所得税制改革需要重点考量的问题

### （一）所得税的征税范围

征税范围与征税对象密切联系在一起，后者是税法确定的产生纳税义务的标的或依据。所得税的征税对象是"所得"或称之为"收入"[①]，收益性是确定可否征税的一个非常基础性的因素。《企业所得税法》中的所谓"应纳税所得"、"不征税收入"、"免税收入"等概念，其实明确了"征税范围"这一概念的重要性，进而也明确了收益不仅具有与征税对象总体相对应的基础地位，而且还是在总体上判断可税性的最基本的因素，同时也是衡量纳税主体纳税能力有无或多少的前提。

1. 收益的可税性

可税性理论作为税法理论的重要组成部分，其研究的着重点是如何在

---

[①] 在中国，所得在立法技术上有所区分，除税法名称外，《个人所得税法》在税目中常常使用"所得"一词，而《企业所得税法》中则常常使用"收入"或"收益"一词，"所得"在征税范围、税目和计税依据等不同逻辑层次上均有使用。

立法上有效界定征税范围，确保国家征税具有可行性和合法性，其核心是对各类收益可否征税做出取舍。① 税法对不同类型收益的选择并非没有意义：现行《企业所得税法》既采用了货币形式收入和非货币形式收入的概念，也采用了销售货物收入、提供劳务收入、转让财产收入、股息、红利等权益性投资收益、利息收入、租金收入、特许权使用费收入、接受捐赠收入和其他收入等概念；《个人所得税法》则采用了工资薪金所得、个体工商户的生产经营所得、对企事业单位的承包经营和承租经营所得、劳务报酬所得、稿酬所得、特许权使用费所得、利息股息红利所得、财产租赁所得、财产转让所得、偶然所得以及其他所得等概念。这些不同概念不仅具有会计学上的实用性意义，而且具有税法上的可税性意义。当然，这些来源和形式不同的收入应属于既得收入、有形收入以及合法收入是自不待言的，问题在于，预期收入、无形收入以及非法收入等相对应的其他收入类型是否也具有可税性，在理论和实践上仍有争议。

2. 预期收入、无形收入和非法收入的可税性

按照中国《企业所得税法》的规定，企业以非货币形式取得的收入，应当按照公允价值确定收入额并进行征税，这为非货币形式收入纳税提供了税法上可税性的立法注脚。② 其实，预期收入、无形收入和非法收入也均具有收益性，从税收公平角度将其纳入征税范围并无不可，人们担心的只是这些收益是否能满足税法上的"可确定性"、"可量化性"或"可计算性"以及"可审查性"等要求，这与税收效率原则又联系在了一起。由于分类标准不同，税法对这些收入考量的侧重点亦不相同。从世界各国的税法规定来看，各国一般都把货币收入、有形收入、既得收入、合法收入纳入所得税的征税范围，而对于实物收入的规定则相对较少，对无形收入、预期收入则基本不列入征税范围。在中国，《企业所得税法实施条例》第9条规定了权责发生制原则的适用，从而使预期收入的不课税问题有了法律依据。该法条强调企业应纳税所得额的计算，以权责发生制为原则。属于当期的收入和费用，不论款项是否收付，均作为当期的收入和费用；不属于当期的收入和费用，即使款项已经在当期收付，均不作为当期的收入和费用。中国的所得税法对无形收入虽未做课税规定，但这并不代表无形收

---

① 参见张守文《收益的可税性》，《法学评论》，2001年第6期。
② 参见《中华人民共和国企业所得税法》第5条、第6条以及《中华人民共和国企业所得税法实施条例》第13条。

入现象不存在,人们宁愿选择闲暇而不选择货币所得,宁愿作家庭主妇而放弃就业,都说明诸如闲暇、家庭服务等也应当作为一种所得,只是这些无形收入因其无形性以及由此带来的较为突出的主观性和不易量化的特点,实际上很难对其征税。

3. 非法收入应该被纳入征税范围

笔者想要强调的是,就中国所得税制的完善而言,非法收入其实应该被纳入所得税的征税范围。原因是:非法收入逃离税法规制只会助长各类违法犯罪行为,加剧收入分配不公的现象;相反,将其纳入征税范围后,不仅能够发挥税收的财政收入保障功能,而且能够发挥税收的收入分配调节功能,更多地发现企业和个人的经济违法犯罪行为线索,有利于打击各类经济违法犯罪行为。从根本上说,收益的合法性判断不是税务机关所能承担的,也不是税法效力所能达成的效果,它更多地依赖于民商法对市场交易行为本身效力的判断以及对财产权实际内容的界定。换言之,从税法角度看,对各类收益征税时,应强调收益来源或依据的"无因性",这使现代国家的税务机关能够回避棘手的"收益合法性"问题,摆脱为做出判断而耗时费力的困扰,从而可以高效率地从事日常的征税工作,这同总体上的可税性原理和效率性要求是一致的。① 有的学者提出,对非法所得征税并不能解决税收流失问题,而且与中国传统的道德观念相背离。因此,应税所得还是应当限于合法收入,对非法所得可以采取没收、罚款等处理方式。② 从应然的角度看,在被依法剥夺之前,非法所得同样具有税收负担能力,因此应当缴纳相应的税款。③ 至于担心其一旦被课税即等于承认其具有合法性,进而导致各种社会丑恶现象会因此而畅通无阻,笔者认为这样的担心其实是多余的。现实情况是,这些非法所得虽然未被征税,但违法犯罪行为并未因此而减少,相反却可能助长了各种违法犯罪行为人的投机冒险。非法所得并不属于税法照顾或者鼓励的对象,无论是免税或者不征税都不会与非法所得发生联系,更何况税法绝不能为非法所得设置比合法所得更为优越的税收待遇。另外,对非法所得课税并不会增加税法的制度成本和税务机构的人力成本,税务机构无须调查每一笔应税所得的合法性即可按规定征税。所得税征税范围的确定并非一成不变,随着经济社会的快

---

① 参见张守文《收益的可税性》,《法学评论》2001 年第 6 期。
② 参见王玮《"应税所得具有合法性"命题不容否定》,《涉外税务》2001 年第 11 期。
③ 参见熊伟《非法所得的可税性》,载《财税法论丛》第 5 卷,刘剑文主编,法律出版社,2004,第 106 页。

速发展变化，对其进行必要的调整是税法与时俱进的一种表现，税目的调整或拓展应成为未来中国所得税制改革的重点。

### (二) 所得的科学分类

对于所得税制中的"所得"这一概念而言，其基本含义和法定分类在税法上有着不同寻常的意义，它既是税法基于量能课税原则而做出差异性税负安排的重要依据，也是税务机构准确计算所得税时的重要方法。然而，虽然所得税建立在所得概念之上，然而所得概念之无法明确，却是所得税法的主要困扰之一。各国的所得税法都规定了哪些属于"所得"，但是几乎所有的国家均未在法律规定中界定"所得"的概念，大部分国家都是在法律中直接使用"所得"这个概念。[①]

1. 所得的含义

事实上，"所得"作为税法上的一个基本概念，其含义应该得到法律的明确界定，以避免实践中对其的理解产生歧义。从历史上看，对所得的定义存在着不同的理论学说，如"增值说"、"来源说"、"信托说"等，不同学说的差异主要在于如何对待资本利得，相比较而言，"增值说"更符合所得税利益衡平的理念。真正意义上的所得意味着通过对财产的利用而获得的效用和通过个人的劳务提供所获得的满足。因此对这些效用和满足加以测定和予以量化是很困难的，所以只好用能把这些效用和满足表示出来的金钱价值来表现（所得）。具体说来，所得分为消费型所得和取得型所得两种类型。其中，前者把用于积蓄的那部分所得从所得的范围中扣除出去，后者则强调经济利益的取得。在范围上所得又可以被区分为限制性所得和包揽性所得。限制性所得把一时性、偶然性、恩惠性所得从所得范围中排除了出去，体现为一种反复利得；包揽性所得则将反复性、连续性的所得和一时性、偶然性的所得一并纳入课税范围之内，体现为一种纯资产的增加。[②] 从中国现行《个人所得税法》的规定来看，其虽未给所得这一概念下明确定义，但从列举的所得类型看，其实际上采用的是包揽性所得的含义，这与日本等国保持了一致。

2. 所得的分类及其整合

亚当·斯密早在其 1776 年的《国富论》中，就将所得依来源分为三

---

① 参见徐蓉《所得税征税客体研究》，法律出版社，2010，第 84 页。
② 参见〔日〕金子宏《日本税法》，战宪斌、郑林根等译，法律出版社，2004，第 139～141 页。

类,即土地、劳力及资本,主张就其来源所产生之地租、工资及资本利润课以所得税。[①] 但也有学者提出不同意见,认为由土地产生之租金的营利基础与资本产生的利润并无差别,因此可将所得归为两类:资产所得与劳动所得。[②] 德国在1891年的所得税法中把自然人的所得区分为资本所得、土地财产所得、经营所得和劳动所得四类。[③] 目前,中国《个人所得税法》所确立的分类所得税制把个人所得区分为11类,这一分类是基于不同所得的性质和来源进行区分的,税率的设定也是基于不同类型所得所具备的不同担税力。

笔者认为,中国《个人所得税法》对个人所得的分类需要整合,从长远看,其更需要与《企业所得税法》进行更高层次的整合。税法上的所得基本上可以分为三大类:一是劳动所得,二是资产所得,三是事业所得。这三种所得之间需要实行差别性税率,但同一类型所得之间的税率不该出现太大差距。例如,个人独资企业、合伙企业与公司一样,其所得都属于事业所得,都同时融合了劳动与资产两大元素,都具有经营性和营利性的特征,因此,应该共同适用《企业所得税法》,适用比例税率,而不是依主体资格而分别适用两部所得税法。另外,目前中国个人所得税法中的个体工商户的生产经营所得、对企事业单位的承包经营和承租经营所得两个税目也同样属于事业所得,但在税率设计上,目前的企业所得税适用比例税率,并且设计了3档税率,而个人所得税则适用累进税率,其中工资薪金所得作为纯劳动所得,其累进税率比个体工商户的生产经营所得、对企事业单位的承包经营和承租经营所得两个税目的累进级距更多、最高税率也更高,加上费用扣除标准也不同,这就导致在所得税负担上的差异性分配,现行税法的这种差异性分配的合理性目前值得质疑。

### (三) 税收公平与量能负担原则的适用

所得税制度直接关系社会财富的合理分配,由于分配风险的不断积聚可能导致分配危机,因此必须注意及时防范和化解社会财富的分配风险。中国社会传统的"均贫富"思想是个人对公平价值追求的一种体现,但不可回避的事实是分配差异是客观存在的,差异性分配在一定条件下也具有合理性。从中国的现实状况看,由于差异性分配所导致的社会不稳定因素

---

① See Adam Smith, *The Wealth of Nations*, W. Strahan and T. Cadell, Bk. V, p. 347.
② 参见葛克昌《所得税与宪法》,北京大学出版社,2004,第52页。
③ 参见夏琛舸《所得税的历史分析和比较研究》,东北财经大学出版社,2003,第77页。

在增加,社会存在不安全性,因此必须在分配领域进行有效调控。① 问题在于,差异性分配不同于"均等性分配",后者的重要假设是主体的无差异性,此类分配往往在形式上看似公平,但通常却会牺牲效率,形成实质上的不公平。

1. 差异性分配的合理性

相对而言,差异性分配对效率关注更多一些,有时更能够体现实质公平。可见,在不同分配形式的讨论上,效率与公平的平衡问题仍然难以逾越,而公平则是社会公众普遍关注的更为核心的所得税价值。在我国强调对差异性分配进行财税法规制,主要目标是使分配差异保持在适度的范围内,而不是完全消除差异。在西方税收思想史上,税收公平的衡量主要依据利益原则和支付能力原则。② 在现代社会中,以所得为标准最能反映纳税人的能力。在人们的工作积极性受到所得课税影响的情况下,所得课税不仅仅要考虑社会收入分配的公平问题,还要考虑效率问题,即考虑到工作与闲暇之间的替代关系。推而广之,应考虑所得课税对储蓄、劳动、投资等的抑制作用。③

笔者认为:个人独资企业、合伙企业、个体工商户、对企事业单位的承包经营和承租经营形式在市场经济中应受到税法的鼓励和支持,因其担税能力较之于公司要低一些,问题是目前的所得税税率设计不利于这些市场主体的生存和发展,未能发挥所得税应有的资源配置功能和公平分配功能;另外,也未向工资薪金所得进行照顾性倾斜,不利于促进自主创业和充分就业。在中国未来的所得税制改革中,必须重视税收公平原则和量能负担原则的适用。

2. 量能课税原则应受到重视

量能原则能确保纳税人对税法的信赖感,以使得税法长期维持其适用效力。正如中国台湾地区学者所指出的,今日租税负担之不公平感,让一般人感到税法实际非依所得税分配租税负担,反而依法律上形式表象及其狡诈来分配。④ 在经历了起码有十几年之久的苦苦期待但屡屡受挫之后,中国百姓对于解决收入分配问题的信心已经下降,对于缓解收入分配矛盾的耐心已经减弱,这种正在下降和减弱的信心和耐心,同正在渐次显现的通

---

① 参见张守文《差异性分配及其财税法规制》,《税务研究》2011 年第 2 期。
② 参见刘剑文《税法基础理论》,北京大学出版社,2004,第 128 页。
③ 参见岳树民《中国税制优化的理论分析》,中国人民大学出版社,2003,第 106 页。
④ 参见葛克昌著《所得税与宪法》,北京大学出版社,2004,第 223 页。

货膨胀压力相碰头，已经使贫富差距逼近社会可容忍的"红线"，因此当务之急是让人们看到希望。① 量能课税原则在所得税立法以及法律适用中，要求立法机关在不同纳税义务人之间进行比较，衡量其担税能力有无异同，立法机关在选择征税范围时，须以纳税义务人的支付能力作为指针，在与整体法律体系的价值保持一致的情况下进行所得税各构成要素的选取和评量，须使所得税法与整体税制保持协调一致，须通过对税目的整合或拓展、税率形式与数量调整等具体制度的设计保证量能课税原则的完全实现。总之，国家征税并不只是单纯考虑获取财政收入，而是要全面实现税收的各项职能，以期在分配收入、配置资源、保障稳定等各个方面发挥税收的杠杆作用。正因为如此，国家在确定税收政策、制定税收法律时，就必须考虑经济、社会等其他一些因素，而并非仅是财政因素。②

### （四）两税合一的正当性

从形式上看，中国现行所得税制是符合税收法定主义要求的，无论是企业所得税还是个人所得税，均由国家立法机关即全国人大通过法律形式进行立法，相较于流转税而言，所得税在立法成果方面已经取得了明显的进步。中国《宪法》规定，公民合法的私有财产不受侵犯，国家依照法律规定保护公民的私有财产权和继承权。由立法机关直接制定所得税法要比授权国务院制定行政法规更具有征税上的合法性，这在一定程度上体现了对公民私有财产权的尊重和保护。

#### 1. 两税分立所存在的问题

当然，如前所述，中国现行所得税制虽然历经了由分到合的过程，但目前仍维持多年来的两税分立状态，企业所得税和个人所得税的制度设计并未充分考虑企业和个人在所得税上应然的不同担税力，也未充分重视不同主体的事业所得所具备的基本共性特征。有的学者提出，由于所得征税的复杂性和按企业所得和个人所得划分纳税的局限性，为了避免重复课税和防止税收空隙与流失，必须注意企业所得税法和个人所得税法的衔接。这种衔接着重表现在两方面：一是两税征收对象、范围和减免优惠项目边缘的衔接；二是两税税率和列支扣除项目边缘的衔接。如果衔接不当则会

---

① 参见高培勇《尽快启动直接税改革——由收入分配问题引发的思考》，载施正文主编《中国税法评论》第1辑，中国税务出版社，2012，第1页。
② 参见张守文《论税法上的"可税性"》，《法学家》2000年第5期。

造成纳税人的税负不公。①

2. 两税合一应成为未来所得税制改革的目标

笔者认为，从中国未来所得税制改革的走向看，两税的衔接固然重要，但我们更应该注意的是两税合一的正当性和可行性问题。以股利所得为例，随着中国经济体制逐步转型为社会主义市场经济形态，民间投资比重已呈现超过国有投资的发展趋势，股份有限公司俨然已成为企业为了扩张经营规模顺应局势所必须积极考虑的组织形态。在此背景下，《企业所得税法》的相关规定如何与《个人所得税法》的相关规定进行一体化整合，涉及在税收层面上股利所得的经济性双重征税如何处理的问题，这在经济层面上影响企业参与市场的组织形态的选择，在筹措财源政策上公司以资本（equity）还是以负债（debt）的方式筹资的选择以及公司对于盈余分配的决策等。显然，这一问题已成为当前亟待解决的问题，值得进一步分析研究。②

从中国台湾地区看，1955年所得税改制，乃就个人及营利事业均采综合而非分类所得税的方式课征，换言之，在1998年以前，所得税法即采营利事业所得税与（个人）综合所得税并行之独立课税制。公司缴纳营利事业所得税后盈余分配予股东时，股东应并计其所得，课征综合所得税；至于独资与合伙组织，独资资本主与合伙人每年度应分之盈余，应并计个人所得税。此种课税制度迭遭争议之处，包括股利所得在公司及股东阶段之重复课税、扭曲企业之财源筹措方式、公司借保留盈余以规避税负、各类所得间之税负不公等。③

从世界范围看，在综合所得税制下，既有将公司纳税人限定在具有法人地位的经济实体范围内的，也有不区分各种经济组织的法律地位，在所得税法上都把它们作为独立的纳税主体看待的。④ 中国的企业所得税主要适用于企业法人，对法人本质的认识是采"法人实在说"理论还是采"法人拟制说"理论，在对所得税是否存在重复性征税的判断上是有区别的。美国和欧洲国家在这一方面即表现出明显的不同，前者采用独立课税制，后

---

① 参见李志萍、刘隆亨《论企税法律制度与个税法律制度的关系及其发展前景》，《法学杂志》2008年第5期。
② 参见高汪渝《中国大陆企业所得税与个人所得税一体化的法律思考》，载《厦门大学法律评论》第16辑，厦门大学出版社，2008，第253页。
③ 参见葛克昌《所得税与宪法》，北京大学出版社，2004，第93页。
④ 参见刘剑文《所得税法》，北京大学出版社，1999，第68~70页。

者则采用合并课税制。一些人认为,法人具有独立人格,非法人组织没有独立人格,因此,对法人及其股东分别课税不属于重复征税,而对非法人组织及其投资人分别课税则存在重复征税问题,事实上,这种认识在税法上属于重大误解。公司法上有"揭开公司的面纱"的制度,税法上有实质课税的原则,虽然中国民法对法人民事权利能力和民事行为能力做出了与自然人不同的规定,并承认法人具有独立之人格,但需要指出的是,税法及其他公法上债权的债务人,均采用实质课税原则,并以经济上的负担能力而非法律上的形式来认定其纳税主体资格,因此,所得税两税合一,并不妨碍私法上公司所享有的独立人格。

### (五) 国际税收协定在减少重复征税方面的补强

#### 1. 税法的国际化趋势

当今全球化进程的一个最直接的后果就是其给国家主权带来了挑战,随着个人行动选择性的增强和自主性的提高,主权国家的税收政策难以独善其身。一国政府对税收工具的运用,其基本目的在于纠正市场失灵、提供公共产品以及实现收入再分配等目标。问题在于这些目标于不同的主权国家是有差异的,从而导致国际税收竞争成为经济全球化中必然出现的一个突出现象,因此税法的国际化是研究所得税制改革所不可忽略的重要问题。

税法的国际化并不是指税法所代表的主权因素在世界贸易组织体制下不复存在,相反,税法的国际化是在经济全球化背景下更好地维护国家主权和利益的方式。它的核心内容即在于,税法应该顺应全球经济一体化的趋势,协调促进经济资源的全球流动与合理满足本国特殊需要的关系,在观念、原则、制度和规则等各个方面充分汲取国际税收法律实践中对中国税法的完善有所裨益之处。[①]

#### 2. 重复征税与国际税收协定的补强

笔者认为,在中国未来的所得税制改革中,必须重视国际税收协定在协调与其他国家税收政策、减少重复征税方面的补强作用。国际劳动力和国际资本的有效配置,客观上要求各个国家的边际收益效率相等。在劳动力和资本的国际流动中,各国不同的所得税税率或差别化的纳税负担都会干扰经济活动的区域决策,从而影响资源的有效使用。以资本的跨国流动来说,根据资本课税对储蓄和投资不同配置的影响,采用居民管辖权原则

---

① 参见刘剑文、熊伟《WTO 体制下中国税法发展的趋势》,《中国法学》2002 年第 3 期。

有助于实现税收的资本输出中性；反之，采用收入来源地管辖权则有助于实现税收的资本输入中性。至于居民管辖权原则和收入来源地管辖权原则两者谁应该优先考虑，或者说两种原则哪一种更有利于提高全世界的福利水平，目前财税理论界并没有一致的结论。这只是从效率的观点来考察资本课税的两种税收管辖权，而优化税制的分析则要从主权国家的税制设置的角度来考察不同税收方式对本国社会福利的影响。①

重复征税不只在国内层面存在，国际重复征税同样不容忽视，它体现了隐藏其后的国家利益分配的冲突，因此，税收管辖权的冲突及其解决需要各国之间的有效协调。各国在所得税领域进行的国际协调，主要通过订立税收协定来实现。从实践看，所得税的国际协调是频繁的、大量的。1963年出炉的经济发展与合作组织《关于对所得和资本避免双重征税的协定范本》与1979年通过、1980年发布的联合国《发达国家和发展中国家间关于双重征税的协定范本》② 即很好地发挥了在国际协调方面的作用，其示范效应明显，国际上的大部分税收协定都是以该两个范本为基础而订立的。③ 另外，根据世界贸易组织最惠国待遇原则，对所有成员的企业和居民要实行同等的税收待遇。也就是说，给予任何一个成员的企业和居民的税收待遇要无差别地给予其他成员的企业和居民。④ 因此，在利用税收协定补强所得税制时，需要注意清理现行的涉外税收法规和双边税收协定，对那些适用于不同成员的带有差别待遇性质、又不符合所谓例外规定的项目或条款予以纠正，避免与最惠国待遇原则的要求相矛盾。

---

① 参见邓力平、陈涛《国际税收竞争研究》，中国财政经济出版社，2004，第71~73页。
② 为避免国家之间对资本和所得的双重课税，经济合作与发展组织的24个成员国于1963年制定了这一协定草案。这一协定草案的修订稿于1977年发表，全文39条，在协定名称和序言之后，分为七章，由五部分构成：第一部分是协定适用的人和税种的范围；第二部是协定用语的定义；第三部分是对所得和财产征税权的划分；第四部分是避免双重征税的方法；第五部分是税务行政管理特别规定和协定生效与终止与程序规定。该范本旨在避免国际重复课税、消除税收差别待遇及通过各国税务部门的情报互换、防止国家之间的偷漏税等问题。联合国范本于1979年12月21日通过，1980年公布，内容共七章29条，分别是第一章协定的范围、第二章定义、第三章对所得的征税、第四章对有关资本的征税、第五章避免双重征税的方法、第六章特别规定以及第七章最后规定。两相比较，前者更强调对收入所得实行居民管辖权，并对有关国际税收的内容做了有利于发达国家的规定，后者与前者体例类似，只是在个别条款中更加注意维护发展中国家的税收利益。
③ 参见张守文《税法原理》，北京大学出版社，2001，第118~119页。
④ 参见高培勇《加入世界贸易组织后的中国税收：两个层面的分析》，载财政部干部教育中心组编《世界贸易组织与财税政策》，中国财政经济出版社，2004，第202页。

## 三　完善中国所得税制的具体建议

"没有任何税比所得税更为民主、更富有人性及社会性"①，此为 Neumark 在《现代所得税理论与实务》一书的扉页所引用之标语。② 从中国当代史看，个人和企业方面的利益分配要求是推动中国改革开放和社会主义市场经济发展的基本动因，国家财政分配则是直接动因。鉴于中国的《个人所得税法》所存在的问题要比《企业所得税法》更多，本着循序渐进的原则，在调整国家、企业、个人三者利益分配关系的进程中，我们需要注意到中国改革开放以来从"重视产品分配"到"重视权利分配"的分配领域的深刻转化，需要关注财政收入与国家经济职能之间的互动关系，③ 需要更多地关注个人所得税制的改革，并通过进一步改革和完善中国的所得税制，更好地解决分配结构失衡的问题，更好地促进经济的稳定增长和社会的良性运行。

### （一）对个人所得税法的建议

#### 1. 建立按家庭征收的制度

个人所得税以所得归属人为中心，特别斟酌和考量纳税人的个别状态和家庭负担，因此被认为最符合量能课税原则。目前中国的个人所得税按个人征收，这种税制客观地造成了已婚已育者所负担的税收与其支出不够匹配。原本应最能体现社会公平的个人所得税，现在却成为社会不公平的源头之一。要确保纳税人对《个人所得税法》的信赖感，长期维持其适用效力，就必须维护个人所得税的量能课税原则。个人生存权保障的优先性需要在《个人所得税法》中得以贯彻，纳税人的家庭抚养、扶养和赡养义务应优先于其纳税义务，从而使得每个人生存权保障的支出得以在家庭所得总额中减除，确保其个人及其配偶、未成年子女、需扶养的兄弟姐妹以及父母生存之必需。

世界各国个人所得税的纳税主体虽为个人，但却形成了个人、夫妻和

---

① Fritz Neumark, Theorie und Praxis der modernen Einkommensbesteuerung, Bern Francke, 1947, S. 1.
② 参见葛克昌《所得税与宪法》，北京大学出版社，2004，第 3 页。
③ 这种互动关系表现在：一方面，财政收入的变化会影响国家职能的履行，当财政收入增加时，国家有条件更好地履行其经济职能，而当财政收入减少时，国家经济职能的实现则会受到制约；另一方面，国家为了更好地实现其相关职能，甚或为了扩大相关职能，必然会有增加财政收入的冲动，并努力通过制度安排来扩大财政收入。

家庭这三种不同的课税单位类型。个人单位主义虽符合现代个人主义的原理以及符合税制的婚姻中立性的要求,但它不可能满足"对合计所得相等的夫妻或家庭课以相等的税负"这一意义上的税负公平主义的要求。个人单位主义的另一弊端是纳税义务人容易通过家庭组合公司的设立,把资产分散给家庭成员而达到使其所得在家庭成员之间进行分摊,从而达到排除高累进税率的适用和避税的目的。① 从公平的角度看,以家庭为纳税主体对非劳动收入如股息、利息、红利会予以较公平地对待,因为以个人为纳税主体时对这些所得的源泉扣缴根本不考虑其实际纳税能力,在以家庭为纳税主体的情况下将这些所得并入家庭总收入再对某些项目进行扣除,能更好地体现综合纳税能力。从效率角度看,对个人征税影响的是个人的投资与劳动力决策,对家庭征税所产生的影响则更广泛。选择以家庭为纳税主体,可以实现相同收入的家庭缴纳相同的个人所得税,并且可以以家庭为单位实现一定的社会政策,如对老年人的减免,对无生活能力的儿童采用增加基本扣除的方法等。②

中国目前正处在新型城镇化的过程中,频繁的劳动力流动与传统的户籍制度之间的关系一直较为紧张,个人所得税属于地方税,其"属人税"的性质与用于认定家庭关系的户口簿的地域管理之间短时期内无法实现统一,这不利于个人所得税的征收。但从未来发展的趋势看,如果改采综合所得税制或者分类与综合所得税制,并实行自行申报纳税,则按家庭进行征收会变得实际一些。

当然,按家庭进行征收时,为真正实现税收公平,个人所得税法还必须建立科学、完善的个人所得税费用扣除标准,综合考虑基于维持本人和家庭最低限度生活的人的扣除,基于同正常人比起来会增加生活费用的残疾扣除、老年扣除、鳏寡扣除,基于降低纳税能力的杂损扣除和医疗费扣除,以及基于不具有担税能力的社会保险费的扣除和鼓励社会公益的捐赠扣除等,同时还要对家庭收入的合算与分摊在税法上做出妥善处理,正确引导社会就业。

**2. 扩大居民纳税人范围**

个人所得税属于地方税。按照现行规定,中国《个人所得税法》参照国际通行做法,确立了税收管辖方面属地和属人双重原则:一方面对居民

---

① 参见〔日〕金子宏《日本税法》,战宪斌、郑林根等译,法律出版社,2004,第145页。
② 参见刘剑文《理性看待个人所得税法改革》,《中国税务》2011年第8期。

纳税人行使完全的税收管辖权，对其来源于我国境内、境外的所得均征收个人所得税；另一方面，对非居民纳税人，则仅对其来源于我国境内的所得行使税收管辖权。

中国判断居民与非居民法律地位的要素只限于住所和居住期限两项。在法国，除住所和居住期间外，个人主要在法国从事经营活动，或者个人的经济利益中心在法国境内，同样可被认定为法国税收居民，而且，只要个人在一个日历年度内在法国居住天数超过183天，其虽然无住所也被视为法国税收居民。俄罗斯判断居民身份的要素只有一个，即在俄罗斯居住183天以上的个人属于俄罗斯居民。美国判断居民的标准稍嫌复杂，其规定外国公民如果是美国合法的永久居民（即持有"绿卡"），或者符合实际停留时间的检验标准，便被视为美国居民。如果按当前日历年度计算，个人在美国停留的时间不少于31天，且个人于当前年份在美国停留的总天数，分别加上前一年在美国停留天数的1/3和前两年在美国停留天数的1/6，等于或大于183天，那么该人便满足了居民身份检验的条件。

从上述各国的经验看，中国在居住期限方面的时间标准偏低，这与"入世"后中国对外开放的现实状况不符。当前，越来越多的外国人进入中国从事各种经营活动，其中相当一部分人在一些大、中城市开始购买高档商品住宅。因此，宜借鉴国外经验，将目前在中国居住不满"一年"的居住期限缩短为6个月或者180天，以避免不必要的税收流失和不公平的税收竞争。同时，我国应通过税收协定的形式，解决和避免与他国在税收居民身份认定上的冲突。①

3. 进一步优化税率结构

中国目前正在深化收入分配改革，其中最重要的还是要改变初次分配不合理的现状，如果希望充分发挥个人所得税收入再分配的作用，就应该加强对高收入群体、行业的税收征管。高收入阶层的收入大部分并不是来自工薪所得，而是财产性收入。

2010年5月31日，中国国家税务总局曾经发文要求加强对五类收入的税收征管，包括财产转让所得，利息、股息、红利所得，规模较大的个人独资企业、合伙企业和个体工商户的生产、经营所得，劳务报酬所得和外籍个人取得所得。2011年4月18日我国又发布了关于切实加强高收入者个人所得税征管的通知，重点强调对高收入者的收入调节以及对高收入行业

---

① 参见席月民《关于完善我国个人所得税法的建议》，《中国经贸导刊》2007年第6期。

和人群的个人所得税监管。我国对个人财产性所得均实行20%的比例税率，这与企业所得税的税率相比明显偏低，不利于引导和鼓励劳动与社会就业，因此应当适度提高财产性所得的税率。

笔者认为，应把财产性所得的个人所得税税率提高到与企业所得税基本税率相一致的水平。与此同时，应当再度降低工薪所得的税率，使工薪所得累进税率中的最高档税率与生产经营所得的税率相当。2000年9月，财政部、国家税务总局根据国务院有关通知精神，制定了《关于个人独资企业和合伙企业投资者征收个人所得税的规定》（财税［2000］91号），明确从2000年1月1日起，对个人独资企业和合伙企业停征企业所得税，对其投资者的生产经营所得征收个人所得税，从而解决了个人独资企业和合伙企业投资者的双重征税问题。但问题在于，个人独资企业和合伙企业均适用个体工商户的生产、经营所得以及对企事业单位的承包经营、承租经营所得的税率，即5%～35%五级超额累进税率，而工薪所得则实行七级超额累进税率，税率为3%～45%。

4. 建立混合所得税制

世界各国采用的个人所得税制大体上可以分为三类，即分类所得税制、综合所得税制和混合所得税制。中国当前分类所得税制的主要缺陷表现在：一方面税基狭窄，不包括在分类列举的种类中的所得就无法纳入税基；另一方面，对不同性质的所得适用不同的税率，无法完整体现纳税人的真实纳税能力，这与税收公平原则明显不符。另外，分类所得税制与源泉扣缴相联系，不利于纳税申报的自觉开展与对公民纳税意识的培养。

为了克服这些缺陷，笔者认为，中国的个人所得税制模式确实需要向混合所得税制转变，适当合并个人所得类型，在征税对象上改采综合与分类相结合的个人所得税制。现行《个人所得税法》所采用的分类所得税制，在个人收入来源日益多元化的今天，显然无法满足对相对隐蔽、不易监控的个人其他收入的征税需要。个人所得分类过多，不但增加了税务机关的工作成本，而且大大增加了纳税人偷、漏、逃税的机会。实行综合与分类相结合的个人所得税制已经成为众多专家学者的共识，其早在2001年制定《国民经济和社会发展第十个五年规划纲要》时就已被确立为改革目标，后因遭遇各种障碍而不得不两次"搬家"，在国家"十一五"规划和"十二五"规划中被反复提出。目前中国在个人所得税征管手段方面的层层改进，正为实行这一税制积极创造着条件。新征管规定中所要建立的个人收入档案管理制度、代扣代缴明细账制度、纳税人与扣缴义务人双向申报制度、与社会各部门配合的协税制度,以及所研发应用的统一个人所得税管理信息系统,对高收入者的重点管理、税源的源泉管理、全员全额管理等,都是题中应有之意。严格意义上的混合所得税制是对分类所得税制和综合所得税制的重叠使用。即对某些种类所得采用源泉征税,到纳税年度终了时再将各类所得汇总,统一计税。不过,在税收实践中,它已被泛化,形成了通常意义上的混合所得税制,即将收入根据不同的来源进行分类,对某些收入项目单独计征所得税,而对某些项目进行合并,适用累进税率计征税收。这种模式能够区别对待纳税人不同种类的所得,兼顾纳税人全面的支付能力,但对税收管理仍有较高的要求,尤其是严格意义上的混合所得税制。

笔者建议,应将现行11种个人所得进行适当合并,可考虑将所得性质和计算是否简便作为合并标准,对同一纳税人的各类所得,先课以分类所得税,然后汇总其该年度综合所得,对在法定限额以上的所得再以累进税率征收综合所得税,从而实行严格的综合与分类相结合的个人所得税制。有人提出,把综合计征和分类计征结合起来,最恰当的方法是把工资薪金所得、生产经营所得、劳务报酬所得、财产租赁所得和财产转让所得5个项目列入综合征税,而对利息股息红利所得和偶然所得等仍实行分类征税。笔者对此意见不敢苟同,笔者认为,在目标税制中把几种性质完全不同的所得项目列入综合征税,适用同一税率,不利于个人所得税在收入分配调节方面的作用的有效发挥,与税收公平原则相悖。相反,实行严格的综合与分类相结合的混合所得税制,可以有效兼顾个人所得税的财政收入功能和收入分配调节功能。因此,笔者建议分别依劳动所得、经营所得、资本所得、知识产权所得和其他财产所得等,对纳税人的不同所得合并归类,并就不同类别的所得配置不同的累进税率和比例税率。

## (二) 对《企业所得税法》的修改建议

### 1. 建立税式支出制度

税式支出概念的提出是税收优惠概念的突破,从税收优惠概念发展到税式支出概念,是财政理论的一次质的飞跃。表面上看,税法对所得税的各项税收优惠规定得十分具体和明确,但在实践中税收优惠却是一个边界不定的开放性概念,其外延总是随着各种税收优惠措施的出台而不断扩张。理论上说,税收优惠是通过税收体系进行的一种间接的财政支出,它会减少政府可供支配的财政收入,与纳入预算管理的直接财政支出并没有实质性的区别。基于这种认识,20世纪60年代以来,西方国家的税收与税法理论出现了一个全新概念——税式支出，这些国家把以各种形式放弃或减少的税收收入纳入税式支出范畴。中国新《企业所得税法》第 35 条将税收优惠具体办法的制定权授予国务院，这种安排属于制度性减免，其第 36 条规定国务院可以制定企业所得税专项优惠政策的特殊情形及其备案要求，这种安排则属于临时性减免。这两条规定授权国务院根据社会、经济发展的需要，通过行政法规灵活行使企业所得税的减免权。而实践中，财政部、国家税务总局等国务院职能部门行使了大部分的减免权。中国目前的财政支出预算中尚无关于税式支出的实践，为防止税收优惠无序扩张，中国需要建立税式支出制度，将所得税的税收优惠纳入预算管理范畴。只有将税收优惠权的行使合理且谨慎地控制在一定范围内，才能减少税收优惠泛滥产生的负面效应。①

2. 完善税收情报交换机制

在国际税收领域的双、多边安排中，相关国家的税务主管当局之间根据跨国公司的申请而正式启动谈判，其中最重要的环节就是税收情报交换。② 税收情报交换在国际实践中通常表现为两种形式：一种是包含在双边或多边税收协定中的税收情报交换条款（the Tax Information Exchange Clause），简称 TIEC 型；另一种是专项的税收情报交换协议（the Tax Information Exchange Agreement），简称 TIEA 型。③ 就企业所得税法的完善而言，税收情报交换是中国作为税收协定缔约国所承担的一项国际义务，也是中国和其他国家之间开展税收征管合作的主要方式。完善税收情报交换机制，目的在于使中国与相关税收协定缔约国家的主管当局能够正确执行税收协定及其所涉及税种的国内法，及时取得各自所需要的税收信息。具体说来，税收情报交换包括了专项情报交换、自动情报交换、自发情报交换以及同期税务检查、授权代表访问和行业范围情报交换等诸多形式。2013 年，中国正式加入了《多边税收征管互助公约》，这标志着中国的税收情报交换工作迈上了新台阶。在所得税领域，避免国际层面上的双重征税，需

---

① 参见叶姗《企业所得税税收优惠的法律分析》，《江西财经大学学报》2008 年第 1 期。

② 这里的情报，包括了税收协定缔约双方主管当局交换的为实施税收协定和税收协定所涉及的税种相应的国内法律、法规所必需的情报，仅涉及税收协定规定的具有所得税性质的税种，企业所得税、个人所得税、对股息、利息、特许权使用费征收的预提所得税。个别税收协定中涉及其他税种的，按相应的协定规定执行。参见叶姗《税法之预约定价制度研究》，人民出版社，2009，第 191 页。

③ 参见李刚《税收情报交换涵义初探》，《国际税收》2014 年第 2 期。

要把握税收情报交换形式的两类性、主体的两重性或三重性、性质的交叉性、目标的双重性和范围的延展性等特征，并从避免法律性双重征税和经济性双重征税两方面入手，注意提高情报交换的效率与公平，不断克服技术障碍，增强税收情报交换工作的实用性、准确性和规范性。

# Income Tax Reform in China: Trend of Development and Institutional Improvement

*Xi Yuemin*

【Abstract】 The income tax system does not have a very long history in China and currently the main issue faced China in carrying out comprehensive reform of the income tax system is how to realize equitable distribution of social wealth between the state, the enterprise and the individual. This article reviews the historical development of income tax in China, summarizing the characteristics of the current corporate and individual income tax systems, analyzing the main issues to be taken into consideration by China in the future reform of the income tax system, including the scope of taxation, the scientific classification of income, application of the principle of equitable taxation and the principle of taxation on capability, the justifiability of income tax integration, the role played by international taxation agreements in reducing repetitive taxation, and puts forward concrete suggestions on the improvement of both corporate and individual income tax systems.

【Key words】Income Tax Reform; Corporate Income Tax; Individual Income Tax

# 互联网时代中国的电子政务与公民参与

李 霞[*]

**【摘要】** 快速发展的互联网使得公民的直接式民主参与成为可能。庞大的网民群体借助信息传播平台实践着民主参与,并有力推动着中国的民主和法治进程。互联网在提供了良好的公共参与平台的同时,却也带来了一些法律上的挑战。一方面,网络环境下的公民参与失范导致了公民参与的非秩序化;另一方面,电子政务发展滞后、政府信息公开力度不够,导致了信息不对称,从而使得公民无法有效参与甚或无法参与。针对这些问题,需要通过法律和其他手段加以规制,促进互联网时代公民参与的健康有序发展。

**【关键词】** 互联网 信息化 电子政务 公共参与

互联网的出现,是一场划时代的"革命"。凯斯泰尔斯曾说:"互联网是这样一种传播媒介:它首次实现了在全球范围、选定的时段内,进行多人对多人的传播。"[①] 这一 1998 年即已被联合国教科文组织定义为"第四媒体"[②] 的事物,为开展社会和政治讨论开辟了一个潜在的、新的公共论坛,并使得公民的直接式民主参与成为可能。在中国,互联网时代也已经以前人所意想不到的速度到来。中国互联网络信息中心(CNNIC)2014 年 7 月 21 日发布的《34 次互联网发展状况统计报告》显示,截至 2014 年 6 月,中

---

[*] 中国社会科学院法学研究所助理研究员,法学博士。
[①] 〔英〕格雷姆·伯顿:《媒体与社会:批判的视角》,史安斌主译,清华大学出版社,2007,第 34 页。
[②] 潘跃华:《Web 2.0 时代的网络新闻传播》,《新闻爱好者(理论版)》2009 年第 2 期。

国网民规模达 6.32 亿，较 2013 年底增加 1442 万人，互联网普及率为 46.9%，较 2013 年底提升了 1.1 个百分点。① 同 1997 年 10 月第一次调查的 62 万网民人数相比，现在的网民人数已膨胀了 1000 多倍。进而，以不可抗拒之势席卷而来的微博、微信更是背弃传统媒体和社交方式，培育着"新常态"的电子公民社会的雏形。庞大的网民群体，凭借技术日新月异的信息传播平台，正积极践行着民主参与，有力推动着中国的民主和法治进程。

进而言之，互联网不仅改变了人们沟通、交流和活动的方式，更是引发了政府管理模式的变革和社会组织结构的变迁。各国政府在信息化和全球化的大背景下，大力发展电子政务，运用信息通信技术穿透行政机关之间的藩篱，这使得政府机关之间、政府与社会和公众之间，能够经由网络进行信息沟通。例如：经过十余年的建设，政府门户网站已然成为政府与公民之间互动的重要平台；政府和公民之间通过政务论坛、政府邮箱、在线咨询、民意征集、网上信访等形式，进行互动交流。② 电子政务"意味着政府信息的公开化，政府有责任与义务以更便利的方式，更容易理解的语言，让民众能够容易地获得政府的信息，从而创造更高的附加值"③。

凡事皆有两面性。互联网在为公民提供良好的参与平台的同时，也带来了一些法律上的挑战：一方面，网络环境下的公民参与失范导致了公民参与的非秩序化；另一方面，电子政务发展滞后、政府信息公开力度不够，导致了信息不对称，从而使得公民无法有效参与甚或无法参与。除此之外，中国现阶段还存在一些特殊的、妨碍公民参与的因素。针对这些问题，需要通过法律和其他手段加以规制，促进互联网时代公民参与的健康有序发展。

## 一 电子政务及其对公民参与的影响

### （一）电子政务的概念

电子政务是"在信息与通讯技术的基础上对传统行政流程的再造和改革"④，是运用信息和通信技术"实现组织结构和工作流程的重组优化，打

---

① 中国互联网络信息中心：《34 次互联网发展状况统计报告》，http://www.cnnic.cn/gywm/xwzx/rdxw/2014/201407/W020140721559080702009.pdf，最后访问时间：2014 年 11 月 1 日。
② 参见李勇、惠鸿曜《电子政务环境下政民交互的特征集管理对策探讨》，《现代情报》2012 年第 32 期。
③ 吴再发：《对推进中国电子政府建设的若干思考》，硕士学位论文，福建师范大学，2005。
④ 周汉华：《电子政务法研究》，《法学研究》2007 年第 3 期。

破部门分割,向社会提供优质、规范、透明的管理和服务"①。这一定义借鉴了世界银行对电子政务的描述:"政府机构运用现代信息和通信技术,转变它与公民、企业、政府部门之间的关系……这些技术可以服务于不同的目的:向公民提供更有效的服务、改进政府与企业的关系,促进公民利用获知的信息更好履行其权利,提升政府的管理效能。"② 相应地,电子政府的实质,就是为了适应新到来的信息社会的需要,由传统"官僚型"的政府转变为扁平的、自动回应式的、高效率的、全天候提供优质公共服务的主体。

电子政务的核心价值不仅在于透明高效的政府治理,还在于社会、民众的良性互动,它将原本需要投入海量资源处理的公共事务,通过数字化的转化,使其自动在虚拟空间中处置,从根本上突破原本自足的治理体系和封闭的决策体系,将处于决策系统外的团体和个人纳入决策的主体甚至置于核心。

### (二) 电子政务对公民参与的影响

电子政务不仅能为公民提供"知情"的平台,还能为其提供"参政"的空间。随着信息技术的不断发展,政府(Government)和公民(Citizen)(G2C)及政府和政府(G2G)之间进行充分交流,会促进民主的进步,并进而使公民和公民(C2C)之间的交流成为可能。也就是说,电子政府建设的不断推进,为"电子民主"的实现准备了更充分的条件。以全球视野分析电子政务的宏观走向并观察各国的具体情形可知,不同国家中电子政务的发育和成熟程度与该国公民参与的现实状况之间存在较大的正相关性。此处将从两个层面分析电子政务对公民参与的影响。

1. 对参与主体的影响:培养参与文化

公民之所以参与到决策过程中来是因为"任何权力必须公正行使,对当事人不利的决定必须听取他的意见"③。"凡生活受到某项决策影响的人,就应该参与到此决策的制定过程。"④ 电子政务时代的公民参与是一种参与

---

① 张锐昕:《电子政府与电子政务》,中国人民大学出版社,2011,第37页。
② 世界银行网站,http://web.worldbank.org/WBSITE/EXTERNAL/TOPICS/EXTINFORMATION-ANDCOMMUNICATIONANDTECHNOLOGIES/EXTEGOVERNMENT/0,contentMDK:20870448~menuPK:6226295~pagePK:210058~piPK:210062~theSitePK:702586,00.html,最后访问时间:2014年4月15日。
③ 〔英〕威廉·韦德:《行政法》,楚建译,中国大百科全书出版社,1997,第95页。
④ 〔美〕科恩:《论民主》,聂崇信等译,商务印书馆,1988,第15页。

式的直接民主。它为公民提供了便捷参与公共事务的渠道。"电子民主和参与"是电子政务的四要素之一。① 电子政务开辟了参与制民主的广阔空间，为公民参与公共事务准备了主观和客观条件，有利于对整个社会公民参与文化的培养。

2. 对公民参与方式的影响

网络社会的逐步形成，对公民的民主参与有着很大的作用，公民通过网络直接参与公共事务的管理与决策等，实现民主过程中公民价值理念、政治观点等的电子交换这将对公民参与产生下列五方面的影响。第一，公民参与更为直接。除却一些例外情形，当今世界的民主基本是一种间接民主，广大公民通过人数较少的代表（人大代表、议员等）来代表自己参与政治生活。然而在网络世界，民众不再需要他人作为代表，而是可以直接表达自己的诉求——此为电子政务时代公众参与的最显著的特征。第二，公民参与更为自由和平等。平等的"网络世界"为所有人提供了均等的公共参与的机会和自由。第三，公民参与更为快捷和便利。第四，公民参与更为廉价。公民参与成本的降低，也是广大民众踊跃参与的原因之一。第五，由于网络实名制尚未真正落地，网络社会的公民参与还具有一定的隐匿性。

## 二 互联网时代的公民参与面临的问题

### （一）网络公众与政府的关系

关于网络公众的定义，可以援引美国公众新闻理论最早提出者卡雷（James Carey）在《新闻与公众对话》的说法："公众是一群聚在一起讨论新闻的陌生人，他们为讨论共同关心的事聚合起来就形成公众。"② 也就是说，公众是对社会负有责任感、参与感和使命感的人群，他们是社会事件的亲历者而非漠然的旁观者，是信息社会的参与者而非一旁的沉默者。

相较传统媒体，互联网更为自由、开放和随意，信息发布更为及时和便捷，信息传播更为快速和普遍，这使得政府难以对信息的发布和传播施加有效控制。尽管如此，总体来看，网络公众和政府绝非对立甚至敌对的

---

① Kuno Schedler, Lukas Summermatter, "E-government: What Countries Do and Why: A European Perspective", *Journal of Political Marketing*, 2003 (2), pp. 255 – 277.
② 转引自李岩《网络"公众新闻"实践与"网络公众的形成"——对"关于突发事件应对法（草案）中有关对媒体的处罚规定的网络讨论分析"》，《当代传播》2008 年第 1 期。

关系，仍是一种良性的互动关系。统计表明，目前92.7%的网民是50岁以下的年轻人。① 尽管屡见互联网上的发言和评论夹杂着一些非理性的因素，表现出一些情绪化的冲动和发泄，但绝大多数公众并非有意制造冲突或恐慌，而是更愿意追求和谐、自由的网络舆论环境。

**（二）公民参与的非秩序化**

1. 公民参与的非秩序化概念

公民非秩序化参与，是与有序参与相对的概念，是指公民以非法甚至违法的方式或采取非法甚至违法的途径参与公共部门的决策（包括立法、执法、司法等），并企图对决策施加影响。②

从现实因素来看，互联网为公民参与提供了可供发挥的舞台，但任何民主政治对公民参与的承受能力都是有限的，因而有序的公民参与成为时代所需。目前的互联网舆论中，"极左"、"极右"的思想仍有市场，甚至在一定时期和范围内有泛滥之势，这误导了少数公众，也在一定程度上扰乱了舆论环境和公共参与空间。就中国而言，市场经济体制的改革进一步深化，随即而至的是利益的多元化，加之电子民主的飞速发展给社会稳定带来了不和谐因素，充分重视公民参与的有序发展变得日益重要。

2. 公民有序参与的特征

第一，首先它应当是一种合法的活动，这是参与的前提和基础。所谓"合法"，包括三个层面的要求：一是指公民的参与活动必须在宪法、法律法规容许的范围内进行，必须符合法律所规定的参与程序、条件和规则；二是指公民参与必须符合互联网自身的规则和行为规范；三是指参与的动机必须是为了追求合法的权利和利益，或避免合法的权益受损。

第二，它应当是一种制度化的、理性的行为。理性是秩序之源。互联网中有序的公共参与者必须秉持理性和克制来享受宪法和法律所赋予公民的权利和自由，履行公民应尽的义务，必须保持冷静和理智来表达合理的利益诉求，参与利益协调，必须自主决定和自愿表达，避免被非理性的情绪和思想所控制和左右，防止被别有用心的势力所利用。

第三，它发生在政府与公民的互相回应和关照中。公民作为参与主体，

---

① 中国互联网络信息中心：《34次互联网发展状况统计报告》，http://www.cnnic.cn/gywm/xwzx/rdxw/2014/201407/W020140721559080702009.pdf，最后访问时间：2014年11月1日。
② 参见杨三涛《电子政务中公众参与法律问题的研究》，硕士学位论文，西南政法大学，2007。

关注自身所处的社会和政治环境,将公共参与看作行使其民主权利、追求合法利益之举。政府则逐渐建立回应机制,以回应公民的合法诉求,并将其实质性地反映在决策的过程和结果中。正如斯塔林所指出的:"回应(responsiveness)是一个组织对公众提出政策变化这一要求作出的迅速反应,也可以说是政府对公众所提出的要求作出超一般的反应的行为。"①

3. 互联网对公民非秩序化参与的影响

互联网作为一个"技术中立"的事物,在为公民有序参与提供了更为便捷的途径和渠道的同时,也不可避免地拓展了非秩序化参与的途径,提升了非秩序化参与的"能力",扩大了它的影响范围的广度和深度。② 可以说,"互联网络的扩张几乎在各个方面都成为国家政治的'克星',它正以自己的节奏甚至摧毁传统意义的政治控制机器,影响公民的政治参与"③,为各国带来了强大的挑战。

### (三) 电子政务发展现状下公民参与面临的问题

除了非秩序化参与外,在我国电子政务发展的现实下,公民参与还面临其他一些特有的问题。

第一,政府信息公开工作滞后。政府(主动或依申请)公开相关信息,是公民充分有效参与公共事务的前提,也是发展电子政务的初衷之一。中国社会科学院信息化研究中心所做的调查显示,现阶段,无论是政府还是电子政务的普通用户,都将政府信息的提供列为政府在线服务功能的第 1 位(列第 2、3 位的是网上办事和民意收集)。④

2008 年 5 月 1 日,被各界寄予厚望的中国的"阳光法案"——《政府信息公开条例》(以下简称《公开条例》)开始实施。《公开条例》实施近 7 年以来,从中央到地方,各级政府依法主动公开或应民众申请公开了大量信息,这为公民有效参与决策和公共事务管理提供了基础。然而客观地说,《公开条例》在各地的实施效果参差不齐。近几年,中国社会科学院法学研究所法治国情调研组持续对国务院部门网站、省级政府网站和较大的市的政府网站等进行观察、验证、统计,测评其信息公开透明度指数。2013 年,这项测评共选取了 55 家国务院部门、31 家省级政府和 49 家较大的市政府,

---

① 〔美〕格罗弗·斯塔林:《公共部门管理》,陈宪等译,上海译文出版社,2003,第 132 页。
② 参见杨三涛《电子政务中公众参与法律问题的研究》,硕士学位论文,西南政法大学,2007。
③ 李永刚:《网络扩张对后发展国家政治生活的潜在影响》,《战略与管理》1999 年第 5 期。
④ 中国社会科学院信息化研究中心:《中国电子政务实施与应用调查报告》,2006。

测评项目包括政府信息公开目录、依申请公开工作情况、政府信息公开年度报告制度的实施情况，以及各类信息（包括工作信息、环保信息、食品安全信息等）的公开情况。测评结果显示：55家国务院部门只有6家及格，及格率不到1/9；31个省级政府中只有7个及格，及格率超过1/5，高于国务院部门。报告认为，国务院部门和地方政府近年来在贯彻实施《公开条例》、推进政府管理透明度方面所付出的努力确有值得肯定之处，但客观来看，仍有部分网站的运行状况不佳，与通过推行电子政务来打造"永不下班的政府"的目标相去甚远，电子政务重复建设的问题比较严重，部分网站缺乏有效信息，信息公开流于形式，部分网站信息的更新严重滞后，基本处于"休眠"状态，还有一些政府网站为公众获取信息增加了难度和成本，非"用户友好型"[①]。上述问题极有可能造成信息的不对称，并使得公民参与的有效性大大削弱。更为严重的是，对于一些敏感事件（例如环境污染、食品安全事件、自然灾害等），若无权威机构及时准确地向公众发布信息、澄清事实，想象将"插上翅膀"任意驰骋，甚或给谣言的传播制造市场，引起或激化矛盾，导致混乱。

第二，电子政务发展缺乏顶层设计，未能实现政务资源共享。公民参与需要大量的信息，这要求各部门的协调配合，克服信息垄断。然而实际情况是，由于电子政务的建设长期以来由单个的部门作为主导，它们较少将纵向不同层级之间和横向不同部门之间的信息共享和协同纳入考量范畴，从而导致信息壁垒和信息孤岛的出现。

第三，重电子，轻政务。电子政务意在通过信息化，实现对政府管理方式和业务流程的"再造"。然而实践中，对于电子政务的要旨、重心和发展趋势等，目前中国相当一部分政府部门还存在认识误区，尚未深刻地认识到电子政务建设"不是'作秀'，而是要真正建设一个内容实用、信息丰富、互动性强、服务快捷的电子政府"，某些政府部门往往耗费大量资源却建成了一些毫无应用实效的"形象工程"。[②]

第四，"重电子建设，轻政务应用"[③]。在信息化领域，常常存在信息化的能力、应用和绩效三者之间的矛盾，这被称为"信息化不等式"，即能力

---

① 参见中国社会科学院法学研究所法治国情调研组《中国政府透明度年度报告（2014）》，载中国社会科学院法学研究所编《中国法治发展报告（2014）》，社会科学文献出版社，2014。

② 参见陈国柱《浅谈我国电子政务存在的问题与对策》，《科技信息》2013年第6期。

③ 周汉华《电子政务法研究》，《法学研究》2007年第3期。

≠应用≠有效。① 具体是指：信息能力建设的水平，不一定与其应用水平相当；信息能力被应用的程度，也不一定对应其信息能力应用的有效程度。这一不等式在电子政务领域尤其凸显。不少地方或部门的门户网站内容丰富、功能强大，而当地上网用户很少，政府网站的访问量少，网站的办事服务、信息收集和反馈功能不彰。② 电子政务轻应用，成为公众对电子政务缺乏热情的重要原因之一。根据 UNDESA 的调查，2010 年我国公众的电子参与度指数（E-participation Index）在全球排第 32 名，较之 2004 年没有进步，比 2008 年（第 20 名）还退后了 12 位。③

## 三 网络时代公民参与的法律保障

网络时代的公民参与，是受到《中华人民共和国宪法》④ 确认和保障的公民的基本权利。但在法律层面，对网络公民参与的法律保障和规制都显不够。突出表现之一是，在经合组织所列举的电子政府建设的外部障碍中，法律障碍高居首位。⑤ 法律方面存在的问题，对推动和规范网络时代的公民参与构成了严重阻碍，因此，对现行法律进行修改和补充十分迫切。

### （一）制定和修改政府信息公开法律法规

在一定范围内，一个社会的自主和承受能力与其信息公开的程度成正比——信息公开程度越高，公众的心理承受能力就越高，公众参与能力也相应越高，社会自主能力越强。⑥

在世界范围内，国家制定以公开为原则、以不公开为例外的政府信息公开法已成为趋势。在中国，第一部全国性的规范信息公开的行政法规——《公开条例》发布于 2007 年，它首先对政府信息进行了明确界定，⑦ 并且明确

---

① 参见汪向东《信息化不等式：能力≠应用≠有效》，《光明日报》2006 年 7 月 20 日。
② 参见汪向东、姜奇平、田铮《电子政务的行政生态学调查》，《中国计算机用户》2006 年第 11 期。
③ 参见肖拥军、姚磊、李宏伟《我国电子政务发展研究》，《中国信息界》2012 年第 2 期。
④ 《中华人民共和国宪法》第 33 条规定：国家尊重和保障人权。其他宪法条款还规定公民享有平等权，选举权与被选举权，言论、出版、集会、结社、游行、示威自由，通讯自由和秘密权，批评、建议、检举、申诉权，参与权等公民基本权利。
⑤ OECD, The E-government Imperative, 48（2003）. 转引自周汉华《电子政务法研究》，《法学研究》2007 年第 3 期。
⑥ 参见范文芳《政府信息公开与保密的守衡》，《河南图书馆学刊》2007 年第 11 期。
⑦ 《政府信息公开条例》第 2 条："本条例所称政府信息，是指行政机关在履行职责过程中制作或者获得的，以一定形式记录、保存的信息。"

行政机关公开政府信息,应当遵循公正、公平、便民的原则。同时,条例对中国政府信息公开制度(分主动公开和依申请公开)进行了建构,具体包括政府信息公开的主体制度、范围制度、发布制度、豁免制度、审查制度、保障制度、监督制度,等等。

客观来看,目前中国的政府信息公开制度体系已初步建立,但还远未成熟,具体表现在以下几点。第一,立法层级过低。除了一部行政法规外,现行有效的均为地方性立法,且立法内容上不是照搬《条例》就是相互借鉴,缺乏地方特色和针对性。第二,立法大多为原则性的粗略规定,可操作性较差。例如,对于政府信息范围的界定、政府信息公开工作和普通工作之间的区分、政府信息公开保密审查机制如何运作、"三需要"和"三安全一稳定"等条款如何适用等,都规定得过于原则,使得政府部门和申请人经常无所适从。

因应这些问题,可以尝试从立法层级、立法观念、立法体系等层面对现阶段中国政府信息公开的制度建构做进一步完善。第一,立法层级。目前主流意见认为,在政府信息公开的立法方面应上升至法律的形式,由全国人大或者全国人大常委会制定《政府信息公开法》。目前最高行政机关制定的《条例》无法涵盖人大、法院、检察院和党的机关的行为规则,这使得大量信息脱出规制范围。并且,从其他国家的立法经验来看,关于政府信息公开的法律法规大多是由立法机关颁布的。第二,立法体系。参考各国立法经验,难以由单一的政府信息公开法典对政府信息公开进行统一规制,而应分步骤、分阶段地进行相关立法。在立法体系架构上,可以由以下几部分构成:(1)关于政府信息公开的法律规定;(2)关于政府信息获取、存储、管理、使用和在政府系统内部分享、传递的法律制度;(3)关于公共数据库的开发和共享的法律制度;(4)关于网络和政府信息安全及个人信息保护的法律制度,如《保守国家秘密法》和《个人信息保护法》,等等。

### (二) 加快制定电子政务法

首先,要制定电子政务基本法。"电子政务法是专门调整现代信息技术在公共行政中应用的范围、条件、方式、地位和效力等事项的法律规范的总称。"[①] 其中,最为重要的当为电子政务基本法,它是整个电子政务法律

---

① 高家伟:《论电子政务法》,《中国法学》2003年第4期。

体系的基础，决定着电子政务的整个法律体系架构。① 目前我国尚无关于电子政务的纲领性（基础性）立法，整个立法层次较低。② 本文主张，要尽快制定《电子政务法》作为基本法，使其涵括电子政务法律体系的基本内容，对电子政务法的立法原则、目的、重要的相关制度等做出明确规定，使其发挥"电子政务宪法"的作用。其次，应加快制定政府网站管理法，以规范网络域名，规范政府网站内容和日常管理，确保网站的可用性和安全性。此外，应选择良好的立法时机，出台关于电子签名、网络安全、政府数据开发利用、征信管理等方面的法律法规。

### （三）修改和完善政府组织法

中国的电子政务主要依循两套系统展开，一是各级政府及其部门的政府上网工程及政府门户网站，二是以"金"字工程为主体的纵向业务应用系统（包括金卡、金关、金桥等）。由于我国现行的政府组织法规（如《地方各级人民代表大会和地方各级人民政府组织法》）等没有对本级政府与实行垂直管理的同级行政管理部门之间的关系予以明确化，各级政府的门户网站难以整合实行垂直管理的部门，从而影响了综合性政府网站作用的发挥，引致信息化过程当中的"信息孤岛"现象。因应信息化的大势和信息资源共建共享的要求，我国有必要对相关组织法做必要修改。

### （四）立法对网络公民参与行为进行规范

针对前文论及的网络非秩序化的参与行为，必须补充和完善相关立法。目前中国尚无针对网络公民参与的制度规范，只有《刑法》的相关条款③和《电子签名法》、《全国人大常委会关于维护互联网安全的决定》、《全国人大常委会关于加强网络信息保护的决定》、《计算机信息系统安全保护条例》、《互联网信息服务管理办法》、《互联网新闻信息服务管理规定》、《信息网络传播权保护条例》、《计算机信息网络国际联网管理暂行规定》，最高人民法院、最高人民检察院《关于办理利用信息网络实施诽谤等刑事案件适用法律若干问题的解释》等法律法规涉及对网络行为的规制。建议立法、行政

---

① 参见张继超《电子政务立法规制研究》，硕士学位论文，黑龙江大学，2011。
② 参见周汉华、苏苗罕《我国信息化法律法规建设六十年》，《电子政务》2009年第10期；蒋琼：《电子政务的法律现状、困境与出路》，《广西师范大学学报（哲学社会科学版）》2012年第2期。
③ 例如《中华人民共和国刑法》第285、286条针对侵入计算机系统和破坏计算机系统的行为做出了规定。

和司法机关在对网络公民参与的特点和规律进行深入分析和研究的基础上，参考其他国家经验，制定规则以规范网络公民参与。

## 结　语

　　网络时代的公民参与，是一个尚待深入研究的主题。这种"电子民主"的兴起，基于两个关键因素——传统民主政治中公民参与度的低下和新兴信息技术的广泛应用。主观上，为了提升决策的民主性和科学性，政府有提升公民参与度的动力，公民也因长期压抑而有着参与的愿望和诉求；客观上，信息技术的发展和应用促进了透明政府和电子政府的建设，进而为公民参政议政提供了更为便捷的渠道和平台。发展至今日，电子民主已经成为建设成熟完善的电子政府所无法回避的客观存在。但仍然需要承认，尽管互联网浪潮为电子民主制造了条件和氛围，但事实上在大多数国家，公民对电子民主的反应仍比较平淡，电子民主的实现仍然是或远或近的未来。

　　那么，电子政务将步向何方？答案已初现端倪。电子政务和治理理论二者产生于相同的背景，即传统政府管理的困境和全新信息化的挑战。只是，电子政务主要致力于从实践层面更新政府的运作模式，而治理理论则从理论层面试图疏解陈旧的公共管理方式和现实社会之间的张力。在治理理论的引导下，电子政务的发展大致要经历四个阶段：以组织为中心的电子政务阶段→以公众为中心的电子政务阶段→以组织为中心的电子化治理阶段→以公众为中心的电子化治理阶段。[①] 电子治理概念的内涵和外延却变得更为广泛，它的要旨是向公民社会充分赋权，提升公民参与的广度和深度，彰显参与和决策之间的相互作用，提升决策过程的透明度等。电子治理的实现是一个复杂的工程，需要法律和公共政策的支持、技术平台的支撑、透明政府的建设，乃至整个社会人文环境的转变。

---

① 参见李春《治理视角：电子政务的另一种解读》，《电子政务》2005年第Z2期。也有学者指出各国电子政务的发展必经的三个阶段是电子政务建设、信息技术应用以及行政流程的再造和改革。参见周汉华《电子政务法研究》，《法学研究》2007年第3期。这是从不同分析视角做出的不同归纳。

# E-Government and Public Participation in the Internet Era

*Li Xia*

【Abstract】 The rapid development of the Internet has made citizens' direct democratic participation possible. With the help of information transmission platforms, the huge population of netizens is able to practice democratic participation and forcefully promote the development of democracy and the rule of law in China. The Internet, while providing a good platform of public participation, has also brought about some legal challenges: on the one hand, the anomies in citizens' participation in the context of the Internet have led to the non-ordering of civic participation; on the other hand, because of the slow development of e-government, the disclosure of government information is inadequate, making citizens' participation ineffective or impossible. In view of these problems, China should take legal and other regulatory measures to promote the healthy and orderly development of civic participation in the internet era.

【Key words】the Internet; Informatization; E-government; Public Participation

图书在版编目(CIP)数据

法治发展与司法改革：中国与芬兰的比较/李林，（芬兰）柳库恩主编. -- 北京：社会科学文献出版社，2016.6

（中国法治论坛）

ISBN 978-7-5097-9198-1

Ⅰ.①法… Ⅱ.①李… ②柳… Ⅲ.①司法制度-体制改革-对比研究-中国、芬兰 Ⅳ.①D926②D975.316

中国版本图书馆CIP数据核字（2016）第108868号

·中国法治论坛·

## 法治发展与司法改革
### ——中国与芬兰的比较

主　　编／李　林　〔芬兰〕尤拉·柳库恩
副 主 编／谢增毅

出 版 人／谢寿光
项目统筹／芮素平
责任编辑／李　晨　郭瑞萍

出　　版／社会科学文献出版社·社会政法分社（010）59367156
　　　　　地址：北京市北三环中路甲29号院华龙大厦　邮编：100029
　　　　　网址：www.ssap.com.cn
发　　行／市场营销中心（010）59367081　59367018
印　　装／三河市东方印刷有限公司
规　　格／开　本：787mm×1092mm　1/16
　　　　　印　张：17.75　字　数：304千字
版　　次／2016年6月第1版　2016年6月第1次印刷
书　　号／ISBN 978-7-5097-9198-1
定　　价／79.00元

本书如有印装质量问题，请与读者服务中心（010-59367028）联系

▲ 版权所有 翻印必究